MONEY DEMAND AND MONETARY POLICY

MONEY DEMAND AND MONETARY POLICY

Douglas Fisher

THE UNIVERSITY OF MICHIGAN PRESS
Ann Arbor

Published in the United States of America
by the University of Michigan Press

Printed in Great Britain

1992 1991 1990 1989 4 3 2 1

Library of Congress Cataloging-in-Publication Data

Fisher, Douglas, 1934–
Money demand and monetary policy / Douglas Fisher.
p. cm
Includes bibliographical references.
ISBN 0-472-10169-2
1. Demand for money. 2. Money supply.
3. Monetary policy.
I. Title.
HG226.5.F57 1989
332.4′6—dc20 89-37216
CIP

TO MY WIFE

CONTENTS

TABLES AND FIGURES

Tables

Figures

PREFACE

Primarily, this is a study of an integrated money-demand and money-supply market employing the concepts of revealed preference and/or demand-systems analysis on both demand and supply problems. This work represents a literature that has developed in the monetary context over the last 15 or so years and one that now offers theoretical and empirical insights on both the nature of what we might call 'the monetary problem' and on most of the major issues involving monetary policy. This is not a particularly well-known literature, on the whole, perhaps because its traditional orientation (rooted in standard aggregation theory) robs it of intrinsic novelty, but in view of the results which help explain such questions as that of the 'case of the missing money', adaptive v. rational expectations, and the like, it needs to be brought to a broader audience, if only for the criticisms and extensions that might occur.

The story begins in Chapter 1 with the aggregation discussion itself, which is bundled with some traditional material on the definition of money. In this chapter and in most of the rest of the book, there are a number of empirical *illustrations*, some of which are quite complicated (as 'systems' analysis can sometimes be). By including illustrations the theory can be fleshed out in an interesting way, and this is a significant reason for taking this approach, but it is equally important to appreciate that many of these findings stand by themselves as results that have some bearing on problems of money demand and monetary policy in the current policy discussion. This is the case in Chapter 1, where the demand-theory inspired Divisia monetary indices are defined – after a theoretical discussion of their 'user costs' (i.e. prices) – and then compared in various theoretically inspired ways. The methods involve revealed preference testing on recent US data and the comparisons are among simple-sum, Divisia and MQ (monetary quantities) aggregates. The comparison is generally to the advantage of the Divisia measures, but the margin of victory is not large.

Chapter 2 is the first of two chapters dealing with money demand, a topic which is itself split up into 'transactions-demand' and 'asset-demand' components across the two chapters. In the transactions material the early emphasis

(in Chapter 2) is on traditional inventory and transactions-costs models with some discussion of the promising 'value of time' hypothesis, in anticipation, possibly, of a literature that has yet to bear fruit. A literature that does show some results, however, is that on the rational expectations approach to money demand; and here, after a theoretical discussion, a full implementation is presented, offering a comparison between the US Divisia and simple-sum monetary aggregates. While the conditions of the rational model do not appear to be fully satisfied in this test, important differences continue to appear among the monetary aggregates. In Chapter 3, then, again following a brief discussion of the traditional material, a formal asset (systems) approach is explained and again illustrated by the US data. Here the empirical implementation involves a comparison between the Translog and the Fourier flexible functional forms as methods for extracting unbiased and statistically precise estimates of the elasticity relationships among financial aggregates. The sets actually considered are those most strongly recommended in the aggregation material of Chapter 1, and the results offer possible insights into why a decent estimate of the demand for money has been so elusive in recent years.

Chapter 4 (through to Chapter 6) begins a trek moving from traditional (helicopter-style) monetary policies right through to the (aggregate) banking sector. In this final set of three chapters, the empirical illustrations are not as numerous as in Chapters 1–3, and there is more use of the survey form of discussion to appraise the literature. This is especially the case when the empirical possibilities are being discussed. Chapter 4 takes up the central question of monetary neutrality – that is to say, of the effect of money on real variables – in a decidedly neoclassical way. The mainstream real-balance and wealth effects are discussed (mostly in a microtheoretical framework) and then some original tests of Lucas's 'two illustrations' of the quantity theory of money are offered on quarterly US data. These do not work out very well. Chapter 4 also carries a discussion of some mainstream money-growth models.

Commercial banking begins to enter the discussion in Chapter 5, where the emphasis is on the influence of monetary policy on both monetary and real variables. Chapter 4 treats the money stock as exogenously determined, but with the appearance of banks (and some recent real business-cycle theories) this is no longer feasible if only because of the presence of regulations within this sector. Chapter 6 goes into banking even more deeply and abandons the discussion of neutrality (for the most part) in favour of a return to microtheoretic topics which are more in keeping with the discussion in Chapter 1. This is a promising line of research, originated separately by Diana Hancock and William Barnett, that has only just begun to pay off empirically. This is, therefore, a very provisional discussion of a topic that I believe will receive a great deal more attention in the near future. Note, especially, that a lot of recent banking material is not discussed here, mainly because it does not fit into the line of thought of the book. *Some* is included, for reference purposes,

but only rarely in this book is anything like a complete survey attempted on any topic. Reference to effective surveys is made, however, at least when I was aware of them.

A number of original empirical tests are reported in this study, and, of course, there are data to go along with them. I had originally hoped to publish the data, but none of it is of my own creation, and , in any case, space limitations prohibit this. The main source was a very good set of real, *per-capita* monetary quantities and user costs generously made available to me by James Swofford and Gerald Whitney. They have my thanks. Other data came from a set supplied by Apostolos Serletis, and this is explained at length in our (1989) paper on 'monetary velocity'. Finally, some use was made of the quarterly data appearing in Robert Gordon's *The American Business Cycles* (1986) as updated (to 1985) by my colleague Jack Wilson. In any case, I will be happy to provide any interested party with a printout of any of this or (at cost) a micro-disk ($5\frac{1}{4}$ or $3\frac{1}{2}$) in DOS-text format (both with full explanations of sources) suitable for use in almost any conceivable software environment.

A number of people have provided significant help in the development of the material for this book, and this is the spot where I can offer my thanks. My largest debts are those to my collaborators on past or ongoing projects; these are William Barnett, Jeffrey Bernstein, Nabil Ewis, Myra McCrickard and Apostolos Serletis, to take them in alphabetical order. For the most part, their contributions are also marked in the study and it is no exaggeration to say that this work would not have been possible without their efforts. Two of my students at North Carolina State University who were particularly helpful were Gary Klonicki and Walter Coleman, both of whom were working on parallel material in the course of their PhD studies; it was extremely helpful to compare notes as we went along. Others who have read parts of the manuscript or provided comments or other contributions of particular importance are Doug Beach, Paul Johnson, Nur Onvural and John Zyren, while Allen MacDowell did those things and also served as my research assistant for several years. Finally, I want to acknowledge the work of my wife, Lois, who edited the last draft of the manuscript and Rosi H. Fudge, who saw the whole project through numerous revisions on word-processing equipment which evolved about as quickly as the manuscript.

Douglas Fisher

1

THE DEFINITION OF MONEY

1.1 INTRODUCTION

In this chapter we will consider a broad treatment of a standard topic in monetary theory – that of 'defining' an entity that is unarguably 'money' from either a theoretical or an empirical point of view. From the theoretical perspective we might wish to be able to settle on an *a priori* definition of money, i.e. settle on a list of characteristics that an item called 'money' should possess, and then turn to the data to determine the properties of the demand and supply of this entity. The empirical perspective can be established in various ways, although two approaches seem to dominate. In the first of these approaches we define some ultimate purpose, e.g. predicting the rate of inflation, and then let 'money' be the financial entity that predicts best. The concern is that *in fact* different purposes seem to require different measures of money, leaving no unique entity called 'money'. This is also a problem in the second empirical approach which favours using the 'revealed preferences' of money-holders to tell us how to define the concept in practice. The latter approach is fully illustrated in the empirical sections of this chapter, while the former surfaces from time to time throughout the book.

The *a priori* method of definition was popular among the classical economists and survives to this day, especially in money and banking textbooks. Even so, what we will discover here is that a theoretical definition of this sort – *nominalism* in technical terms – is not always fruitful in the monetary context because money is basically valued for what it does and not for what it is. This implies that at the very least we will need to extend the discussion of the definition of money to include the 'definition' of the underlying structure of an economic problem (usually a demand problem, but in this study also a supply problem). Specifically, in this context what we might want to do is define (i.e. set up) the utility function and the associated constraints of a consumer demand problem. The 'defined' measure of money, then, would emerge as one for which the statistical performance of the entire programme is satisfactory. Needless to say, both supply and demand are generally necessary to the process of definition if this is the way we intend to proceed.

We will look at this sort of work in later chapters after we have considered various structural definitions.

There are a number of more specific problems that condition the way we will approach the subject matter of this chapter. The problems that arise concern the following facts:

1. The measures of moneyness which we normally consider are inevitably aggregates.
2. Any measure we can conceive of is a joint product.
3. The broad characteristics of money are similar to those of a variety of other 'non-money' financial assets.
4. Technical change in the financial services industry affects the characteristics of money and 'non-money' in their various forms.
5. The actions of the government in picking and then attempting to influence specific definitions tend to 'force' these definitions both practically and in the sense of identifying (statistically) their demand functions.

In a nutshell, the aggregation (i.e. index number) problem in 1 and 2 , the substitutability problem in 3 and 4, the money-supply problem in 2, 3, 4, and 5, and the nature of the policy response in 5 surely preclude a purely abstract resolution to the problem of the definition of money. But there are still many important theoretical issues, as we shall see in the remainder of this chapter.

In the sections that follow in this chapter we will begin by looking over the *a priori* literature on the definition of money in order to narrow the scope of our search as much as possible. What we will do, after a brief pass at an older and more traditional literature, is set the structure of an economic problem that includes the decision to hold money. The two structures we will discuss in detail are those of the transactions and the asset approaches to money-holding. At a more fundamental level, though, the problem of the definition of money is an aggregation problem. Formally, an aggregation problem is a matter of linking microeconomic structure to macroeconomic 'empirical' definitions. We will, in this discussion, first consider some important theoretical issues and then look at some original empirical tests on the US data. The data themselves will be constructed along the lines recommended by the literature on aggregation. The objective, again, is to ferret out a useful definition of money from the point of view of the demanders of monetary services. As we shall see, though, there are still some ambiguities in this work, some of which will be addressed in later chapters.

1.2 *A PRIORI* DEFINITIONS

The precursors of the modern structural approaches to defining money, by-and-large, are the classical and neoclassical economists who sought to establish the functions or characteristics of money. According to John Stuart Mill (1848), the medium of exchange can be defined in terms of 'the principal

inconveniences which we should experience if we had not such a medium' (p. 483). He suggests the following:

1. 'The first and most obvious would be the want of a common measure for values of different sorts.'
2. 'The inconveniences of barter are so great, that without some more commodious means of effecting exchanges, the division of employments could hardly have been carried to any considerable extent.'
3. 'To the qualities which originally recommended them, another came to be added . . . they are among the least influenced by any of the causes which produce fluctuations of value.' (pp. 483–5)

Indeed: 'Money is a commodity, and its value is determined like that of other commodities, temporarily by demand and supply, permanently and on average by cost of production.' (p. 488) This point of view survives to this day in textbook discussions.

1.2.1 Transactions costs

In the classical scheme just mentioned, money is thought of as, simultaneously, a medium of exchange and a store of value (i.e. both as a transactions intermediary and as an especially liquid asset). As a medium of exchange, money is presumably valued because it lowers net transactions costs, although the next step, modelling and measuring exactly what costs are lowered, brings in many new problems. While Mill defines money so that an empirical implementation is reasonably obvious, neoclassical economists continued to try to think their way through this problem. For example, Wicksteed proposes that:

> As soon as this custom begins to be well established it will automatically extend and confirm itself, and the commodity in question will become a 'currency' or 'medium of exchange', the special characteristic of a medium of exchange being that it is accepted by a man who does not want it, or does not want it as much as what he gives for it, in order that he may exchange it for something he wants more. (1933, Vol. I, p. 136)

More conventionally, but also in somewhat the same circular manner, consider Yeager's suggestion that: 'Nothing is more ultimate than money. Instead of going out of existence, unwanted money gets passed around until it ceases to be unwanted.' (1968, p. 50) That is, the special attribute of nominal money balances as a medium of exchange is that they are indestructible in this role – unless the inflation rate reaches infinity – as long as they are 'acceptable'. In turn, I. Fisher argues:

> Any property right which is generally acceptable in exchange may be called 'money'. Its printed evidence is also called money. Hence there arise three meanings of the term money, viz. its meaning in the sense of wealth; its meaning in the sense of property; and its meaning in the sense of written evidence. From the standpoint of economic analysis the property sense is the most important. (1922, p. 5)

With this scheme, Fisher was obliged to doubt the moneyness of bank deposits since they were not especially useful as stores of value (bank failures being one consideration) and seemed generally unacceptable without the support of legal tender status. The point is generally moot, however, since legal tender status (and deposit insurance or other guarantees) have provided the legal structure that makes these dubious entities money after all.

In recent years the literature attempting to define the role of money in lowering transactions costs has passed through the filter of the Keynesians v. monetarists debate. Post-Keynesians and neo-Keynesians (e.g. Davidson, 1972 and Goodhart, 1975) have suggested that money-holding might better be directly related to uncertainty and to the resulting costs of obtaining information. This has a decidedly modern ring to it, particularly with the arrival of 'rational expectations' on the scene. However, we must be clear as to what has produced the uncertainty. For one thing, as Brunner notes:

> Uncertainty with respect to the price-level clearly presupposes money, otherwise there would be no price-level to be uncertain about; . . . Similarly, uncertainty about the timing of payments and the non-synchronous nature of payments schedules only imply the existence of an inventory problem but do not explain the concentration of these inventories on a small subset of assets. (1971, p. 6)

But information costs are another matter; indeed, Brunner and Meltzer base their case for the existence of money on its special ability to provide information to transactors. In particular, 'it is the uneven distribution of information, and not the existence of an undifferentiated uncertainty, that induces individuals to search for, and social groups to accept, alternatives to barter' (1971, p. 786). Even so, this is almost a 'unit of account' definition of money because it emphasizes that calculating in money terms reduces the 'matrix of prices' needed in order to be fully informed about relative values: 'The gain from the use of a unit of account is analogous to the gain that comes from introducing a common unit of measure such as height, weight, or temperature.' (1971, p. 787) This establishes, in one particular way, why money exists in the first place, although not why changes in its quantity might affect the economic system after the system is fully monetized.

In spite of these concerns, the 'information approach' can be made into a generic optimizing problem which solves for the optimum quantity of money, assuming that money already exists. In such a structure we can argue that an economic agent normally uses resources to obtain information ('invests in information') and then to engage in market exchanges. Since he includes this calculation in his own optimizing decisions, under certain conditions: 'The production of information is optimized when the loss in welfare due to the use of endowed resources in the production of information is matched by the gain in welfare associated with more information.' (Brunner, 1971, p. 9) The latter are associated both with the marginal utility of an improved trading position and with reduced uncertainty. On net:

> There are many stages of development between double-coincidence barter and a fully monetary economy. At some stage, a few assets are used with dominant frequency in transactions . . . Thus, money as a medium of exchange, as a transaction dominating asset, results from the opportunities offered by the distribution of incomplete information and the search by potential transactors to develop transactions chains that save resources. (Brunner and Meltzer, 1971, p. 793)

In this sense, the Brunner and Meltzer model seems particularly useful in describing the transactions demand for money in a sufficiently general way to capture many of the more specific devices that have been proposed in the literature.

Transactions models of money utilization are often very specific in the set-up stage of the problem. The prototype is the inventory-theoretic model in which 'inventories' (i.e. 'stocks') of financial assets are held, with reference (usually) to some cost-minimizing behaviour. By far the best-known of these is Baumol's (1952) version. The motivation in this early paper is, as noted, that of an inventory-control problem. The general idea is to impose a cost of liquidating one's inventory of short-term non-cash assets (which earn an interest rate of i) in addition to the interest cost foregone by holding non-interest-bearing money. The former cost is met by assuming that each withdrawal of M dollars from the bank requires the payment of a brokerage fee (b). In common-sense terms, these could be justified in terms of the cost of making trips to the bank or, even, the time used up in converting one's assets into cash. They could also be explicit brokerage fees or 'substantial penalties for early withdrawal'. If we assume that an individual pays out T dollars per unit of time, then T/M represents the velocity of cash, i.e. the number of times cash must be raised, and $b(T/M)$ the money cost of these trips. The individual's average cash holding over the interval of time in question will be $M/2$, and the cost of these holdings is $i(M/2)$ where, as noted, i represents the interest earnings foregone by holding cash. Thus, the total costs of 'liquidity' will be the sum of the two components, as given by Equation (1.1):

$$\frac{bT}{M} + \frac{iM}{2} = C \qquad (1.1)$$

The foregoing is actually an individual choice problem where the size of M, the cash balance, is the decision variable. It 'defines' money as a liquid asset, the optimal holding of which will minimize transactions costs.[1]

1.2.2 The asset approach to monetary definition

A dichotomy that we will be exploiting throughout this study is that of the contrast between transactions and asset (or utility function) approaches to the demand for money. This dichotomy begins in the definitional literature, at least in the way we are setting this up. Patinkin (1965) argues that (by

assumption) money does not reward the holder with any cash return and that while it deteriorates at the rate of inflation, so do all other assets denominated in money terms. Because these observations do not lead to any way to distinguish money from other non-interest-bearing assets (even including stores of consumer goods), Patinkin proposes the idea of a 'non-pecuniary' (and generally unobservable) return to money which is an expression of the direct services to consumers. He also provides a parallel rationale for the use of money as an input in the firm's production function. In Patinkin's work, to be precise, money is entered as an argument in the utility function, not because of any direct utility or because of any utility associated with spending money, but because of the utility associated with actually holding money. This utility is explained as the result of what happens when an individual runs out of cash:

> Assume also that an individual who runs out of cash during the week can meet the situation in one of two ways. Either he can default temporarily on any payment that he is called upon to make – a course of action that is assumed to generate some embarrassment for him; or he can replenish his balances by achieving an intraweek redemption (at their maturity value) of the bonds he holds – an action which is assumed to necessitate some extra bother on his part. (pp. 79–80)

The debate here is between putting nominal money into both the utility function (along with the price level) and the budget constraint, or putting it into the budget constraint only. This is a very controversial topic, as we shall see.

Patinkin, as just described, provides a rationale for putting money into the utility function, and in this he is following Samuelson (1974), whose view is that money is not like any other commodity and that we should insert money and the vector of money prices directly into the utility function to capture its role as an 'exchange intermediary'. The presence of the vector of money prices ensures that money will play a role roughly consistent with neoclassical thinking on the role of money (i.e. will render it 'neutral' under certain conditions). The Samuelson utility function is

$$u = U(x_1, \ldots, x_n, M, p_1, \ldots, p_n) \tag{1.2}$$

which, to complete the process of (neoclassical) definition, is assumed homogeneous of degree zero in money prices ($p_1, \ldots, p_n$) and the quantity of money (i.e. doubling these will leave the utility level unchanged); here $X_1, \ldots, X_n$ are commodities and M denotes the nominal quantity of money. This is a neutrality proposition. Patinkin's contribution, then, is to establish a special case of Samuelson's definition by replacing the list of money prices with P, the aggregate price level. It is, in a sense, the parallel macroeconomic version of Samuelson's microeconomic definition.

While Samuelson's usage is consistent with thinking of money as different from other commodities, the definitional procedure is actually so general in this case that it does not permit any of the standard neoclassical restrictions

when the properties of the resulting demand structure are analysed.[2] In particular, then, if we define the problem in the way just stated, there would be little benefit from the theoretical exercise in that little assistance exists in the form of theoretical restrictions for the (empirical) study of the role of money. An alternative, initially the work of Lloyd (1971) and Morishima (1973), is to define a utility function which is *weakly separable* in the following way:

$$u = U[\phi(x_1, \ldots, x_n), M, p_1, \ldots, p_n] \quad (1.3)$$

Here, by weak separability, we mean that the marginal rate of substitution between x_1 and x_2 is independent of changes in M and the separate money prices, although the level of satisfaction from the consumption of goods $\phi(\cdot)$, taken as a whole, is not. This function (U), which embodies the notion (as discussed above) of money being useful not for itself but for what it can purchase, is then assumed to be homogeneous of degree zero in M and $p_1, \ldots, p_n$. However, and this is really the main point, this formulation provides negative own-substitution effects and a symmetric substitution matrix. Indeed, the model possesses the properties that the sum of price-weighted substitution effects is zero and that the substitution matrix is negative semidefinite. All these properties provide potential restrictions for empirical exercises. These are, indeed, the standard restrictions of neoclassical theory.

While Equation (1.3), as a definition of (the role of) money, is comfortably neoclassical and provides a rationale for money-holding which distinguishes money from non-money, there is nothing in the formulation which precludes one from putting *any* commodity into money's position. This, then, would not seem to bring us down to things like M1 or M2, except arbitrarily, and so Clower (1967), among others, has proposed an additional restriction in the context of Equation (1.3), in the form of a second budget constraint. Assuming that individuals have net cash uses as a result of their net *purchase* of commodities $(1, \ldots, k)$, they would be constrained by

$$\sum_{i=1}^{k} p_i(x_i - x_{0i}) + M - M_0 = 0 \quad (1.4)$$

where M_0 is initial nominal money balance and the $x_i - x_{0i}$ are all positive (x_{0i} are initial endowments of commodities). At the same time, individuals will have net cash *receipts* which result from their selling of commodities in excess of their needs. This second constraint is

$$\sum_{i=k+1}^{n} p_i(x_i - x_{0i}) + m = 0 \quad (1.5)$$

and is again in nominal terms. Equation (1.4), then, is the expenditure constraint, while Equation (1.5) is the 'income' constraint in this dual-constraint framework. Here, money-holding arises because initial balances do not match expenditures (the result would be negative, typically), while m

is produced directly as a result of income-generating transactions. The utility function which goes with this conception is

$$u = U[\phi(x_1, \ldots, x_n), M, m, p_1, \ldots, p_n] \tag{1.6}$$

and, provided the utility function is homogeneous of degree zero in M, m and $p_1, \ldots, p_n$, the entire list of neoclassical restrictions can be demonstrated (see Bernstein, 1978*a*). This model thus goes at least part way towards combining the properties of the transactions and utility-function approaches to defining the role of money, although, of course, the transactions approach is not in the specific form of the inventory model.

Another line of attack employing the utility-function approach builds on the idea that money is not desired for itself, but for its *characteristics*; this time, however, it is usually financial characteristics that are stressed. The financial model generally employed in this context is the 'mean-variance', and one of the attractive features of this approach is that it also provides an easy rationale (and some theoretically inspired constraints) for simultaneous-equations tests of the demand for financial assets (including, of course, money). This approach takes the view that money is one among a number of assets and that the wealth-holder makes his choices among these assets on the basis of their perceived characteristics. If, as in the finance literature on capital assets, we suppose that the characteristics of most interest to the wealth-holder are the expected return (E) on each asset and the variation (V) in the expected return, then the former would provide utility and the latter disutility, taken by themselves. Of course, assets are not considered individually but are taken as 'portfolios', in which case there is the additional possibility of exploiting the covariation among assets to lower risk (*ceteris paribus*).

To be specific, the wealth-holder can be presumed to be attempting both to combine various assets into potential portfolios and then to pick the best of these portfolios, the best being the one which maximizes his expected utility. What we have said amounts to the assumption that the representative wealth-holder will maximize a utility function such as Equation (1.7).

$$u = U(E, V) \qquad (U_1 > 0, U_2 < 0) \tag{1.7}$$

The next step in the process of defining the role of money in this paradigm is to set down some specific utility function – preferably a quadratic – which is, at the same time, consistent with assets whose returns are normally distributed (and hence can be described completely by the first two moments of their distributions). Such a utility function, utilizing π for the expected return, is

$$u = a - c\exp(-b\pi) \tag{1.8}$$

where a, b and c are positive constants. The problem becomes that of finding measures for the mean and the variance of the portfolio of assets, where each of the assets is normally distributed. Necessarily, then, in this multivariate problem, there is a variance–covariance structure to consider, since covari-

ation between expected asset returns can raise or lower portfolio variation, depending on its sign. The result is a simultaneous-equations problem, where the resulting demand for asset functions is well-structured in the sense that appropriate restrictions are applied at the estimation stage. That is, symmetry, negative own-rate effects, and Cournot and Engle aggregation all hold in this model and can be imposed and/or tested for their significance. Here money does not enter the utility function directly but is only one among a number of assets which possess return and risk in varying degrees (and with varying degrees of interaction among them). This might seem a less objectionable rationale than the direct utility-function approach, and it has the significant advantage that the powerful apparatus of demand-systems analysis can be applied. But we must still measure the yield on money – and money is still primarily a 'transactions asset' – in order to implement this approach. Furthermore, as we shall see, it is possible to employ the *general* demand-systems approach without resort to the restrictive mean-variance paradigm, and so this method has generally been used in the literature to explain what is going on, rather than to provide direct tests. This is a pity since it would provide a good empirical benchmark but, in any case, we will return to the model and spell out some of the details in Chapter 3 as the starting point for our discussion of the better-received demand-systems models just referred to.

1.2.3 The equivalence of transactions and utility approaches

In the preceding two sections we have operated on the assumption that transactions-cost and utility-function approaches are broadly incompatible with each other and thus present a choice to the researcher looking for a specific starting point for his monetary analysis. In one sense this is patently absurd since if duality holds for the representative consumer, then the appropriate 'dual' to the consumer's utility function is the cost function from a 'household production function' structure – and transactions-costs would play a direct role there. But this is too casual a comment to stand by itself – and feelings run high on this issue – so it is just as well to step back a little and consider the dispute over money's utility before discussing an important recent paper by Feenstra (1986) which actually solves for such a duality.[3]

The objection to inserting money directly into the utility function has come primarily from the Keynesians and neo-Keynesians. We have already noted that money 'falls out' of many of the inventory models and that this has established what is almost a prejudice in this literature against anything that looks as if it arises from a framework in which money provides direct utility. Clower, whose work (1967) begins this alternative tradition, may well be reacting to the fact that the Samuelson–Patinkin model will not provide a distinctive role for money, but the resulting paradigms go deeper than that. One procedure, as we have seen, is to invoke weak separability, but another is

to force money into the constraints, 'we now define a money economy as a system involving at least one money commodity but a non-transitive exchange relation' (p. 206). The particular non-transitivity he suggests is the 'cash-in-advance' constraint, whereby consumption expenditures in period t are constrained by the cash available at the start of the period (presumably having been generated in the previous period). In this framework: 'The distinction between money and other commodities is thus a matter not of degree but of kind.' (p. 207) In the Samuelson–Patinkin framework, on the other hand, it is clearly a matter of degree. In any case, if one allows agents to choose the frequency of sales and purchases as well as the timing of transactions, 'commonly accepted comparative-statics propositions about the demand for money are of dubious validity except in cases that are too specialized to be of serious practical interest' (Clower and Howitt, 1978, p. 450). Feenstra, as we shall see, does not agree.

The cash-in-advance constraint has survived as a device for modelling monetary dynamics, thanks largely to the work of Lucas and Stokey (1987) and Sargent (1987). But money-growth models continue to use a utility-function methodology in spite of what is now almost a tradition of dissent in this literature. There are two sorts of money-growth model for which there is a developed literature. One is monetarist in style, with adaptive expectations and with monetary non-neutrality (as a consequence). The standard work here is by Sidrauski (1967*a*), and there are other papers by Fischer (1977), Turnovsky (1977*a*, 1977*b*), and many others who continue the line of research. The second line taken is that of assuming 'perfect foresight' and generating results relevant to the neutrality debate. The initiating paper here is by Brock (1974) and there are later contributions by Fischer (1979), Obstfeld (1984), and others, which pursue the topic. Here it turns out to be important to stability and uniqueness – and certainly to neutrality – whether or not money and consumption goods are separable from each other. We will discuss some of the broad findings of this literature below and in Chapters 2 and 3, with much of the explicit growth material contained in Chapter 4. We should note that separability has already been an issue in our discussion and will even present us with an empirical dimension later in this chapter.

Returning, then, to Feenstra's (1986) discussion, let us go back to the question of the conditions under which we can regard the two approaches to defining money as equivalent. What Feenstra does is construct a general class of liquidity-cost functions and then demonstrate an exact duality between this class and a broad class of utility functions (containing real balances). We are interested in the details of this derivation since it will tell us what functions are included in these sets and also in some of the theoretical conclusions. The chief casualty of this general approach seems to be the separability of the money-holding decision from the consumption decision. In view of the difficulty, reported below, of establishing this separability on recent empirical data, this may not be perceived as too great a cost to pay, at least ultimately.

The framework for the transactions and precautionary models is that of liquidity costs (usually transactions costs).[4] Let the consumer maximize the intertemporal utility function

$$\sum_{t=0}^{\infty} \delta^t U(c_t) \tag{1.9}$$

where δ is a discount rate, subject to

$$c_t + \phi(c_t, m_t) + b_t + m_t = w_t + [(1 + i_{t-1})b_{t-1} + m_{t-1}]\left(\frac{P_{t-1}}{P_t}\right) \tag{1.10}$$

The 'sources' on the right-hand side of Equation (1.10) consist of wage (and non-interest) income in w_t and the value of real bond-holdings (incremented by the nominal interest rate (i) carried over from period $t - 1$). The expression

$$(1 + i_{t-1})\left(\frac{P_{t-1}}{P_t}\right)$$

is equal to $(1+r_{t-1})$ where r_{t-1} is the real interest rate and P_{t-1}/P_t is the inverse of the inflation rate. The function $\phi(c_t, m_t)$ is, of course, the real liquidity cost function, and its properties are what this exercise is all about. Presumably, consumption raises real liquidity costs and money-holding reduces them (so that $\phi_c \geq 0$ and $\phi_m \leq 0$); it is also reasonable to assert that there are constant or rising real liquidity costs from consumption ($\phi_{cc} \geq 0$) and constant or diminishing real benefits from money-holding ($\phi_{mm} \geq 0$). As for the cross-effect, Feenstra assumes a diminishing marginal rate of substitution between money benefits and consumption costs (so that $\phi_{mc} \leq 0$).

To make money seem different from consumption, Feenstra applies the following restriction:

$$\phi(0, m_t) = 0$$

This asserts that if there is no consumption there will be no liquidity costs; this is certainly reasonable. Furthermore, but on a slightly less general note, he assumes that the 'subfunction' on the left of Equation (1.10) is itself quasiconvex with non-negatively sloped expansion paths.

Feenstra demonstrates (in detail) that the Baumol (1952)–Tobin (1956) model, the Barro integral constraint model (1976), and Whalen's precautionary demand model (1966) are all special cases of the general liquidity structure just laid out. What we then need to do, in order to understand how the two approaches mesh, is establish exactly what is meant by the 'functional equivalence' of the foregoing with the utility-function approach. For the utility-function approach let the consumer be assumed to maximize

$$\sum_{t=0}^{\infty} \delta^t V(x_t, m_t) \tag{1.11}$$

subject to $x_t + b_t + m_t = y_t$. Here y_t is just the right-hand side of Equation (1.10) and x_t is real consumption. Clearly, Equation (1.9) is equivalent to Equation (1.11) in an economic sense if it generates equal utilities for all c_t, m_t and x_t, i.e. if $U(c_t) \equiv V(x_t, m_t)$. The budget constraints, in turn, are equivalent if $c_t + \phi(c_t, m_t) = x_t$, where x_t is 'gross consumption'. Combining these ideas, then, the equivalence between the two approaches would hold if the following is true for the utility functions:

$$U(c_t) \equiv V[c_t + \phi(c_t, m_t), m_t] \tag{1.12}$$

for all c_t, m_t. In effect, this is a working definition of equivalence for the two structures.

Feenstra takes one further step to eliminate U in Equation (1.12). Defining the utility function $W(x_t, m_t) \equiv U^{-1}[V(x_t, m_t)]$, Equation (1.12) can be rewritten as

$$c_t \equiv W[c_t + \phi(c_t, m_t), m_t] \tag{1.13}$$

This device simplifies the structure while permitting us to recover $V(\cdot)$ if we wish.[5] In effect, $U(c_t)$ has been replaced by the realization c_t, while the function U has been retained in the definition of $W(\cdot)$.

To establish equivalence, we must impose conditions on W, the derived utility function from the 'utility of money' problem. In a fashion parallel to that in the general transactions model, money here is assumed to generate positive or zero utility ($W \geq 0$) and to provide no utility if consumption is zero [$W(0, m_t) = 0$]. Consumption also provides positive marginal utilities ($W_x > 0$), but this is assumed to be bounded from above ($W_x \leq 1$). The conditions on the second derivatives are conventional ($W_{xx} \leq 0$, $W_{mm} \leq 0$, $W_{xm} \geq 0$); finally, the function W is assumed to have quasi-concave Engel curves with non-negative slopes.[6] The overall result is very straightforward: 'If the liquidity costs $\phi(c_t, m_t)$ satisfy [the first set of assumptions] then there exists an equivalent utility function $W(x_t, m_t)$ satisfying [the second set of assumptions], and conversely.' (Feenstra, p. 281) We have pointed out that the Baumol–Tobin/Barro/Whalen models all meet this condition – moving from transactions to utility functions – and Feenstra provides demonstrations. More to the point, perhaps, $W(\cdot)$ is certainly a general enough utility framework for most tastes, so this is a satisfactory general result.

To see how this might work, consider the Baumol–Tobin example. Feenstra demonstrates that this satisfies the first set of assumptions. The next task, then, is to generate a set of utility functions directly and to verify that they have the properties of the second set of assumptions. In the *B–T* model real average liquidity costs are $kc_t/2m_t$ as in the first part of Equation (1.1) above. In this case x_t, total expenditures, are

$$x_t = c_t + \frac{kc_t}{2m_t} \quad \text{or} \quad c_t = \frac{x_t}{1 + (k/2m_t)} \tag{1.14}$$

The utility function $V(\cdot)$ is then

$$V(x_t, m_t) = U(c_t) = U\left(\frac{x_t}{1 + (k/2m_t)}\right) \tag{1.15}$$

This function directly meets the conditions for the consumer's optimum.[7] This is hardly the most general transactions model available (see Feenstra for more general results), but at least it shows how the theorem is applied.

This is a very useful demonstration, since it certainly narrows the range of dispute among the transactions v. asset approaches and leaves the researcher generally free to pick his strategy depending on the nature of the problem at hand. In particular, the following hold, as Feenstra demonstrates:

1. Neutrality propositions (in the form of linear-homogeneity restrictions) apply across structures that satisfy both sets of conditions.
2. Models with money in the (household) production function will produce nearly identical results with those having money in the utility function.
3. Clower's cash-in-advance structure is a special case of a utility function with real money balances in it.[8]

This last is interesting since part of Clower's motivation for using the cash-in-advance constraint is to avoid placing money in the utility function.

1.2.4 Money in the production function

The 'supply side' analogue of putting money into the utility function is, of course, that of giving it a role to play in the production process. Roughly speaking, these formulations stand as generalizations of the inventory-theoretic models already introduced in this chapter, but in any case, they are structured at a level of generality that fits in well with the definitional material of this chapter. Our discussion here is drawn from a paper by Fischer (1974) which generalizes the inventory-theoretic models of Baumol (1952), Tobin (1956), and Miller and Orr (1966, 1968). Here we begin by defining a production function of the form

$$y = f(K, L_p) \tag{1.16}$$

where L_p defines the labour used in production. The business firm is constrained by Equation (1.16) and by three other relations which define the role of money in the precise way that this literature favours. The first of these, in Equation (1.17), divides total labour effort into 'productive' and 'transactions' components:

$$L_p + L_T = L \tag{1.17}$$

The second constraint, Equation (1.18), relates the time spent on transactions directly to the number of transactions (n):

$$L_T = \beta n \tag{1.18}$$

and the third, Equation (1.19), relates average money-holdings to the ratio of net operating revenues (revenues less production costs) to the number of transactions:

$$\bar{M} = \frac{R}{n} \tag{1.19}$$

Here, it should be noticed, $n = R/\bar{M}$ is, in effect, the velocity of money in this model. After combining the constraints and substituting into Equation (1.16), we have the overall constraint of

$$y = f\left[K, L - \left(\frac{1}{\beta}\frac{\bar{M}}{R}\right)^{-1}\right] \tag{1.20}$$

Thus money is 'in' the production function not in its own right but as a result of collapsing and substituting in the constraints. This formulation is then employed in a profit-maximizing framework to produce a demand for money for the business firm; this profit-maximizing expression is

$$\pi = Pf\left[K, L - \left(\frac{1}{\beta}\frac{\bar{M}}{R}\right)^{-1}\right] - w_K K - w_L L - w_m \frac{\bar{M}}{R} \tag{1.21}$$

where the w_i are the money prices attached to the three inputs. Indeed, as will be pointed out in detail in Chapter 6, while L and K interact through the production mechanism, L and M do so through the transactions process; here, M and K do not interact at all.

1.3 EMPIRICAL APPROACHES TO THE DEFINITION OF MONEY

As the foregoing has demonstrated, the way we define money in an *a priori* sense depends a great deal on the theoretical problem at hand. In telling our story we have insisted on having money 'definitions' precede the derivation of any demand for money function (we did not derive these explicitly). That is, we have laid out our *a priori* search in terms of the definition of a utility/production structure and then provided the statement of (or the 'definition of') a role for transactions balance or liquid financial assets, either as a direct contributor to utility and/or as an entity in the constraints. This approach has many detractors, especially if money somehow winds up in the utility function, and so an alternative approach has been made available in the index number (or aggregation theory) literature. This literature is 'micro-foundations': that it goes back to first principles while at the same time it has a macropolicy-dimension since monetary policy must work with a carefully-defined definition of money. We will begin with the policy discussion, actually, and play, for the first time, the 'money supply' theme of this study.[9]

In any complete discussion of monetary policy we begin by defining both the objectives and instruments of policy. For the instruments (e.g. open-

market operations) there do not seem to be any serious conceptual problems, but for the objectives, since the concepts discussed are generally aggregates, e.g. of the rate of change of consumer prices, unemployment rates, and the rate of growth of real gross national product (GNP), we generally need to consider further the basic index number problem that arises when (constructed) aggregates are used for policy purposes. Here we are not interested in the actual objectives, of course, but there is a financial variable – the quantity of money – which turns out to be central to the policy discussion because it is an intermediate variable in the usual policy scenario. By 'intermediate' we mean that it appears in a financial market that is directly affected by, say, open-market operations and through which policy influences reach the objective variables (e.g. reach unemployment, inflation, etc.).

In a sense, the monetary aggregates (e.g. M1, M2) are basically indicators of what we might provisionally call the stock of 'moneyness' in the economy. We are, then, led to adopt an empirical approach to the resulting definitional problem because of the heterogeneous nature of monetary products. Indeed, transactions accounts and savings accounts have different blends of the underlying characteristics of money – as mediators in exchange or as stores of value – and so a viable approach would be to utilize received consumer theory in the search for a useful 'indicator' of monetary services. Upon identification of the entity, we could then propose to control it by means of a direct policy instrument. This is the policy interest discussed in this chapter.

1.3.1 The aggregation of monetary assets

The present practice in most countries is to classify certain bank and public sector financial liabilities arbitrarily as either 'narrow' money (M1) – that is, balances that can be used for transactions purposes – or 'broad' money (M2, M3), where the latter usually include M1 plus savings (and time) deposits and other accounts on which drafts usually cannot be written directly. On occasion very large denomination deposits are included in monetary measures, even though it is admitted that the users are generally not individuals but business firms looking for a competitive return on funds that are accumulating frequently for some financial purpose. All these measures (M1, M2, etc.) are frequently redefined by the authorities, usually because the monetary measure shows – or is expected to show – 'erratic' behaviour in the face of institutional or technological changes (such as the introduction of automatic transfers among accounts). Indeed, the dominant reasons for this have recently been financial innovations that have, it seems, changed the basic characteristics of various financial commodities and, it is often alleged, actually increased substitutability among many of these entities.

The aggregates just described are the most straightforward conceivable, being merely simple sums of their components (e.g. $M1 = C + D$). They are also incredibly naïve measures of the stock of moneyness and, one hardly exaggerates, it is an act of almost boundless faith to construct aggregates

merely by adding together the various components, without employing index number theory in their construction. It might be hoped, of course, that for a certain time and place we might find a suitably close relation between the components, but, for the USA at least, 'the simple sum M1 aggregate is the only official monetary aggregate whose behaviour even remotely approximates that of a well-designed index number' (Barnett, 1984, pp. 165–6). Even M1 is not always effective from this point of view (and the authorities often put weight on M2 and M3 if M1 looks particularly shaky for any reason) and so policy mistakes will occur that can materially reduce the effectiveness of policy, to be polite about it.[10]

The issue at hand is substitutability among the potential assets since: 'It is well known in aggregation theory that aggregation by simple summation is valid only when aggregating over goods that are perfect substitutes.' (Barnett, 1984, p. 165) The main problem with the simple-sum index is that in aggregation theory, while a quantity index should actually measure the income effects of a relative price change, it should, at the same time, be unresponsive to substitution effects which the index should internalize. However, the simple-sum index cannot produce that decomposition unless the component assets are *perfect* substitutes.[11] It seems that these relative prices do, indeed, actually change significantly (see the discussion in Chapter 3). Friedman and Schwartz put the problem as follows:

> This [summation] procedure is a very special case of the more general approach . . . In brief, the general approach consists of regarding each asset as a joint product having different degrees of 'moneyness', and defining the quantity of money as the weighted sum of the aggregate value of all assets, the weights for individual assets varying from zero to unity with a weight of unity assigned to that asset or assets regarded as having the largest quantity of 'moneyness' per dollar of aggregate value . . . The more general approach has been suggested frequently but experimented with only occasionally. We conjecture that this approach deserves and will get much more attention that it has so far received. (1970, pp. 151–2)

Provided that it is recognized that non-linear weights would be needed (because even weighted aggregation implies perfect substitutability), this is a reasonable 'call to action'.

We can approach this topic either by means of a system of demand equations for the various assets – measuring the relevant elasticities of substitution and plotting the behaviour over time – or, for practical purposes, by means of the construction of the 'ideal' indices of monetary quantities (the Divisia or Fisher ideal indices), where ideal indices are those that are based on (i.e. approximate) the true indices suggested by microeconomic (aggregation) theory. We will pursue both these topics in the remainder of this section, admitting, of course, that 'demand theory' has invaded the definitional problem. It has intruded, basically, because we are employing economic analysis in order to arrive at a monetary 'definition' for policy purposes. However, we will not get into the specific properties of the macroeconomic

demand for money in this discussion, but will reserve that topic for later chapters.

The representative consumer can be assumed to maximize

$$u_t = U_t(\mathbf{c}_t, \ldots, \mathbf{c}_{t+T}; \mathbf{x}_t, \ldots, \mathbf{x}_{t+T}; B_{t+T}) \tag{1.22}$$

where **c** and **x** are vectors of consumer goods and financial commodities (the former flows, the latter stocks) and B is a long-term bond that has no moneyness to it (it is used to facilitate the transfer of wealth among time periods); T defines the agent's horizon. The suitable constraint, of course, is a dynamic one, but rather than complicate things, we can invoke the standard collapsibility theorem (see Barnett, 1981); i.e. if a multiperiod utility function is maximized subject to some appropriate set of intertemporal wealth constraints, assuming that optimal plans are revised every period, there exists a one-period utility function that if maximized subject to a single wealth constraint yields a set of demand functions that trace out the time path. This produces the following problem for the current period:

$$u_t = U(c_1, \ldots, c_n; x_1, \ldots, x_n) \tag{1.23}$$

with

$$\sum_{j=1}^{n} p_j c_j + \sum_{i=1}^{m} \pi_i x_i = M'_t \tag{1.24}$$

where M'_t defines current resources and π_i is the nominal 'user cost' associated with the ith financial commodity.[12] This last is based on the representative non-money asset (B_{t+T}) that appears in Equation (1.22), and, for the ith nominal asset is

$$\pi_{it} = \bar{p}_t\left(\frac{r_t^* - r_{it}}{1 + r_t^*}\right) \tag{1.25}$$

where r_t^* identifies the expected yield on the bond (B), r_{it} is the yield on the ith asset, and $\bar{p}_t$ is the true cost-of-living index. This is one way of getting at the marginal opportunity cost of holding a monetary asset – comparing it with an alternative asset (B) that actually provides no 'pecuniary' services. If the individual uses money and foregoes interest, then the foregone interest is the user cost (which is equal, at the margin, to the value of the pecuniary services). Although this idea will be made more precise in Chapter 3, it should be emphasized that this concept is derived directly from an intertemporal choice problem and is not just an arbitrary opportunity cost (Barnett, 1978).

If we do not wish to estimate the larger demand system implied by Equations (1.23)–(1.25), we can further assume weak separability between the financial assets and the consumption goods; this, at least, is what the literature usually does.[13] We can, then, estimate (simultaneously) a set of monetary-demand equations for the components of M1, M2, etc., where the

structure of the problem is to maximize

$$u_t = U_t(x_{1t}, \ldots, x_{mt}) \tag{1.26}$$

subject to

$$\sum_{i=1}^{m} \pi_{it} x_{it} - M_t = 0 \tag{1.27}$$

where M_t represents the resources devoted to this class of commodities.[14] The simultaneity will be recognized by imposing the standard restrictions of consumer theory, and the aggregation across consumers can be checked by testing the significance of the aggregation on various proposed collections of financial commodities (e.g. currency, demand deposits, and Negotiable Order of Withdrawal accounts); the separability is also testable, either by direct means (in this chapter) or in conjunction with a specific functional form (see the discussion in Chapter 3).[15] If all goes well, i.e. if the coefficients are well determined, etc., and if the aggregation across consumers goes through, then the derived elasticities of substitution among the financial commodities can be examined to determine those that might reasonably be aggregated. We will look at work on this topic in Chapter 3.

1.3.2 Index number approaches

In this literature – whether or not the aggregation across consumers has been checked – the results generally suggest that the elasticities are too low (and too unstable) for simple-sum aggregations, even of M1, to be safe indicators of what final users think money is.[16] The implication is that the index must be constructed using a weighted average, where, we will argue, the weights are those suggested by superlative index number theory.

The superlative index approach to defining a monetary indicator is based on economic theory; its purpose is to achieve as rigorous a measure of moneyness as possible, given that we can never expect to construct a perfect measure. The basic problem here is studied under the congruent headings of the 'composite goods theorem' or 'the index number problem'. In order to construct an aggregate that obeys the laws of microeconomic theory (negative substitution elasticities, symmetrical preferences, etc.), the following is a necessary and sufficient condition: 'A collection of physical things can always be treated as if they were divisible into units of a single commodity so long as their relative prices can be assumed to be unchanged, in the particular problem at hand.' (Hicks, 1946, p. 33) In short, when prices change (the only interesting case), those changes must be equiproportionate among the elements of the aggregate.[17] Failing this, at some level (statistically), the constructed entity will have no meaning in economic theory and will be a treacherous element in any policy design as a target, as an indicator, or (of course) as the dependent variable in a demand for money function. The problem is that of an 'unstable' definition (Barnett, 1980) which can translate

into an unstable policy (or demand for money function) quite apart from any destabilizing actions of economic agents.

The current procedure used by the authorities in all countries with monetary policies is that of constructing the simple-sum aggregates we described above. We have argued that this is most likely to produce unsatisfactory numbers and we have also suggested that empirical studies sometimes confirm this. The next best approach would be to construct arbitrary weights based on budget shares at some base period (a Laspeyres index); the problem in this case is that after a price change, because of the substitution effect, the old budget shares will not reflect the actual economic decisions taken when setting new prices. The theoretical answer is to employ aggregation theory in which aggregator functions are constructed; in the case of consumers this aggregator function is in effect a representative utility function. What we do is estimate the parameters of the utility functions – assuming, arbitrarily, some specific functional form – in order to be able to construct weights for the price index at relative prices that differ from the original ones; the quantity index is the 'dual' of this price index. The problem is that the true utility/aggregator function is unknown, as are the details of its best parameterization, so that the appearance of instability of the index can re-enter the problem.[18] The Laspeyres index, in this case, can be interpreted as a linear approximation of the true but unknown aggregator function, but it is not necessarily a very good approximation although it could easily be better than the simple-sum 'index' generally employed by the monetary authorities. 'Better', in this case, means for 'practical purposes'.

It is here that we might consider a formulation in terms of 'ideal' statistical index number theory; this approach is designed to provide higher-order approximations to the underlying aggregator functions. The statistical approach, to put the cart before the horse, has the following properties:

1. The index numbers do not depend upon any unknown parameters.
2. There is no need to specialize the underlying utility function.
3. The statistical index is a function of both prices and quantities.[19]

Among the potentially large class of superlative indices, the Fisher ideal and the Divisia stand out. Of these two the Divisia has a particularly straightforward interpretation; for one thing: 'Hulten . . . has proved that in continuous time the Divisia is always exact for any consistent (. . . weakly separable) aggregator function. Hence, no index number can be better than the Divisia in continuous time.' (Barnett, 1981, p. 221) Even so, the Divisia has problems, the most notable of which being that it requires the underlying preference function to be homothetic (i.e. have unitary income elasticities for the various commodity demands). There are alternatives, such as McKenzie and Pearce's (1976, 1980) 'money metric', but so far these have not been implemented in the monetary literature.

The Divisia is constructed as follows. For M_{it} being the quantity of financial asset i at time period t, then the share of M_{it} of total 'expenditures'

in the class of financial assets is (in discrete time)

$$S_{it} = \frac{\pi_{it} M_{it}}{\sum_{j=1}^{n} \pi_{jt} M_{jt}} \tag{1.28}$$

Here π is the user cost defined in Equation (1.25). In continuous time the Divisia index would be the line integral of the differential

$$\mathrm{d}\log M = \sum_{i=1}^{n} S_i \,\mathrm{d}\log M_i \tag{1.29}$$

In discrete time we could approximate Equation (1.28) with

$$S_{it}^{*} = \frac{S_{it} + S_{it-1}}{2}$$

and then the Divisia would be constructed from

$$\log M_t - \log M_{t-1} = \sum_{i=1}^{n} S_{it}^{*}(\log M_{it} - \log M_{it-1}) \tag{1.30}$$

It is this formulation (the Törnqvist approximation) that has the theoretical and statistical backing to measure 'moneyness', once we have settled on a class of representative assets. It should be noted again that the weights here (in Equation (1.28)) depend on both prices and quantities and that the prices are user costs, reflecting, in effect, the opportunity costs of holding monetary financial assets relative to some benchmark non-monetary asset.

Does using a Divisia index make a difference to money as a target, as an indicator or as an input into, e.g. the demand for money? For some problems it does. Barnett (1980) shows that some apparent shifts in the demand for money in the USA are removed if a Divisia rather than a simple-sum index is employed. In a test of the velocity function for the USA, however, Fisher and Serletis (1989) do not find substantial differences, at least among the transactions measures; a variation on that paper is discussed in Chapter 5. In another test, this time of money as a potential target, Barnett and Spindt (1979), show that the information content of the Divisia dominates the simple sum. Barnett (1984) shows that the differences as indicators between Divisia and simple-sum estimates of M1 and, especially, M2 and M3 are considerable on recent US data. This should alarm anyone who relies on any of these money stock indicators for almost any conceivable purpose.

While we are on the topic of monetary indices, we might briefly consider an entry due to Spindt (1985), who recommends the use of a velocity-weighted monetary index. Spindt suggests that the natural way to think of money is provided by the equation of exchange ($MV = PQ$) since it recognizes the role of money as a means of payment. Of course, a number of liquid assets function as means of payment; indeed, Spindt argues that there are six in the US data.[20] Each of these turns over a number of times ($V_i = PQ/M_i$) during the payments period, and this turnover is a good indicator of the asset's use

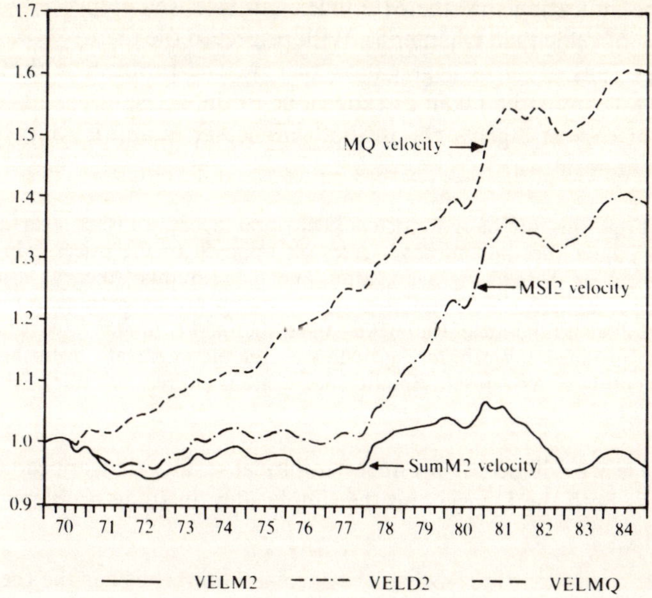

Figure 1.1 Velocity in the USA.

as a means of payment. Quite naturally, then, a direct way to measure the quantity of the aggregate 'means of payment' is to weight each of the six components by its 'velocity share'. The following formula, employing the Fisher ideal index, reproduces the formula for Spindt's MQ or monetary quantities index. Thus

$$\frac{Q_t}{Q_{t-1}} = \left[\frac{\sum_{i=1}^{n} w_{i,t-1}(x_{it}/x_{i,t-1})}{\sum_{i=1}^{n}(x_{i,t-1}/x_{it})} \right]^{1/2} \tag{1.31}$$

where

$$w_{it} = \frac{v_{it}x_{it}}{\sum_{k=1}^{n} v_{kt}x_{kt}}$$

and v_{it} is the turnover rate of monetary asset i during period t. As Spindt says, 'money is what money does' and what it does is 'turn over' as it services the flow of monetary payments.

Whatever other claims can be made about the MQ index, one thing seems clear: it is different. Spindt demonstrates this on US monthly data and so do we in Figure 1.1, employing quarterly US data. When faced with a necessary choice like this, economists generally resort to one or both of the following: they investigate the theoretical foundations of the proposal, or they evaluate its effectiveness in an empirical context (such as one in which 'money is what money does'). Spindt does not really do either of these things, but there is at

least some indication that the MQ index can fare well empirically (see the discussion of velocity in Chapter 5). With respect to the theory, however, the MQ index runs afoul of aggregation theory. The problem is that money turnover rates must be taken as exogenous to the decision unit, and this is simply not correct; agents choose both monetary quantities and turnover rates.[21] The result is:

> Without rigorous internally consistent behavioral theory, a Fisher ideal index in monetary quantities and turnover rates (as opposed to the prices, which fall directly out of the existing aggregation and index number theory) is just an arbitrary combination of component quantities and turnover rates. An infinite number of such functions of monetary quantities and turnover rates exist, and they can produce any arbitrary growth rate for the aggregate from the same component data. As a result, Spindt's aggregate is entirely arbitrary. (Barnett, 1987, p. 163)

Even so, as we will see, it produces empirical results that appear to be as effective as both the Divisia and the simple sum (in some problems (on the US data)).

1.3.3 The revealed preference approach to monetary aggregation

The foregoing uses microeconomic theory to support the construction of monetary aggregates and does so in a way that reduces the need to parameterize the construction. That is, the Laspeyres and Paasche indices use base or final period weights (i.e. parameters) and thus are vulnerable on this account. The Divisia, on the other hand, provides a theoretically satisfactory (second-degree) non-parametric measure in that the weights are variable (they are price shares in the case of monetary quantity indices). However, there is another way to proceed which leans even more heavily on the theory of consumer choice; this is to employ revealed preference theory to design a test that (ideally) gives us information on definition in a very broad sense. In particular, we can use the actual monetary data and their respective user costs to see which grouping of the many potential monetary assets has been used by money-holders in practice. In a word, we seek to find well-behaved, consistent (in a revealed-preference sense) sets of assets and then, among these sets, to locate separable groupings, if they can be shown to exist. One of these subsets could, conceivably, be a standard measure of money (e.g. M1) although, in fact, this is not the case, as we shall see.

What we would try to do then, is to identify (define?) a set of primary assets, such as currency + demand deposits, time deposits, and consumer goods, for which the general axiom of revealed preference (GARP) is satisfied at some reasonable level of statistical significance, and then identify subsets, such as the following two:

I. Currency + demand deposits + time deposits
II. Consumer durables

for which consumer goods are weakly separable from the others, or, at least, approximately so. This structure would justify the separation of the financial allocation decision from the consumption decision, the use of a systems approach to study the demands for the two (or more) financial products in Set I, as well as the construction of an ideal index of financial services from the same set. These are interrelated topics and will be the subject of the rest of this section and substantial parts of Chapters 3, 5, and 6, in a variety of subject areas.

The most obvious advantage in taking the actual market data generated by the consumers of financial services and applying revealed preference theory is that the approach is non-parametric. As we will see in Chapters 2 and 3, pursuing the *a priori* approach of Section 1.2 gets the researcher involved in picking a specific function with which he then must live, in the sense that it will be jointly tested with his primary hypothesis. Even the so-called flexible functional forms (of Chapter 3) have some level of parameterization, which is why, after all, they are sometimes referred to as semi-non-parametric functional forms. But while the GARP test imposes no functional form restrictions, it is not without problems, as we shall see.

The original work on the revealed preference approach is by Afriat (1967), although we will be using Varian's (1983) technique and, more specifically, his computational package (NONPAR) when we turn to the numbers. In this formulation, a vector of goods $\mathbf{x}^i$ is directly revealed to be preferred to a second bundle $\mathbf{x}^j$ written $\mathbf{x}^i \, R\mathbf{x}^j$ if

$$\mathbf{p}^j\mathbf{x}^j \leq \mathbf{p}^j\mathbf{x}^i$$

for $i, j = 1, \ldots, n$ (i.e. what we are saying here is that the set of choices $\mathbf{x}^i$ is revealed to be preferred to $\mathbf{x}^j$ if the expenditures on $\mathbf{x}^i$ exceed or are equal to those on $\mathbf{x}^j$, evaluated at the original set of prices, where i and j vary over all possible combinations). In practice, then, all pairs in the data (which are, of course, finite) must be evaluated in order to see if the expenditures on $\mathbf{x}^i$, evaluated at $\mathbf{p}^j$, are greater than those on $\mathbf{x}^i$, evaluated at the same price (for all i, j). Recall, in thinking about this, that a typical application is an economic time series so that i, j refer to dates (not necessarily consecutive dates). As we shall see, the number of violations (reversals of the inequality) can be considerable if the data sets contain assets held by different sorts of economic agents (as possibly in consumers v. business firms).

To see how Varian's GARP test might look in practice, consider the set of 'primary' financial products shown in Table 1.1.[22] We note that M1 consists of assets 1–6 and M2, 1–18, less a consolidation calculation. Each of these assets has an associated price (i.e. user cost). The data set also includes data on various categories of consumption and leisure (the former evaluated at their respective price levels and the latter at the wage rate, both discounted as in Diewert (1974*a*)). In the following results, *per capita*, real, seasonally adjusted quantities represent the quantity, and user costs, calculated according to Equation (1.25), represent the price.

Table 1.1 Money-stock definitions, US data

No.	Code	Description
1	CUR	Currency plus travellers cheques
2	DDCON	Household demand deposits
3	DDBUS	Business demand deposits
4	OCD	Other checkable deposits less NOW accounts
5	SNOWC	Super NOW accounts at commercial banks
6	SNOWT	Super NOW accounts at thrift institutions
7	ONRP	Net overnight repurchase agreements at banks
8	ONED	Net overnight Eurodollars
9	MMF	Money market mutual fund shares
10	MMDAC	Money market deposit accounts at banks
11	MMDAT	Money market deposit accounts at thrifts
12	SDCB	Savings deposits less MMDAs at banks
13	SDSL	Savings deposits less MMDAs at Savings and Loans
14	SDSB	Savings deposits less MMDAs at savings banks
15	SDCU	Savings deposits less MMDAs at credit unions
16	STDCB	Small time deposits at commercial banks
17	STDTH	Small time deposits at thrifts
18	STDCU	Small time deposits at credit unions

Table 1.2 Results of GARP test, US monetary components (1970–1 through 1985–2)

Set of components		Assets	Violations
I	Assets in M1	1+2, 3, 4, 5+6	36
II	Assets in M2	1+2, 3, 4, 5+6, 7, 8, 9, 10, 11, 12, 13, 14+15, 16, 17, 18	37
III	M1+durable consumption	1+2, . . . , 5+6, durable consumption	23
IV	M2+durable consumption	1+2, . . . , 18, durable consumption	11

Note: The summed assets had identical or nearly identical user costs.

The first test employed is Varian's (1983) GARP. The procedure supplied by Varian provides an overall judgement as well as a list of the observations that fail to satisfy the general axiom of revealed preference. For the items listed in Table 1.1 we provide a sample of some of the more interesting experiments in Table 1.2. Noticeable in these results are the relatively large number of failures of the non-parametric GARP test for the conventional collections for M1 and M2 and the improvement of the results when durable consumption and its user cost are added into the set. This is not surprising from a theoretical point of view (see Chapter 3), perhaps because financial asset holding ought to be thought of as being embedded in a dynamic consumption framework.

Numerous studies have indicated that business demand for money should be distinguished from consumer demand. Indeed, we are thinking specifically of the representative consumer in our revealed preference structure here, and would think it likely, *a priori*, that the inclusion of financial products

Table 1.3 Conventional monetary aggregates, GARP tests, without business-type deposits (US data)

Set	Identity	Assets included	Violations
I	M1	1+2, 4, 5, 6	5
II	M2*	1+2, 4, 5, 6, 10, 11, 12, 13+14, 16, 17	24
III	M1+durable consumption	1+2, 4, 5, 6, durable consumption	4
IV	M2+durable consumption	1+2, . . . , 17, durable consumption	2
V	M2+3 consumption components	1+2, . . . , 17, durable, non-durable, services	0

*The assets dropped were DDBUS, ONRP, ONED, MMF, and SDCU. The choice was based on the performance of the remaining variables.

primarily of interest to business firms (DDBUS, Repurchases, Eurodollars) would weaken the results of a search that depended on the existence of a stable utility function for the representative 'consumer' of financial services. An obvious next step, then, is to drop these products from the list, thereby abandoning the conventional M1 and M2 framework. These results appear in Table 1.3. These results indicate considerable improvement in the number of violations as non-competing (DDBUS, ONRP, ONED) or marginal (MMF, SDCU) accounts are dropped from the GARP test. Indeed, the last set passes the GARP test; this is achieved by adding in the other components of total consumption so that the full consumer environment is evaluated. It is this collection that we will work with in what follows.

The set of assets in Group V of Table 1.3 has 13 components and represents too large a set of individual assets for many empirical purposes. In particular, one of our objectives is to arrive at a set which can be used in later parametric tests (rational expectations in Chapter 2 and Translog and Fourier expenditure systems in Chapter 3) where, for estimation purposes, limits on the number of assets considered need to be imposed. In the specific systems literature there are (at least) two ways in which these tests might be structured, either by 'like-assets' across institutions or by 'like-institutions' across assets. A like-assets combination which might provide some power in the GARP framework is exhibited in Set I of Table 1.4. Once again the power of the consumption terms is illustrated (in the reduction from 48 violations to 4) but at 4 violations, this particular collection of like-assets is not quite as effective as the grouping in Sets III through VI, the first being a grouping by 'like-institutions' and the second by 'like-assets' in a slightly different way. More importantly, the arrangements in Sets IV and VI provide groupings that actually pass the GARP test so that a reasonably sized group (of four or five assets) is achieved without throwing anything away. We also need to have zero violations in order to conduct weak separability tests (so long as we continue to use Varian's NONPAR procedure).[23] These tests (as follow) were performed on both of the two zero-violation sets, although in the empirical work in Chapters 2 and 3, only Sets V and VI are actually used,

Table 1.4 GARP tests of groupings of monetary assets

Set	Components	Violations
	Like-assets (1)	
I	CUR+DDCON+OCD, SDCB+SDSL+SDSB, STDCB+STDTH, MMDAC+MMDAT+SNOWC+SNOWT	48
II	SET I, DUR+NONDUR+SERV	4
	Like-institutions	
III	CUR+DDCON+OCD, SDCB+STDCB, SDSL+SDSB+STDTH, MMDAC+MMDAT+SNOWC+SNOWT	29
IV	SET III, DUR+NONDUR+SERV	0
	Like-assets (2)	
V	CUR+DDCON+OCD, SNOWC+SNOWT+MMDAC+MMDAT +SDCB+SDSL+SDCB, STDCB+STDTH	36
VI	SET V, DUR+NONDUR+SERV	0

partly for economy and partly because the arrangement by 'like-assets' provides a more reasonable arrangement, in view of the very high correlations among the user costs of most bank liabilities.

The theory we have sketched out above suggests that one approach to the demand for financial assets is to separate financial assets from other commodities (and, of course, to separate the decision temporally). We will follow this design, but before we do that, we are in a position to check the separation formally, since data which pass the GARP test just employed can be tested directly for violations of weak separability (as defined above) using Varian's NONPAR software. Thus, if the data for $\{x_1, x_2, x_3\}$ satisfy GARP, then there exists a utility function $U(x_1, x_2, x_3)$, and there may be a weakly separable utility function $V(\cdot)$ in $U(x_1, V((x_2, x_3))$.[24] GARP will still be satisfied by $U(\cdot)$, but $V(\cdot)$ not only must satisfy GARP but must also be homothetically weakly separable (as discussed above). This, then, would provide a necessary condition for separability. There is a sufficient condition provided in these tests, as well, but it is, as conceded by Varian, too restrictive in the sense that failure to meet it does not necessarily mean that the weak (homothetical) separability does not hold.[25]

We can, because the groups IV and VI in Table 1.4 passed the GARP test (with 0 violations), test for possible separable sets of assets. The sets of assets in Group IV, to install a new notation, are the following:

CUR+DDCON+OCD	X_1
SDCB+STDCB	X_2
SDSL+SDSB+STDTH	X_3
MMDAC+MMDAT+SNOWC+SNOWT	X_4
DUR+NONDUR+SERV	X_5

A natural grouping for this collection is indicated in Line I of Table 1.5; this separates X_1 and X_5 from the savings deposits. The utility function we are

Table 1.5 Weak separability tests: like-institutions

	Arrangement	Pass GARP?
I	1, (2, 3, 4), 5	No
II	(1, 2, 3, 4), 5	No
III	1, (2, 3, 4, 5)	Yes

Table 1.6 Weak separability tests: like-assets

Arrangement	Pass GARP?	Pass Afriat?
A1, (A2, A3, A4)	No	No
(A1, A2, A3), A4	No	No
(A1, A2), (A3, A4)	No	No
A1, (A2, A3), A4	No	No
(A1, A4), (A2, A3)	No	No
A1, A2, (A3, A4)	Yes	No

suggesting is

$$U[X_1, V(X_2, X_3, X_4), X_5]$$

As can be seen in Table 1.5, this arrangement fails to satisfy GARP, and consequently we cannot establish weak separability in this case. The second grouping of assets attempts to separate the consumption aggregate from the financial commodities; this, too, is unsuccessful. What does work, satisfying the necessary GARP test, is an arrangement in which savings-assets groups and the total consumption group are taken to be weakly separable from the transactions grouping. This suggests that separability for M1 (as long as it does not include NOW accounts and business deposits) may be (statistically) superior to M2 (or even broader aggregates). In any case, the customary assumption of the separability of the consumption decision from the financial assets decision is not apt in this experiment, so long as it is necessary to include small time deposits in the analysis.

We also checked the second group (based on 'like-assets') for its possible separability arrangements. With the following nomenclature:

CUR + DDCON + OCD	A1
SNOWC + SNOWT + MMDAC + MMDAT + SDCB + SDSL + SDSB	A2
STDCB + STDTH	A3
DUR + NONDUR + SERV	A4

we find weak separability in only one case (Table 1.6). This suggests that either a 'transactions' measure (A1) or a non-term savings asset collection (A2) might be useful as measures of moneyness, but that broader measures including term deposits (STDCB, STDTH) may not be separable from consumption expenditures. These results are similar to those of Swofford and

Whitney (1987), although not exactly so (see below). If the theory is structured in this way, then aggregation beyond A1 and A2 would not be advisable. At any rate, the entire group of 13 assets in A1 and A2 is also an interesting collection and will receive more attention in Chapters 2 and 3. In the latter case we will estimate the systems of demand equations which are appropriate for this collection. In Chapter 2, on the other hand, when we search out the possibility that these numbers are generated 'rationally', a Divisia index number is constructed across the assets in A1 and A2.

1.4 EMPIRICAL STUDIES OF MONETARY INDEX NUMBERS

Swofford and Whitney, who initiated the line of research involving GARP tests in monetary studies, have published several such tests on annual and quarterly US data (1987, 1988). For the quarterly data, ONRP, ONED, LTDCB (large time Deposits at Commercial Banks) and LTDTH (large time deposits at thrifts) are included in the full set that passed GARP, while on the annual data the full set of 27 items in the Federal Reserve's collection passed GARP (the set tested also included three types of consumption and leisure). With regard to the quarterly tests, Swofford and Whitney (1987) still find that it is difficult to locate a group of monetary assets that is weakly separable from the components of consumption (and leisure) although a collection consisting of consumer M1 (CM1), OCD and the four types of savings deposits (SD) satisfies the necessary (but not sufficient) conditions for separability. The best arrangement, satisfying both necessary and sufficient conditions for weak separability (of $V(\cdot)$), is

$$U[V(DUR, NDUR, SERV, LEIS), CM1, OCD, SD, STD]$$

Here STD represents the three distinct small time deposits listed as Nos. 16, 17 and 18 in Table 1.1. Note that the monetary assets are not separable here, taken as a group. If we want separability for monetary assets, then it appears that STD must be excluded from the collection. This is approximately what we have shown in our own explorations, on the same data.

A second set of results is available in a paper by Belongia and Chalfant (1989), who work with more recent data; they provide a three-pronged attack on the problem of selecting a monetary aggregate. Arguing, first, that the data must pass the condition of 'admissibility', which the GARP test searches for, Belongia and Chalfant locate three groupings that satisfy the necessary conditions; these are M1A (currency plus demand deposits), M1 (as it is currently defined) and M1+ (M1 plus the interest-bearing checking deposits presently counted in M2). These categories are then summed either as simple-sum or Divisia aggregates and are compared in the St Louis equation. The winner of the six, on performance grounds, is Divisia M1A. A final test attempted for the six potential indexes is that of their 'controllability'. This involves searching for the measure that is most closely related

to the *monetary base* (itself presumably directly controlled). Only the simple-sum and Divisia M1A measures perform well, with a clear lead going to Divisia M1A. These results, too, are not inconsistent with the examples given above, although they are drawn from a somewhat different time period.

Considering the empirical comparisons of the index numbers of monetary quantities, we have, in fact, a rapidly burgeoning literature. The main topic concerns an assessment of the relative merits of Divisia v. summation monetary quantity indices. To some extent, the agenda for this research was set in a paper by Barnett, Offenbacher and Spindt (1984) who compare the empirical performance of the Divisia and the sum-monetary aggregates in terms of various policy criteria, such as causality, the information content of an aggregate, and the stability of conventional money-demand equations. They conclude in favour of the Divisia monetary aggregates, especially at broad levels of aggregation, but they do not find a single aggregate, whether Divisia or not, that is uniformly best over all possible uses. This ambiguity continues to be a feature of the empirical comparisons of monetary index numbers, as we shall see.

A second study done at the Board of Governors by Lindsey and Spindt (1986) evaluates the performance of the MQ, Sum, and MSI indices over the first half of the 1980s. They show that while MQ grew considerably faster than SumM1 and SumM1-A (which itself excludes other checkable deposits), it was intermediate to these two indices in terms of the predictability of money-demand growth and in terms of the prediction of nominal GNP growth. SumM1 was worse and SumM1-A was better, in each case. With regard to the MSI indices, the money-demand growth predictability was worse than with SumM1, SumM1-A and MQ (for MSI1) and with SumM2 and SumM3 (for MSI2 and MSI3). As an indicator of nominal GNP growth, MSI1 does outperform MQ, SumM1 and SumM1-A, but by far the best indicators for GNP growth in the 1980s are SumM3 and SumM2, in that order.

Clearly, then, these results are not encouraging for the case for ideal index numbers, although one must remember that the period 1980–85 offers somewhat unusual and possibly inconsistent monetary policy actions by the Federal Reserve. This would affect both the identification of the simple money-demand function employed and the stability of the indicator relation between money and income. The results, that is to say, might be 'correct' for a badly mis-specified model, providing a sort of 'second best' guide for policy.[26] Even so, as Lindsey and Spindt certainly make clear, having first one and then another index work best, as the questions and the time period vary, does not provide a very firm footing for policy actions.[27] This seems a 'robust' finding, if anything is robust in this emerging literature.

Another, less structured, way in which comparisons of the monetary aggregates might be generated is by means of their time-series properties. A study by Christiano (1986) looks at the US monetary base (MB), MQ, SumM1, SumM2, MSI1, and MSI2 monthly data for the 1970–85 period.[28]

Christiano is concerned with whether a break in the monetary series occurs in 1979 (after the change in the Federal Reserve's operating style) and with the 'out-of-sample' forecasting performance of various macroeconomic variables by the various measures in the 1980s. He also addresses the question of whether the data are better defined as trend-stationary (TS) or difference-stationary (DS). Most investigators prefer the latter method of achieving stationarity and so does Christiano, on the record.

What happens, then, in Christiano's comparisons is that for MB and MQ – in DS form – there actually is no break in the series in 1979, while for all other formulations there is. With regard to the forecasting performance, DS versions of the monetary data consistently predict output, prices, money, the interest rate, and the exchange rate better than do Translog versions. Across monies, the biggest gains for using the DS-transformed data in forecasting depends somewhat on which variable is being predicted, with differencing improving the forecasting performance of MSI1 the most and MQ and M1 the least in the comparisons attempted. This is therefore yet another way in which the data are shown to have different properties when different aggregations are compared.

One of the possible ways of improving on the foregoing is to employ a notion of causality in place of the structural-type test favoured in the 'indicators' studies described above. In this respect, Serletis (1988*b*) investigates the relationship between Sum, Divisia, and MQ money and prices and income using the notion of Granger (1969) causality. This is achieved by evaluating empirically (using Dickey–Fuller, 1979, unit-root tests similar to those in Nelson and Plosser, 1982) whether the variables are trend-stationary or difference-stationary and by conducting causality tests using Akaike's (1970) final prediction error criterion. Generally, the data have to be differenced, and when they are, the Granger-causality test results do not reveal a single uniformly best monetary aggregate. The MSI aggregates, however, generally perform better, especially MSI2 and MSIL, in explaining the growth rates of prices and nominal income in the USA. The data cover the 1970–85 period on a monthly basis.[29]

Comparisons of money demand and income prediction naturally raise questions concerning the recent behaviour of velocity (by some measures it has declined through most of the 1980s) and how this might be related to the choice of a monetary indicator. Lindsey and Spindt (1986) point out that the different measures of money show sharply different velocity patterns; indeed, no decline is visible in the SumM1-A velocity, while the alleged decline is sharpest in SumM1.[30] While the MQ figures show less of a deviation from trend (than SumM1 and SumM1-A), the velocity growth rates of all the indices show what is described as erratic behaviour and not very close association with interest rates. MSI indices are not immune to these difficulties, either. There is a Granger-causality literature for the velocity question also, beginning with a test by Hall and Noble (1987). They conjecture and demonstrate that the *volatility* of the growth rate of SumM1 Granger-causes the growth rate of velocity for the 1960–84 US data. We will return to

these questions in Chapter 5 where we report on this literature and conduct some tests of our own, following the line of attack in Fisher and Serletis (1989).

NOTES

1. To derive the optimal balance, differentiate Equation (1.1) to get $dC/dM = -(bT/M^2) + i/2$. This can then be solved for M^* directly.
2. In this model own-substitution effects are not necessarily negative and the matrix of substitution effects is not symmetrical. Basically, these results occur because of the wealth effect of changes in money prices (or the price level) on utility.
3. There is a proof of this proposition in Arrow and Hahn (1971) in a general equilibrium framework, while Fischer (1974) provides a proof in the context of a production (and money) problem.
4. Feenstra is at pains to refer to the costs as 'liquidity costs' rather than as transactions costs, simply because his formulation is consistent with a standard version, due to Whalen (1966), of the precautionary demand for money. We will use his designation with an occasional reminder that most interest lies in the transactions results.
5. That is, $V(x_t, m_t) = U[W(x_t, m_t)]$ for $U' > 0$, $U'' \leq 0$ (i.e. V is an increasing, concave function of W).
6. We obtain V as an increasing concave function of W which does have the nuisance result that $V_{xm} < 0$ is a possibility unless sufficient concavity is assumed.
7. For example, if $U(c_t) = \log c_t$, then $V = \log x_t - \log(1 + k/m_t)$ is separable in x_t and m_t. This satisfies the condition that V_{xm} (or W_{xm}) have $V_{xm} \geq 0$ (it is zero).
8. The specialization is that there be a zero elasticity of substitution between goods and money. This is not required of the Lucas–Stokey (1987) version of this model in which there are cash goods and credit goods.
9. We should point out that nowhere in this study will we be discussing the 'macromonetarist' approach to the definition of money associated with Friedman and Schwartz (1970) and Laidler (1969) among others (see the survey in D. Fisher, 1978). Laidler, for example, argues that we have identified money if the entity in question has a stable demand function defined over some relevant empirical range (of M, i, Y). Friedman is content, in the same context, to link M to Y alone, but in either case the approach has foundered on empirical demonstrations of the instability of the proposed relationships and on a certain amount of justified suspicion as to the statistical properties of estimators that are fished out of the pool of data on the basis of their t-values (see Cooley and Leroy, 1981). In effect, we have nothing to add to the earlier discussion, apart from the new reference.
10. Consider the following simple correlations among the prices of the six components of the US SumM1 index for 1976,3 to 1985,2.

	CUR	DDCON	DDBUS	OCD	SNOWC	SNOWT
CUR	1.00					
DDCON	1.00	1.00				
DDBUS	0.72	0.72	1.00			
OCD	0.99	0.99	0.65	1.00		
SNOWC	0.63	0.63	0.10	0.71	1.00	
SNOWT	0.61	0.61	0.08	0.69	0.99	1.00

This implies the following sub-aggregations:

CUR + DDCON + OCD
SNOWC + SNOWT
DDBUS

but not a combination of all six components in view of the often very high correlations among the assets. Note that the prices here are 'user' costs, and the data are those of Swofford and Whitney as described below. Data for the period 1970–1 to 1985–2 show a similar pattern but present a problem since not all six assets existed until 1976–3.

11. These numbers would be formally correct if the components of the monetary aggregate were perfect substitutes (i.e. if all indifference curves/isoquants were linear with slopes of -1).
12. The explanation of the theory used in this section is based on Barnett (1978, 1981).
13. Again, by weak separability, we mean (Phlips, 1974, pp. 68–9):

    It is a necessary and sufficient condition for a function to be separable, that the marginal rates of substitution between any two variables belonging to the same group be independent of the value of any variable in any other group.

14. If we wish to do any further grouping of the assets here, say $U(x_1, x_2, g(x_3, \ldots, x_m))$ where g is the weakly separable function, then the function g must actually be *homothetically* weakly separable from the other entities. Homothetically implies the additional restriction that the separable functions be monotonic transformations of homogeneous functions of their inputs. That is, in practice the groupings are preserved for different income levels. For a discussion see Samuelson and Swamy (1974).
15. This involves the usual Cournot and Engel aggregations and restrictions on the diagonal and off-diagonal terms of the substitution matrix. The set of restrictions that usually fails to hold (empirically) is that involving the symmetry of the substitution effects.
16. Two examples of this methodology on this problem, arriving at these conclusions, are provided by Ewis and Fisher (1984, 1985); the consumer technology in these studies is Translog and Fourier, respectively. Other studies offering similar conclusions are by Barnett (1980, 1981) and Offenbacher (1979), while in an earlier paper Chetty (1969) arrives at a different conclusion. For an extension of the substitution framework to the topic of currency substitution – that is to say, to the open economy – see Ewis and Fisher (1984) and, especially, Sims and Takayama (1980). The latter has a nicely worded explanation of the theoretical argument (which involves duality theory).
17. The standard proof of this is in Green (1964). Another way to put this condition is that the utility function of the representative consumer 'requires the goods over which it is defined to be perfect substitutes in identical ratios. In other words, the components of the quantity index must be indistinguishable to the consumer' (Barnett, 1980, pp. 14–15).
18. In practice one has to select a particular functional form and therein lies the problem since the particular forms have different, non-general, characteristics. Contemplate, for example, the differences between the Cobb–Douglas and the constant elasticity of substitution (CES) functions with respect to their treatment of the elasticity of substitution.
19. A pure price index exhibits only price effects, while a quantity index contains only quantity effects; thus the non-parametric approach suggested here has the disadvantage that no such simple interpretation can be given to it. Properties 1 and 2 are advantages, of course.

20. These are currency, demand deposits, other checkable deposits, money market mutual funds, telephone transfer mutual funds and money market deposit accounts.
21. In the 'dual' to this problem, money quantities must be taken as exogenous. This, too, seems unreasonable.
22. We are going to use these data at a number of points in this study. The monetary quantities are the monetary services index (Divisia) of Farr and Johnson (1985*b*) as processed by Swofford and Whitney (1987, 1988). The latter have put the quantities in real, per capita form and have calculated the appropriate user costs ($\mathbf{p}^j$ above) for each asset. They are quarterly and run from 1970–1 to 1985–2. Space considerations do not permit their publication here, but they are available from the author at cost, for whatever purposes.
23. Note that satisfaction of the conditions for weak separability (and GARP) imply that the composite goods theorem applies (see Varian, 1983, Theorem 4, p. 106).
24. It is important to realize that a very large number of groupings of the data pass or come close to passing the GARP test. There is no escaping the fact that this is art, not science. The results that follow are, consequently, more of an illustration, although they are interesting nonetheless.
25. The sufficient condition available in the NONPAR procedure is never satisfied in any of these tests and is, in any event, considered to be unduly restrictive for empirical purposes. In the following tests, due to limitations of the software, only weak separability is tested for. It holds rarely enough, anyway. Note that Varian's program tests for homotheticity of the utility function rather than the less restrictive requirement (which is all one needs) that the subgroup function V be 'homothetically separable'.
26. The money-demand model used in this study is the Goldfeld (1973) specification, approximately, with real GNP, the 3-month Treasury bill, and prices as arguments.
27. Lindsey and Spindt suggest that a problem with the MSI index is the use of an occasionally inappropriate benchmark asset. This asset is usually the Baa bond yield, although when the yield curve slopes downward, the benchmark is actually one of the assets in the set of monies (in order to avoid a negative user cost). There is also some sign in the 'system studies' described below that problems in calculating 'own rates' of return on cash assets may be damaging the estimates of this relationship (and, presumably, rendering inefficient any index based on the flawed own-rate numbers).
28. We note, according to Farr and Johnson (1985*a*), that the new MSI (Fisher) numbers and the old (Divisia) have similar autocorrelation and cross-correlation properties (with GNP).
29. The nominal income measure is the same as that employed by Christiano (the consumer price index times the industrial production index).
30. In a parallel study on monthly data, Christiano (1986), using an industrial production index proxy for nominal income, reports that the break in the velocity series is a break from trend. When changes in the log of velocity are graphed against time, no break is visible in the series.

2

TRANSACTIONS AND RATIONAL APPROACHES TO THE DEMAND FOR MONEY

2.1 INTRODUCTION

In recent years there have been two broad areas that have received the most attention in the demand for money literature. One of these is a series of developments in the transactions-cost approach to money-holding and the other is a special area of work on the asset theory involving the use of demand-system analysis. The former is the main topic in this chapter, while the latter appears in Chapter 3. This chapter begins with a discussion of what are now the standard transactions-demand paradigms – of Saving (1971), Dutton and Gramm (1973) and Niehans (1978), especially. This is a traditional approach to the subject and covers a wide range of theoretical possibilities, including some modest extensions into dynamic topics. It will take up roughly half our space. On a less conventional level, but still operating in a broadly neoclassical framework, we will spend the rest of the chapter on some work in a partly parallel literature on the rational expectations approach to the demand for money. Here we will consider the results of some empirical tests on the rational hypothesis, utilizing the data dissected in Chapter 1.

In our discussion of the transactions literature, we will go over a sample of theoretical results bearing on the role of money in reducing the costs of carrying out transactions in goods, financial, and input markets. The smaller part of this work is in terms of the inventory-theoretic model, while a still-growing effort is in terms of increasingly general transactions paradigms. Here work by Saving (1971) and Niehans (1978) will be featured. In a sense, much of the work in this section is devoted to making more precise what one might mean by the 'medium of exchange' function of money. In these models money is given a role to play in a world in which there exist frictions in trading, frictions which produce transactions costs (and thereby use up scarce resources). The demand for money, then, arises as part of the natural solution of a problem in which economic agents maximize utility (subject to a constraint on their resources). In particular, as a medium of exchange, certain forms of money permit exchange to be conducted more efficiently (at

a saving of resources), and as units of accounts the same forms provide lower accounting costs generally. It will be these formal perceptions that motivate much of the following discussion.

There is another branch of the transactions literature that once flourished (in the early 1970s) and has survived into the 1980s, mainly as a possible explanation of the poor fits of conventional money-demand functions. This is the 'value of time' approach to the demand for money which specifies the role of money as that of saving time in carrying out transactions. This becomes an economic problem in various ways – for example, 'leisure time' could be entered directly into the utility function of a representative individual – and then a problem can be solved in which a demand for money function falls out. This function would have as one of its arguments the opportunity cost of time; this is most often taken as the wage rate in the empirical studies of this hypothesis. In discussing this topic in this chapter, then, we will look at several extant (transactions) versions of this 'value of time' hypothesis and comment on the surprisingly strong empirical support that it has received.

A third recent literature is dealt with in this chapter and this involves rational expectations in the demand for money. This is most obviously a topic in the 'asset theory' of money and thus might be considered part of Chapter 3; but, as it turns out, the way this material has evolved, since it has been drawn from a transactions-oriented, but unspecified, microfoundations literature, much of what has been done to date is just as comfortable under the general heading of the 'transactions demand'. In this respect we will be able to take advantage of some insights generated in the earlier parts of this chapter (and in Chapter 1) to restructure the rational expectations material to some extent. It is, in particular, convenient to think in terms of dynamic-consumption, money-holding plans and liquidity constraints, and since these are the methodological props of much of the recent transactions literature, the position of the entire rational expectations package here is economical, at least up to a point. We note, before proceeding with the more traditional transactions literature, that there are some original estimations for this topic, involving recent US data. Finally, of course, 'rational expectations' will resurface in our policy discussions, especially in Chapter 5.

2.2 BASIC INVENTORY-THEORETIC MODELS

The modern form of the transactions approach goes back to I. Fisher (1922). The Fisherian proposal is to suppose that individuals hold a fixed proportion of the expected money value of their transactions in the form of money. If individual demands can then be aggregated in some satisfactory way, we might expect an aggregate proportionality between the quantity of money demanded and total value of transactions in the economy. This proportionality might then be rescaled if another variable (income) is substituted for transactions, and it might well be itself variable if interest rates (let us say as

an opportunity cost factor) affect money-holding. In Baumol's (1952) early revival of the transactions theory, explicit transactions costs are introduced – in the form of the sum of

(a) penalty or brokerage costs attached to converting other assets to cash; and
(b) interest earnings foregone by holding non-interest bearing cash.

Both a direct proportionality between the quantity of money demanded and transactions (or, by some writers, income) and an inverse proportionality with the interest rate are then readily established. This model was introduced in Chapter 1.

Recalling that T represents the dollars paid out per unit of time and that T/M represents the number of times cash must be raised, then, for a brokerage cost of b, the money cost of these trips to the bank is $b(T/M)$. Since the individual money-holder has average cash-holdings of $M/2$ and loses interest at rate i on these balances, his total costs are given by

$$\frac{bT}{M} + \frac{iM}{2} = C \tag{2.1}$$

When differentiated and solved at the optimum, this expression yields a demand for money function of

$$M = \left(\frac{2bT}{i}\right)^{\frac{1}{2}} \tag{2.2}$$

The model just discussed is very simple, and so a minor industry has developed in an attempt to provide more reasonable environments for monetary analysis. One obvious thing missing from the framework just specified is a cash flow for the individual (or the firm) arising from the sale of his services (or from the sale of the firm's output). Actually, in his original paper Baumol produces a cash-flow solution but this appears in a more elegant version by Brunner and Meltzer (1967). They assume that the firm (or individual) generates a cash flow from the sale of its products and uses up this cash flow on payments for inputs, investments on securities, and residual money balances. This seems more realistic. Then, if the spending unit runs out of money during the period, it will have to sell (or withdraw funds) from its savings account. This produces an additional cost to the firm; indeed, there are two explicit transactions costs in the Brunner–Meltzer framework – the cost of deposit activity and the cost of withdrawals – as well as two parts to the opportunity cost in the form of

(a) interest foregone for the initial money balances; and
(b) lost interest on anything withdrawn later from the firm's investments (or from the individual's savings).

While this model is certainly more complex than the first Baumol model, it is not really intrinsically different. At any rate, both models conclude that

money-holding is directly related to the volume of transactions (with an elasticity less than unity) and inversely related to the interest rate. In this basic literature, the latter is generally defined to be the return on an alternative asset.

There is no uncertainty in the transactions framework discussed to this point, and yet the alleviation of uncertainty might be the way we would want to motivate optimal money-holding in the first place. The prototype uncertainty model is one of business demands for money (Miller and Orr, 1968) in which the cash flow of the firm is itself the stochastic variable. Miller and Orr assume a two-asset problem in which cash is non-interest-bearing. If p measures the probability of the cash balance increasing by m dollars during an hour (an hour $= 1/t$), and $q(= 1 - p)$ measures the probability of its decreasing by the same amount in the same period of time, then, assuming a Bernoulli process, over n days the distribution of changes in cash balances will have a mean and variance as given by Equations (2.3) and (2.4):

$$\mu_n = ntm(p - q) \tag{2.3}$$

$$\sigma_n^2 = 4ntpqm^2 \tag{2.4}$$

This distribution approaches the normal as n increases. Miller and Orr assume that $p = q = \frac{1}{2}$, in which case $\mu_n = 0$ and $\sigma_n^2 = nm^2t$; furthermore, they assume the usual cost-minimizing objective for the money-holding unit. The result is a demand for money of

$$m^* = \frac{4}{3}\left(\frac{3\gamma}{4i}\sigma^2\right)^{\frac{1}{3}} \tag{2.5}$$

which is in the precise form in which the inventory model is often found. Here

$$\sigma^2 = \frac{\sigma_n^2}{n} \tag{2.6}$$

and so increased variance in the cash flow produces larger money-holdings. This certainly seems reasonable.

We might also have a stochastic interest rate in the problem, and while the portfolio approach might seem a more natural way to introduce uncertainty into the money-holding problem, there is an interesting version in Niehans (1978) which fits nicely into the structure both here and later. Generally, of course, it might be expected that increased interest-rate uncertainty would induce larger (precautionary) money-holdings, and, indeed, this is what the empirical literature suggests (see the discussion of velocity in Chapter 5, below). As Niehans puts it:

> with uncertain interest the . . . increase in cash balances would clearly reduce risk. It follows that a risk averter, weighing net return against risk, will always find it advantageous to hold a larger cash balance and a smaller bond portfolio than in a riskless situation. (p. 53)

Thus, as might be expected, the existence of risk – along with the assumption of risk aversion – defines a role for money. On the other hand, this precision does not necessarily carry over to the effect of increased uncertainty on money demand.

Following Niehans, let us define 'net revenue' as the difference between interest income and transactions costs, where the interest income is

$$\frac{1}{2}i\left(Y - \frac{M^2}{Y}\right)$$

the transactions costs are

$$C = 2\gamma(Y - M)n$$

where Y is income and n is the number of trips to the bank. Combining these expressions for cost and earnings we directly obtain net revenues as

$$NR = \frac{1}{2}iY - \frac{1}{2}i\frac{M^2}{Y} - 2\gamma(Y - M)n$$

From this arrangement, letting $m = M/2$ and $b = B/2$ define average bond holdings, we have asset 'proportions' of

$$\lambda = \frac{m}{a} \quad \text{and} \quad \beta = \frac{b}{a} \qquad (\lambda + \beta = 1) \tag{2.7}$$

With these concepts we can write an expression for net revenue per unit of assets ($\pi = NR/a$) of

$$\pi = \beta i - 4\gamma n[1 - (1 - \beta)^{\frac{1}{2}}]$$

From this structure, when we introduce interest-rate uncertainty directly, we would be interested in the expected earnings (of the 'portfolio') as in

$$E(\pi) = \beta E(i) - 4\gamma n[1 - (1 - \beta)^{\frac{1}{2}}] \tag{2.8}$$

which implies an expected standard deviation of

$$\sigma_\pi = \beta\sigma_i$$

Here the risk is shown as a linear function of β (for a given σ_i) – which implies that increased holding of the risky asset increases overall risk (linearly). This makes sense. However, the effect of the complicated term in Equation (2.8) is to produce a non-linear opportunity locus (in E/V space) for the representative money-holder and an ambiguous effect of increased interest-rate risk on money-holding. The conclusions Niehans arrives at are as follows:

1. A risk averter will hold more cash in an uncertain environment than in a certain environment.
2. In general the effect of an increase in risk (in σ_i) is actually ambiguous.

For point 2, in particular, while higher risk leads to the substitution away from the risky asset and towards cash (so that a properly compensated

money-demand curve would show increased liquidity), the income effect could dominate the substitution effect and produce a negative effect on cash holding, even under risk aversion. This can happen because the higher risk shifts the opportunity locus. Indeed, in the presence of uncertainty, the interest-elasticity of the demand for money is also theoretically uncertain, a result that can be arrived at in other ways. Incidentally, this exercise repeats a result that appears in Tobin's mean-variance paper (1958), but note that here we are operating in an inventory-theoretic setting.

In this section, then, we have illustrated the flexibility of the basic transactions models in this brief introduction to the topic. What we will do in the remainder of the chapter is consider variations and extensions, with some considerably more detailed structures to follow. Notable in this respect will be an excursion into rational expectations, where we will be required to return to our discussion of the empirical definition of money as we try to get our data into a testable form.

2.3 GENERAL TRANSACTIONS MODELS

The two main approaches that we will consider here, as a way of generalizing the theoretical structure of the somewhat limiting inventory versions of the transactions-cost models, are the work of Saving (1971) and, again, of Niehans (1978).[1] The models are dynamic-consumption-and-money-holding in their basic structure, and they tend to model money-holding in the form of 'money-requirements' constraints. The solutions tend to be very general and do not always possess useful empirical properties, although the overall framework is a very useful one for thinking about the role of money and for concocting empirical strategies.

In Saving's version of the transactions model, the approach is to deal with the dynamic consumption plan of an individual where money is not inserted directly into the utility function (or into the production function) but is instead given the role to play of saving time for other activities (consumption or leisure). If we assume that individuals wish to maximize utility over a horizon running from the present to the end of their horizon (h), then Equation (2.9) might represent a typical dynamic utility function:

$$u = U(c_t, L_t) \qquad (t = 0, \ldots, h) \tag{2.9}$$

Here L_t represents the percentage of total time devoted to leisure, stated as an alternative to consuming goods. The individual will have a real income constraint, given by Equation (2.10); t here represents the dynamic income path, and W_t is the percentage of total time spent on earning income, whatever the source:

$$y_t = F(W_t, t) \tag{2.10}$$

It will take time to carry on economic activity, of course, and so a further

constraint is necessary to divide up the available time:

$$L_t + W_t + T_t = 1 \tag{2.11}$$

The three uses are leisure, work and transactions (consumption) activities.

To complete the model it is appropriate to specify a transactions-time 'production' function. We can assert that an increase in income or consumption will increase the frequency or size of transactions. This accounts for the first two arguments of Equation (2.12). Note that v designates a set of the average holdings of n monetary assets (such as currency, demand deposits, other checkable deposits, etc.).

$$T_t = G(y_t, c_t, \bar{m}_t^v) \qquad (G_1, G_2 > 0; G_3^v < 0, v = 1, \ldots, n) \tag{2.12}$$

The components of the third term are expressed as real balances, and they are naturally assumed to have negative influences, taken individually, since larger money balances would be expected to reduce transactions time. Finally, assume that each individual is faced with a dynamic budget constraint as in Equation (2.13); note the presence of initial real-bond and money-holdings (designated as b_0 and m_0, respectively):

$$\sum_{t=0}^{h}\left(\frac{1}{1+i}\right)^t y_t + b_0 + m_0 = \sum_{t=0}^{h}\left(\frac{i}{1+i}\right)^t\left(c_t + i\sum_{v=1}^{n}\bar{m}_t^v + \sum_{v=1}^{n}\delta_{\bar{m}_t^v}\bar{m}_t^v\right) \tag{2.13}$$

Here, in the right-hand term we list the average real balances of each of the k types of money, along with the opportunity costs (in the form of interest foregone) and storage costs, with the latter defined by δ; δ could, for one thing, measure the effect of inflation on the value of nominal assets.

To solve this system for the demand for money, Saving asserts that it is reasonable both to take the optimal paths for consumption and leisure as predetermined and to use these optimal amounts as parameters in the analysis of the demand for money.[2] The results of the separation of leisure and consumption decisions from money-holding decisions are that we no longer need to operate in an expected utility framework and that a simple net wealth-maximization framework will provide the optimal collection of monetary assets. This concept of net wealth would be the result of subtracting the right-hand side from the left-hand side of Equation (2.13) with the optimal value of consumption ($\hat{c}$) as a parameter. We would also have to constrain this equation with the three relations given in Equations (2.10), (2.11), and (2.12). After suitable substitutions we would arrive at the following two-equation system:

$$W^* = \sum_{t=0}^{h}\left(\frac{1}{1+i}\right)^t F[1 - (\hat{L}_t + T_t), t] + b + m - \sum_{t=0}^{h}\left(\frac{1}{1+i}\right)^t\left(\hat{c}_t + i\sum_{v=1}^{n} m_t^v + \sum_{v=1}^{n}\delta_{\bar{m}_t^v}\bar{m}_t^v\right) \tag{2.14}$$

$$T = G\{F[1 - (\hat{L}_t + T_t)], \hat{c}_t, \bar{m}_t^v\} \qquad (2.15)$$

By maximizing Equation (2.14) subject to Equation (2.15), we obtain the following first-order conditions for the average holdings of the various monetary assets, taken at the optimum:

$$\frac{(\partial F/\partial W)_t(\partial G/\partial \bar{m}^v)_t}{1 + (\partial G/\partial y)_t(\partial F/\partial W)_t} - i - \delta_{\bar{m}_t^v} = 0 \qquad (v = 1, \ldots, n) \qquad (2.16)$$

The expression in Equation (2.16) is the marginal return to holding stocks of the various forms of money. The term in the denominator of this expression reflects the fact that all the time saved on transactions cannot be converted into income because increased income itself requires increased transactions time. These equations, plus Equations (2.10), (2.11), and (2.12), comprise a system of $n+3$ equations, for n financial assets, T, W, and y. Unfortunately, not much can be signed in these equations. Indeed, only the effects of storage costs (inflation?) on the demand for financial assets has a deterministic (negative) sign. Even as structured as this exercise is, no more can be produced, and the whole framework suffers, in effect, from its generality. It does, though, do two things. It provides an explanation of how money-holding might be modelled – as saving transactions time and hence being entered into a constraint rather than into the utility function – and at the same time it suggests why money yields utility at the margin (via its effect on leisure time). Indeed, and transparently, the constraint(s) might be substituted directly into the utility function, following suitable separability assumptions, in order to get a 'direct' utility model for money that does not violate commonsense.

Since each of the constraints in this problem is monotonic in T, W, and y, it is straightforward to deduce demand functions for the monetary assets. Finally, note that it would be appropriate, given the discussion in Chapter 1, to employ the user costs defined there for the monetary assets in such an analysis, should it be done empirically. No such estimates exist for this framework, at least employing the constraints mentioned here.

A second version of the general transactions model is the work of Niehans (1978). We will look at a simplified version of this, with some broader conclusions tacked on at the end. While Niehans claims a general solution to the problem of integrating 'value' theory and the theory of money by the careful specification of the transactions constraint, his actual contribution may well lie in the area of using an appropriate mathematical technique (dynamic non-linear programming with linear constraints) and in the detail of his model. In this model, the consumer maximizes

$$u = U(x_1, \ldots, x_t, \ldots, x_h) \qquad (t = 1, \ldots, h) \qquad (2.17)$$

where h defines the consumer's horizon. There are, further, three sets of constraints facing the consumer, each set containing constraints for each of the k periods. The first of these sets is for commodities for period t

(represented as s_t^{g} in the following):

$$s_{t+1}^{\mathrm{g}} - s_t^{\mathrm{g}} = (x_t^* - x_t) + (z_t^{\mathrm{g}} - y_t^{\mathrm{g}}) - \delta s_t^{\mathrm{g}} \\ - c^{\mathrm{g}}(z_t^{\mathrm{g}} + y_t^{\mathrm{g}}) - c^{\mathrm{b}}(z_t^{\mathrm{b}} + y_t^{\mathrm{b}}) \qquad (2.18)$$

Here the one-period change in commodity stocks depends on the fixed endowment supply (x_t^*) v. the demand (x_t) for commodities, on the difference between purchases (z^{g}) and sales (y^{g}) of commodities, on storage costs (δ) for commodities and on brokerage costs in commodity (c^{g}) and bond (c^{b}) markets. The second constraint in the problem refers to changes in the stock of bonds, as in

$$s_{t+1}^{\mathrm{b}} - s_t^{\mathrm{b}} = z_t^{\mathrm{b}} - y_t^{\mathrm{b}} \qquad (2.19)$$

This merely defines the difference between bonds bought and bonds sold in each period. The third constraint involves stocks of money (which could in principle be divided into elementary bundles as in our empirical discussions in Chapter 1).

$$s_{t+1}^{\mathrm{m}} - s_t^{\mathrm{m}} = p_t^{\mathrm{g}}(y_t^{\mathrm{g}} - z_t^{\mathrm{g}}) + p_t^{\mathrm{b}}(y_t^{\mathrm{b}} - z_t^{\mathrm{b}}) + is_t^{\mathrm{b}} + \pi s_t^{\mathrm{m}} - T_t \qquad (2.20)$$

Here we convert to money terms via p^{g} and p^{b}, i is the nominal interest rate on bonds and π is the own-rate of interest on money (in practice, it could be expected inflation). The T_t term measures tax payments.

Still following Niehans, we can form the Lagrangean for this system as in

$$L = U(x_1, \ldots, x_h) - \sum_{t=1}^{h} \lambda_t^{\mathrm{g}}[(s_{t+1}^{\mathrm{g}} - s_t^{\mathrm{g}}) - (x_t^* - x_t) - (z_t^{\mathrm{g}} - y_t^{\mathrm{g}}) \\ + \delta s_t^{\mathrm{g}} + c^{\mathrm{g}}(z_t^{\mathrm{g}} + y_t^{\mathrm{g}}) + c^{\mathrm{b}}(z_t^{\mathrm{b}} + y_t^{\mathrm{b}})] - \sum_{t=1}^{h} \lambda_t^{\mathrm{b}}[(s_{t+1}^{\mathrm{b}} - s_t^{\mathrm{b}}) \\ - (z_t^{\mathrm{b}} - y_t^{\mathrm{b}})] - \sum_{t=1}^{h} \lambda_t^{\mathrm{m}}[(s_{t+1}^{\mathrm{m}} - s_t^{\mathrm{m}}) - p_t^{\mathrm{g}}(y_t^{\mathrm{g}} - z_t^{\mathrm{g}}) \\ - p_t^{\mathrm{g}}(y_t^{\mathrm{g}} - z_t^{\mathrm{g}}) - is_t^{\mathrm{b}} - \pi s_t^{\mathrm{m}} + T_t] \qquad (2.21)$$

Here the Lagrangean multipliers are the discounted marginal flow values of goods, bonds and money.

There are, in this framework, both flow and stock marginal conditions to consider. The flow equilibrium:

> conditions state that exchange takes place up to the point where the marginal rate of substitution between goods (or bonds) and money is equal to their price after transactions costs. It is because of this wedge between market prices and marginal values, due to transactions costs, that assets may be diversified. (Niehans, 1978, p. 73)

For example, for the exchange between money and commodities the marginal condition is

$$\frac{\lambda_t^{\mathrm{g}}}{\lambda_t^{\mathrm{m}}} \geq \frac{p_t^{\mathrm{g}}}{1 + c^{\mathrm{g}}} \qquad (\text{for } y_t^{\mathrm{g}} \geq 0) \qquad (2.22)$$

which would be in the usual form except for the presence of transactions costs in goods markets. There is a similar condition for bonds. One of the major implications of this result is that the flow demand for money does not go to zero until the economy reaches its bliss point (when the numerator on the left-hand side of the expression just given goes to zero). There is, then, no satiation with money in this model. Another implication is that p_t^g, i.e. the price level, is the appropriate opportunity cost for money *flows*.

There is also a series of first-order conditions for the stocks of all commodities and assets. These involve the opportunity costs and represent the gains in utility from holding the asset for one period (as opposed to the instantaneous gains from exchange in the flow dimension). For money, then, the marginal stock condition at any time can be written as

$$[(1 + \pi)\lambda_t^{m} - \lambda_{t-1}^{m}]s_t^{m} = 0 \tag{2.23}$$

in which case

$$\frac{\lambda_t^{m} - \lambda_{t-1}^{m}}{\lambda_t^{m}} \leq -\pi \qquad (\text{for } s_t^{m} \geq 0) \tag{2.24}$$

This expression yields the marginal value of holding the stock of money for one period, where $-\pi$ (minus the expected inflation rate) is the 'own-rate on money'. (Money does not pay interest in this framework.) This value actually can go to zero so that there is potential satiation in the model.[3] Note that the numerator on the left-hand side of the second expression is the gain in utility from one period's holding of the asset and that the price on the right is potentially an interest rate.

From this analysis Niehans concludes:

> This provides precise answers to the old question whether 'the' value of money is the inverse of the price level or the rate of interest: both are, in principle, valid measures, but one relates to flows while the other relates to stocks. (p. 77)

This has long been implicit in the literature, but Niehans' discussion puts the matter across formally. Niehans also emphasizes that the relevant interest rate in the stock demand is actually not a rate on an alternative asset *per se*, but is instead the difference between time preference and the interest rate on money.[4] In the final analysis, then, money produces utility at the margin, short of the bliss point, in much the same way that stocks and flows of consumer goods do. There is, though, no need to think of money as an input in a utility function, although money does have its derived 'marginal utility'.

2.4 THE VALUE OF TIME HYPOTHESIS

The discussion to this point in the chapter has to some extent been on the topic of the 'value of time', although that idea has not been made explicit. For example, the inventory-of-money model really could be interpreted as

placing a value on economic agents' time in the form of what we are loosely referring to as 'brokerage costs'. This is especially obvious if these concepts are interpreted as equal to the number of 'trips to the bank' (as in Barro, 1976), involving fixed units of time (and distance). Laidler (1985) notes that in studies by Dutton and Gramm (1973), Karni (1974*a*), Diewert (1974*a*) and Phlips (1978), the wage rate has a positive effect on the demand for money, and he concludes:

> one would like to see the importance of the wage variable investigated across a far wider variety of specifications of the demand-for-money function than these before concluding definitely that this work has unearthed another important factor influencing money holding, but the results cited here are nevertheless highly suggestive and open up an interesting line for future research. (p. 144)

But the theoretical foundations of this work are not explained by Laidler, and so we will go into the matter further here, by way of trying to promote activity in this area. It involves what has become known as the 'value of time' approach to money demand.

There is a small literature on the inventory approach to the value of time (see Karni, 1974*a*, *b* and 1975*a*, *b*) that utilizes the simplest form of the square-root rule to arrive at a prediction for the effect of the wage rate (and other variables) on the demand for money. In particular, if income is divided between labour income (time worked times the real wage) and other income and if the brokerage costs of converting savings to money consist partly of wage payments, then a general demand for money function of the following form can be derived.

$$M^{d} = f(Y_{NL}, h, i, w) \qquad (2.25)$$

Here Y_{NL} is the non-labour income, and h, the hours worked. The theoretical predictions are for

(a) a negative and small interest elasticity; and
(b) somewhat surprisingly, a labour-income elasticity of the demand for money *a priori* higher than the 'other income' elasticity.

The wage rate has a positive effect. Karni confirms this in single-equation, log-linear tests on US (1974*a*) but not on UK data (1975*b*).

A much more general effort in this literature is based directly on Saving's (1971) paper and is the work of Dutton and Gramm (1973). Dutton and Gramm observe 'if the use of money saves transactions time, it increases the amount of leisure. This suggests an additional determinant of the demand for money, the consumer's valuation of time, i.e. the wage rate' (p. 652). The wage rate measures leisure because: 'In equilibrium the marginal valuation of an hour of leisure must be equal to the wage rate'. (p. 652) This is the same justification employed by Karni, of course, and is to be understood as a joint decision involving leisure, goods and money-holding. This effect operates independently of the effect of changes in income (of which the wage rate is a component).

Dutton and Gramm assume that the consumer maximizes the following utility function in which the rates of real consumption of goods and services (c), leisure (L) and end of period real assets (a_1) are the arguments,

$$u = U(c, L, a_1) \tag{2.26}$$

with a_1 defined as a proxy for future consumption and leisure. The consumer is also constrained by a dynamic income constraint of

$$y = wN \tag{2.27}$$

In this general framework, then, there are three additional constraints. The first of these is for the consumer's allocation of time. The consumer spends time on leisure and on work, but the special wrinkle here is his time spent carrying out transactions (T). The constraint is

$$L + W + T = 1 \tag{2.28}$$

The second constraint models the determinants of transactions time. That is, an increase in income or in consumption will tend to increase the frequency and the size of transactions and hence tend to use up more transactions time. On the other hand, the larger the holdings of money balances, stocks of consumer goods or income is, the smaller will be the time used in transactions. The result is the function

$$T = G(y, c, \bar{m}, \bar{y}, \bar{c}) \qquad (G_1, G_2 > 0; G_3, G_4, G_5 < 0) \tag{2.29}$$

The third constraint is an accumulation equation which shows how a_1 is computed:

$$a_1 = (y - c) + \int_0^1 i(1 - t)(y - c)\,dt + (1 + i)a_0 - \sum_{j=1}^{3} \left[\mathrm{i} + \delta_j + \int_0^1 i(1 - t)\delta_j\,dt \right] J \tag{2.30}$$

Here J is the quantity of the asset indexed by j. In this expression i defines a nominal interest rate, the first integral measures earnings on one-period bonds held, while the summation term (Σ) measures the costs of holding the stocks of the three entities (m, c, y). The item δ_j is the storage cost (possibly equal to the inflation rate in the case of money), and the second continuous integral measures the interest lost because the storage costs are paid continuously.

The consumer choice problem is then to choose c, L, a_1, y, $\bar{y}$, $\bar{m}$ and $\bar{c}$ so as to maximize Equation (2.26). The Lagrangean is

$$V = U(c, L, a_1) - \lambda_1 \left\{ a_1 - \left[\left(1 + \frac{i}{2} \right)(y - c) + (1 + i)a_0 + \sum_{j=1}^{3} \left(i + \left(1 + \frac{i}{2} \right)\delta_j \right) J \right] \right\} - \lambda_2 \{ y - w[1 - L - G(y, c, \bar{m}, \bar{y}, \bar{c})] \} \qquad (j \equiv J = \bar{m}, \bar{y}, \bar{c}) \tag{2.31}$$

The first-order conditions include

$$U_c = \lambda_1 \left(1 + \frac{i}{2} \right) \frac{[1 + w(G_y + G_c)]}{1 + wG_y} \tag{2.32}$$

which states 'that the marginal utility of consumption must equal its opportunity cost in terms of the marginal utility of asset acquisition foregone and the transactions time cost incurred valued at the wage rate' (Dutton and Gramm, 1973, p. 654), and

$$U_L = \frac{\lambda_1 (1 + i/2)w}{1 + wG_y} \tag{2.33}$$

which states that the marginal utility of leisure must equal the wage rate, valued in terms of the marginal utility of 'end of period' assets. The first-order conditions also include

$$U_{a_1} = \lambda_1 \tag{2.34}$$

which defines the marginal utility of end-of-period assets.

Putting aside the remaining first-order conditions (the choice variables remaining are the stocks defined above), we note that the demand for money derived from this system (utilizing all the first-order conditions and constraints) is

$$\bar{m} = M(w, i, a_0, \delta_{\bar{m}}, \delta_{\bar{y}}, \delta_{\bar{c}}) \tag{2.35}$$

From the full system, which is displayed in Dutton and Gramm, the expression for the influence of wages on the demand for money in Equation (2.35) is

$$\frac{\partial \bar{m}}{\partial w} = \frac{\lambda_2 (G_c D_{c\bar{m}} + D_{L\bar{m}} + G_y D_{y\bar{m}} + G_{\bar{m}} D_{\bar{m}\bar{m}} + G_{\bar{y}} D_{\bar{y}\bar{m}} + G_{\bar{c}} D_{\bar{c}\bar{m}})}{D} + \frac{[1 - L - G(y, c, \bar{m}, \bar{y}, \bar{c})] D_{\lambda_2 \bar{m}}}{D} \tag{2.36}$$

where D is the system determinant (negative definite) and the D_{ij} are cofactors. Under certain conditions, then, Equation (2.36) can be signed, and, when it can be, it is positive. There is no presumption, in view of the offsetting effects in this expression, that it will be a statistically significant or a large effect, and the proper way to estimate this effect is in a multiple-equation framework with all the entities and constraints included. Even so, single-equation log-linear tests by Dutton and Gramm show highly significant effects, with wage rate elasticities as high as 1.27% (and none lower than 0.76%, in various tests). This is not the test their theoretical work suggests and should not be taken as strong evidence in favour of their hypothesis; as Laidler (1985) says, however, it is suggestive.

2.5 RATIONAL EXPECTATIONS AND THE DEMAND FOR MONEY

For monetary economists, rational expectations has had its biggest impact on policy issues and, in particular, on questions of why monetary policy might not influence real variables if economic agents construct their real spending plans rationally. The emphasis in this literature has been on consumption, investment and government spending – and this is how we plan to treat the subject in Chapter 5. While the demand for money is often given roughly parallel treatment in (non-rational) general equilibrium models of the economy, when it comes to policy effects in general and rational expectations in particular, the demand for money more or less disappears from the discussion. Apparently, by a kind of revealed preference, money does not matter to most economists working on macropolicy problems whether expectations are rational or not (since this is a continuing tradition). Since the variables which influence the standard model of the demand for real money balances – nominal interest rates and real income or wealth – are the same ones that influence the real consumption decision and since the most general derivations of the demand for money emanate from a dynamic-consumption and money-holding context, this is not an especially obvious strategy. It is, in the first instance, the *assumption* of the separability of the consumption and money-holding decisions that has produced this perception, although acceptance of the general tradition of monetary neutrality also plays a part.

Section 2.5.1 will lay out the standard rational-expectations money-demand model as it has been developed and tested in the (small) literature on this subject. Here it will be apparent that there are significant policy issues should rationality fail to hold. In Sections 2.5.2 through 2.5.4, then, several attempts are made to see

(a) whether rationality holds on US data; and
(b) to what extent the non-separability implied by the standard demand-for-money literature is really valid in this context.

The experiments will be on a number of monetary quantities (as laid out in Chapter 1) in order to investigate this aspect of the robustness of the results.

2.5.1 The theoretical argument

The basic reason that rational expectations has been introduced into the money-demand literature is that the demand for money is frequently modelled with permanent income as an argument in that function (instead of, for example, the level of income). The difference between the two measures of income often appears to be empirically uninteresting at the single-equation level but, even so, the possibility exists that a rational rather than an adaptive

description of permanent income might produce some gain in the efficiency and predictability of the demand for money. It could also suggest another path that monetary 'non-neutrality' might take (if rationality fails). Further, there is some evidence that consumption itself might not follow a simple random walk (e.g. in studies by Flavin, 1981, and Muellbauer, 1983) and if this is (partly) due to the existence of a 'liquidity constraint' on consumption, then both the separability and neutrality assumptions used on the demand for money (and implicit in consumption studies) may not hold. Indeed, it can be generalized that if they fail for consumption, they can also be expected to fail for the demand for money, at least under Walras's law, so this seems to provide a sufficient motive to look into these matters. Indeed, to turn this around yet again, a failure of money demand has the same implications for the consumption literature, on the whole.

A version of the short-run demand for money that shows some of these factors can be derived as follows. Suppose that actual changes in the real stock of money arise in two ways:

(a) because the long-run desired stock of money (m_t^{d}) is unequal to the actual stock; and
(b) because some savings (S) are held in the form of money.

With Equation (2.37) describing the demand for money in the long run, then actual changes in the stock of money can be described as in Equation (2.38):

$$m_t^{\mathrm{d}} = \gamma y_t^{\mathrm{e}} - \delta i_t + u_t \tag{2.37}$$

$$m_t - m_{t-1} = c(m_t^{\mathrm{d}} - m_{t-1}) + \mathrm{d}s_t + v_t \tag{2.38}$$

Then, since savings are equal to income less consumption, we can substitute $y_t - c_t$ into Equation (2.38);[5] this substitution is the source of the interaction between the consumer sector and the monetary sector. We can also substitute Equation (2.37) into Equation (2.38) and the final result is ($w_t = u_t + v_t$)

$$m_t - m_{t-1} = c(\gamma y_t^{\mathrm{e}} - \delta i_t - m_{t-1}) + \mathrm{d}(y_t - c_t) + w_t \tag{2.39}$$

In order to deal with the consumption factor in Equation (2.39) we can argue that consumption is a function of expected (permanent) income and the interest rate (nominal, here, for convenience); the relationship is

$$c_t = \beta y_t^{\mathrm{e}} + \mu i_t \tag{2.40}$$

Combining Equations (2.39) and (2.40), the short-run demand for money becomes

$$m_t = (1 - c)m_{t-1} + \mathrm{d}y_t - (\mathrm{d}\mu - c\delta)i_t + (c\gamma - \mathrm{d}\beta)y_t^{\mathrm{e}} + error_t \tag{2.41}$$

We can

(a) estimate this equation directly using a proxy for expected income;
(b) assume that the term on expected income is zero (an absolute-income hypothesis);

(c) employ the Koyck (or some other) lag for expected income; or
(d) assume rational expectations for expected income (and, for that matter, for the interest rate).

The last is indeed where we will go, roughly. Note, though, as this theoretical derivation should make clear, that the money-holding decision is not independent of the consumption decision because of the need to satisfy the flow constraint for the consumer; this appears in Equation (2.41) in the form of the parameter d (which brings in the structural parameters β and μ).[6] In the following material we will assume that money-holding and consumption are functionally separable, for the most part, and we will work with data (as discussed in Chapter 1 which approximately meet this criterion).

Before launching into the economics, however, we need to provide a little time-series statistical background. If an economic time series can be represented by a moving average of order one (MA(1)), then it can be written as

$$m_t = e_t + \beta e_{t-1} \tag{2.42}$$

where e_t is white noise. For $\beta \neq 0$, the successful estimation of a moving-average parameter will smooth the original series. Indeed (Wold's theorem), any stationary time series can be described by a deterministic part and by a moving-average component (series) of possibly infinite order. Without the deterministic part, a moving average of order q is given by

$$m_t = e_t + \beta_1 e_{t-1} + \beta_2 e_{t-2} + \ldots = \sum_{i=0}^{q} \beta_i e_{t-i} \tag{2.43}$$

This is a useful fact if the q required is quite small (since moving-average processes are difficult to estimate) because it provides a possible decomposition of the data into a deterministic (*permanent*) and a stochastic (*transitory*) part.

If an economic time series depends on its own past values, as is frequently claimed to be the case for data generated under rational expectations, then it might be represented as an autoregressive process of order one (AR(1)) as in

$$m_t = \delta_1 m_{t-1} + e_t \tag{2.44}$$

Again, e_t is white noise. Many economic time series are at least AR(1) and, as we will see, the monetary quantities may well have this characteristic.[7] The generalization of Equation (2.44) is

$$m_t = \delta_1 m_{t-1} + \delta_2 m_{t-2} + \ldots + e_t = \sum_{i=1}^{p} \delta_i m_{t-i-1} + e_t$$

where the AR process is of order p. Indeed, and even more generally, both processes can occur together, as in the ARMA(p, q) model of

$$m_t = \sum_{i=1}^{p} \delta_i m_{t-i} + \sum_{j=0}^{q} \beta_j e_{t-j} \tag{2.45}$$

where, as before, e_t is white noise. Finally, and most generally, it is possible to have an ARIMA process, where the differences of the data (of order n) are taken. This would be denoted as ARIMA (p, n, q) where n is the number of times the data are differenced (one time in the data, below).

Returning to the economics, and following MacDonald and Peel (1986), the money-demand hypothesis can be framed as follows.[8] Let the demand for real money balances be defined as

$$m_t^d = \alpha_0 + \alpha_1 y_t^p + \alpha_2 i_t + u_t \tag{2.46}$$

where real-money balances and permanent real income are calculated in the logarithms and i_t is a nominal long-term interest rate. This function, as we have seen, is standard in both the asset- and transactions-theory literature and so we will accept it here, at least for the time being. If we difference Equation (2.46) and assume that permanent income is an unbiased random walk as follows (allowing, however, for $\beta_0 \neq 0$)

$$y_t^p = \beta_0 + y_{t-1}^p + e_t \tag{2.47}$$

we have

$$\Delta m^d = \alpha_1 \beta_0 + \alpha_2 \Delta i + \alpha_1 e_t + u_t - u_{t-1} \tag{2.48}$$

Permanent income would take the form of Equation (2.47) if it were constructed from rational predictions of future income (Hall, 1978). If, then, the nominal interest rate approximately follows a Martingale process (Mishkin, 1978*a*; Pesando, 1979) of

$$i_t - E(i_t | \Omega_{t-1}) = v_t$$

then

$$\Delta m^d = \alpha_1 \beta_0 + \alpha_2 v_t + \alpha_1 e_t + u_t - u_{t-1}$$

which is a moving-average process of order one.[9] Here v_t is the white noise term from the Martingale on interest rates. This error term can be consolidated into a single term, k_t, which is thus also a moving-average process of order one under the assumed conditions.

$$\Delta m_t^d = \alpha_1 \beta_0 + k_t \tag{2.49}$$

Thus, changes in money demand are also a moving-average process of order one, assuming that interest rates follow a Martingale and permanent income is predicted rationally.

The framework just specified is long run in nature; in the short run, institutional factors might still suggest that the quantity of money adjusts adaptively to changes in its arguments. A standard form for the short-run adjustment mechanism is the AR(1) representation of

$$m_t - m_{t-1} = \delta(m_t^d - m_{t-1}) \tag{2.50}$$

We may, then, combine Equations (2.49) and (2.50) to obtain

$$\Delta m_t = (1 - \delta)\Delta m_{t-1} + \delta k_t' + \delta \alpha_1 \beta_0 \tag{2.51}$$

Writing this out in level form we have

$$m_t = (2 - \delta)m_{t-1} + (1 - \delta)m_{t-2} + \delta k_t + \delta \alpha_1 \beta_0 \tag{2.52}$$

Recalling that k is itself a moving-average error term (of order one), we have here an ARIMA(1, 1, 1) model.[10] If $\delta = 1$ (if adjustment is instantaneous), then the process would be ARIMA(0, 1, 1) – the *long-run* case – and if it were a random walk (i.e. if there were no moving-average component), it would be ARIMA(0, 1, 0). This set of possibilities permits one to compare specifications empirically.

There is one further matter of a theoretical nature to discuss here, and that involves the *ad hoc* structure of Equation (2.46). In the discussion so far in this chapter we have suggested that a rigorous theoretical derivation of the demand for money is conceivable, parallel to, and from the same structure as that for the consumption function. If consumption is a function of rationally predicted permanent income and the long-term rate of interest, then, following Hall (1978), consumer expenditures should appear as a random walk as in

$$\log c_t = \gamma_0 + \log c_{t-1} + \eta_t \tag{2.53}$$

If we invoke the transactions theory as described above,[11] then the demand for real-money balances (by consumers) can be written as

$$m_t^{\mathrm{d}} = \beta_0 + \beta_1 \log c_t + \beta_2 i_t + \xi_t \tag{2.54}$$

Combining these yields our earlier Equation (2.46). Thus, dependence on consumption, so long as consumption itself is a random walk due to its dependence on rationally predicted permanent income, provides us with a second rather interesting interpretation of what might be behind the standard demand-for-money model in Equation (2.46). It is, in any case, consistent with the stories told earlier in this chapter. Note that the separability problem is not disposed of, since money-holding could still be constrained by consumption.

The empirical literature on rational expectations in the money-demand function is really quite sparse. Bomhoff's (1980) four-equation theoretical model (in which all variables are forecasted rationally), ends with the equation

$$\Delta \hat{m}_t = (1 - \theta L)a_{1,t} \tag{2.55}$$

for the demand for money. Here the hat identifies a rate of change (of the money stock), and θ represents the moving-average process; L is the lag operator. The process is an ARIMA(0, 1, 1) in this case. Estimates of this model prove to be relatively stable on the Dutch data, especially over the 1955–76 period. The inflation rate is Bomhoff's primary interest, however.

An American study of an earlier vintage is that of Schmidt (1978), who also works with expectations of income, an interest rate and the inflation rate. Schmidt compares two models of the demand for money

$$m_t^* = f(y_t, i_t, \pi_t^e)$$

$$m_t^* = g(y_t^e, i_t^e, \pi_t^e)$$

where the predictions are assumed to be generated rationally. Here the money stock is measured in the level figures. In his tests Schmidt generates optimal predictions of each of the variables and then inserts these into a standard money-demand model that has a lagged dependent variable as an additional argument. In the ARIMA model both expected inflation and the expected nominal interest rate enter significantly, with the latter apparently exerting an independent effect. The two-stage procedure followed here, in which separate forecasts are obtained and then substituted into the money-demand function, is broadly consistent with what was discussed in this section under the heading of 'rational expectations', but the absence of an MA (moving average) term in the OLS (ordinary least squares) tests run is notable. In a more recent paper devoted largely to other issues, Roley (1985) estimates a random-walk money-demand equation. This function, which includes only innovations in other variables (interest rates, inflation and income) as arguments, actually performs quite well over the 1974–83 period (that of the 'missing money' in the USA), but not from 1959 to 1973. Since Roley is looking for something that holds true over the entire 1959–83 period, he does not pursue this topic. His monetary aggregate, incidentally, is SumM1.

There is a related literature on money demand which involves rational forecasts of the money stock in a 'buffer stock' environment. The general idea (Carr and Darby, 1981) is that (part of) money-holdings could act as a shock absorber in consumer portfolios, mainly because other entities which could bear some of the shock are relatively 'sticky' in the short run; these would be income, consumer prices and even interest rates. This seems to be an idea that would be especially suitable for definitions of money that include money-market deposit accounts and the like (possibly up to the savings deposits in the US monetary aggregates). The money-demand equation proposed by Carr and Darby is

$$(m - p)_t = \sum_i b_i x_{it} + \alpha(m - m^a)_t + u_t \tag{2.56}$$

where m and p are logarithms of money and prices. The term m^a is anticipated money. To reflect rational expectations, it is supposed that the following ARIMA process generates the money stock:

$$m_t = \sum_i g_i z_{i,t-1} + v_t \tag{2.57}$$

where $\{z_i\}$ is a set of information variables known at time $t-1$. m^a, then, is the

predicted value of money from Equation (2.56), whereby $m - m^a$ in Equation (2.56) is v_t from Equation (2.57). The errors in the two equations are assumed to be independent of each other.

In their original empirical tests on US data, Carr and Darby claim that this formulation is successful, but their result (the equation was estimated in 2SLS (two-stage least squares)) was challenged by MacKinnon and Milbourne (1984) who argue that if the money stock is also endogenous, then $m - m^a$ will be correlated with u_t – 2SLS-estimating procedure or not – and propose an alternative estimating equation that solves for the reduced form (in m) of Equation (2.56). In comparison tests, the Carr–Darby test provides a significant influence for unanticipated money, while the MacKinnon and Milbourne test does not. These are replicated on British (M1) data by Cuthbertson (1986) who finds little support for either formulation in a series of tests. In a recent empirical paper on the UK (M1) data, Cuthbertson and Taylor (1987) propose a less sophisticated method of estimating anticipated money, based on the Kalman filter (see Harvey and Todd, 1983), and this time the buffer-stock notion is strongly supported.[12]

2.5.2 Some empirical preliminaries: US data

Chapter 1 worked over a set of US data that are available on a disaggregated basis for monetary analysis; these are the data prepared by Swofford and Whitney (1987) from the official Federal Reserve numbers of Farr and Johnson (1985*a*, *b*). In this section we are going to backtrack somewhat, returning to the traditional monetary aggregates (SumM1 and SumM2) in order to compare their performance with the Federal Reserve's Divisia numbers (MSI1, MSI2-Monetary Services Index), with Spindt's MQ (velocity-weighted) index and with the data from Chapter 1 that has been subjected to GARP pretesting. We will, in the first instance, employ MacDonald and Peel's (1986) test procedure, so that a separate description of their work on the British data will not be necessary.

First, the data must be put in a form that is econometrically acceptable. The concern here is the stationarity of the process that generates the data (because it will tend to produce non-stationary patterns in the data). By *stationarity* we mean that a stationary series has

$$\mathrm{COV}(x_t, x_{t-k}) = \mu_k$$

for all k; this would be violated for

$$\mathrm{COV}(x_t, x_{t-k}) = \mu_{k,t}$$

In a nutshell, dependence on time of the autocorrelations in the series in question provides for non-stationarity. Indeed, trend in the basic series (or in its variance) is the likely and usual proximate cause of non-stationarity in economic time series (although seasonal factors are also frequently mentioned in this context). In this section we propose to judge stationarity in

terms of both formal test procedures (in particular, by Dickey–Fuller tests) and less rigorous, but nevertheless revealing, time series plots of various sorts. Some samples of the latter will be included, mostly to illustrate the method.

Beginning with the time series plots, let us consider the means of transforming the US MSI1 data in order to induce stationarity in the series. The MSI1 data are the Fisher-ideal index number version of the traditional M1 (i.e. SumM1) numbers (look back to Table 1.2). If we graph the trend-dominated MSI1, which is published in the form of an index number, it would tend to run off the page, strongly suggesting non-stationarity; this is the case in Figure 2.1.

The reason that trend is a culprit is that it provides a proxy for trend-related influences on money demand and since trend is (by itself) of no particular interest for the cycle-related stories we are interested in, the obvious thing to do is to detrend the logarithms of the data (we often work in logarithms in these studies, in order to control for changes in the variance of the data). That is, we would use as our measure of money the residuals from the following regression:

$$\log M = \alpha + \beta T$$

This is most frequently done in the literature, usually implicitly by running a regression in logs and including trend as a regressor. In any case, if we were to detrend the data directly, we would get the pattern of residuals shown in Figure 2.2. This is not as bad as the raw series, in the sense of exploding to the borders of the diagram, at least up to 1980 or so, but it fails to provide a transformation of the raw data that is unambiguously stationary.

Frequently recommended in such cases (e.g. Nelson and Plosser, 1982) is the use of differenced data – of either raw M or the logs of M, whatever the measure of M. In Figure 2.3, then, the latter does actually appear to produce a stationary series on the quarterly US MSI1 series, at least in the sense that the series tends to return to zero (and the deviations do not get any larger over time, probably on account of the logarithmic transformation). We note, especially, that the cyclical character of the data seems intact, an important consideration if topics such as what happened to the 'missing money' in the USA are to be investigated.

Before going on to the formal comparison of the various measures, let us briefly return to the discussion of Chapter 1, and recall that none of the standard measures (SumM1, SumM2, MQ, MSI1 or MSI2) satisfies the general axiom of revealed preference (or, more accurately, their components do not, when taken as a collection). In Chapter 1, when we examined sets of monetary assets, those labelled A1, A2 and A3, we found that a set of A1, A2 and A3, when taken with total consumption expenditures (identified as A4), actually did pass GARP. We propose to use an amended version of these entities to construct an alternative aggregate.

Earlier we established that A3 (time deposits at financial institutions) is apparently not separable from consumption expenditures, so that the

Residual plot

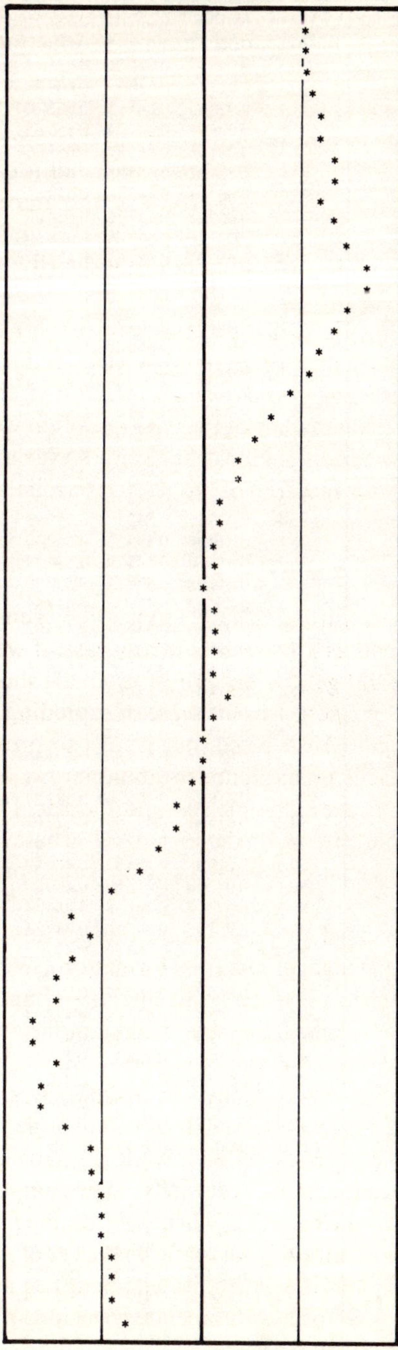

obs	*Residual*	*Actual*	*Fitted*
70.1	0.185 78	1.872 06	1.686 29
70.2	0.172 18	1.858 47	1.686 29
70.3	0.181 98	1.868 27	1.686 29
70.4	0.192 69	1.878 98	1.686 29
71.1	0.213 89	1.900 18	1.686 29
71.2	0.224 94	1.911 22	1.686 29
71.3	0.234 47	1.920 76	1.686 29
71.4	0.239 02	1.925 30	1.686 29
72.1	0.214 34	1.900 62	1.686 29
72.2	0.238 00	1.924 29	1.686 29
72.3	0.259 85	1.946 14	1.686 29
72.4	0.289 59	1.975 88	1.686 29
73.1	0.297 09	1.983 37	1.686 29
73.2	0.282 22	1.968 51	1.686 29
73.3	0.263 55	1.949 84	1.686 29
73.4	0.241 28	1.927 56	1.686 29
74.1	0.199 52	1.885 81	1.686 29
74.2	0.164 42	1.850 71	1.686 29
74.3	0.123 51	1.809 80	1.686 29
74.4	0.096 24	1.782 53	1.686 29
75.1	0.058 96	1.745 24	1.686 29
75.2	0.056 51	1.742 80	1.686 29
75.3	0.047 25	1.733 53	1.686 29
75.4	0.033 44	1.719 73	1.686 29
76.1	0.013 54	1.699 82	1.686 29
76.2	0.018 25	1.704 54	1.686 29
76.3	0.009 46	1.695 75	1.686 29
76.4	0.017 40	1.703 68	1.686 29
77.1	0.020 44	1.706 72	1.686 29
77.2	0.010 98	1.697 27	1.686 29
77.3	0.014 38	1.700 67	1.686 29
77.4	0.034 26	1.720 55	1.686 29
78.1	0.018 00	1.704 29	1.686 29
78.2	0.000 92	1.687 21	1.686 29
78.3	−0.007 95	1.678 34	1.686 29
78.4	−0.013 64	1.672 64	1.686 29
79.1	−0.034 76	1.651 52	1.686 29
79.2	−0.048 92	1.637 36	1.686 29
79.3	−0.071 32	1.614 96	1.686 29
79.4	−0.108 67	1.577 62	1.686 29
80.1	−0.166 45	1.519 84	1.686 29
80.2	−0.221 69	1.464 59	1.686 29
80.3	−0.197 80	1.488 49	1.686 29
80.4	−0.211 20	1.475 09	1.686 29
81.1	−0.245 10	1.441 18	1.686 29
81.2	−0.243 37	1.442 91	1.686 29
81.3	−0.275 88	1.410 41	1.686 29
81.4	−0.268 99	1.417 29	1.686 29
82.1	−0.246 71	1.439 58	1.686 29
82.2	−0.259 10	1.427 19	1.686 29
82.3	−0.264 60	1.421 69	1.686 29
82.4	−0.222 32	1.463 97	1.686 29
83.1	−0.203 24	1.483 04	1.686 29
83.2	−0.189 00	1.497 29	1.686 29
83.3	−0.181 50	1.504 78	1.686 29
83.4	−0.176 94	1.509 35	1.686 29
84.1	−0.169 57	1.516 71	1.686 29
84.2	−0.166 64	1.519 65	1.686 29
84.3	−0.166 28	1.520 01	1.686 29
84.4	−0.165 39	1.520 90	1.686 29
85.1	−0.141 34	1.544 95	1.686 29

Figure 2.1 Real MSI1.

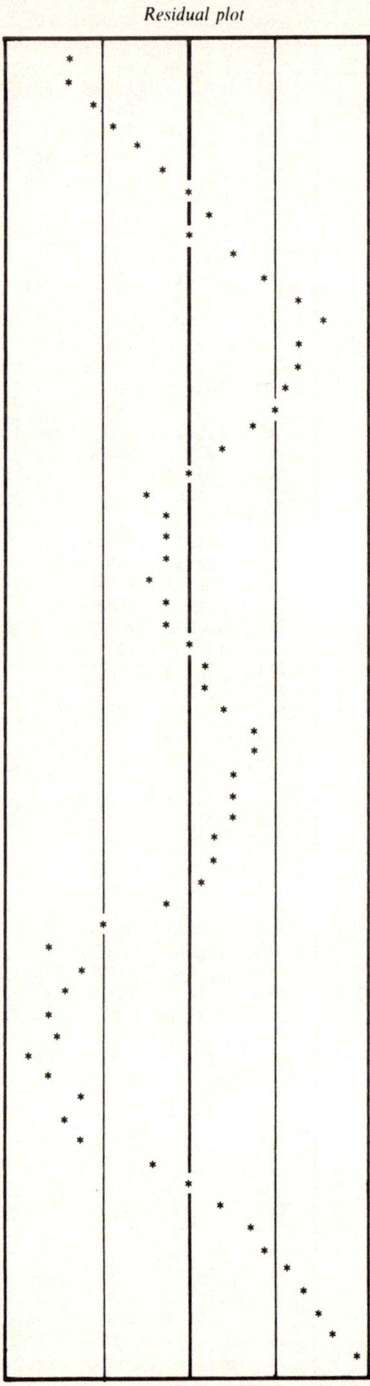

obs	Residual	Actual	Fitted
70.1	−0.057 57	0.627 04	0.684 61
70.2	−0.059 27	0.619 75	0.679 02
70.3	−0.048 42	0.625 01	0.673 43
70.4	−0.037 11	0.630 73	0.667 83
71.1	−0.020 30	0.641 95	0.662 24
71.2	−0.008 91	0.647 74	0.656 65
71.3	0.001 66	0.652 72	0.651 06
71.4	0.009 62	0.655 08	0.645 46
72.1	0.002 31	0.642 18	0.639 87
72.2	0.020 28	0.654 56	0.634 28
72.3	0.037 16	0.665 85	0.628 69
72.4	0.057 92	0.681 01	0.623 09
73.1	0.067 30	0.684 80	0.617 50
73.2	0.065 37	0.677 28	0.611 91
73.3	0.061 43	0.667 75	0.606 31
73.4	0.055 54	0.656 26	0.600 72
74.1	0.039 23	0.634 35	0.595 13
74.2	0.026 03	0.615 57	0.589 54
74.3	0.009 27	0.593 21	0.583 94
74.4	−0.000 32	0.578 03	0.578 35
75.1	−0.015 86	0.556 89	0.572 76
75.2	−0.011 67	0.555 49	0.567 16
75.3	−0.011 41	0.550 16	0.561 57
75.4	−0.013 81	0.542 17	0.555 98
76.1	−0.019 86	0.530 52	0.550 39
76.2	−0.011 50	0.533 29	0.544 79
76.3	−0.011 08	0.528 12	0.539 20
76.4	−0.000 82	0.532 79	0.533 61
77.1	0.006 56	0.534 57	0.528 02
77.2	0.006 60	0.529 02	0.522 42
77.3	0.014 19	0.531 02	0.516 83
77.4	0.031 41	0.542 64	0.511 24
78.1	0.027 50	0.533 15	0.505 64
78.2	0.023 02	0.523 07	0.500 05
78.3	0.023 34	0.517 80	0.494 46
78.4	0.025 54	0.514 41	0.488 87
79.1	0.018 42	0.501 70	0.483 27
79.2	0.015 41	0.493 09	0.477 68
79.3	0.007 22	0.479 31	0.472 09
79.4	−0.010 58	0.455 92	0.466 49
80.1	−0.042 30	0.418 60	0.460 90
80.2	−0.073 73	0.381 58	0.455 31
80.3	−0.051 95	0.397 76	0.449 72
80.4	−0.055 41	0.388 72	0.444 12
81.1	−0.073 07	0.365 46	0.438 53
81.2	−0.066 27	0.366 67	0.432 94
81.3	−0.083 47	0.343 88	0.427 34
81.4	−0.073 00	0.348 75	0.421 75
82.1	−0.051 81	0.364 35	0.416 16
82.2	−0.054 86	0.355 71	0.410 57
82.3	−0.053 13	0.351 84	0.404 97
82.4	−0.018 23	0.381 15	0.399 38
83.1	0.000 31	0.394 10	0.393 79
83.2	0.015 46	0.403 66	0.388 20
83.3	0.026 05	0.408 65	0.382 60
83.4	0.034 67	0.411 68	0.377 01
84.1	0.045 13	0.416 54	0.371 42
84.2	0.052 66	0.418 48	0.365 82
84.3	0.058 48	0.418 72	0.360 23
84.4	0.064 66	0.419 30	0.354 64
85.1	0.085 95	0.434 99	0.349 05

Figure 2.2 Real MSI1 – detrended logs.

Residual plot

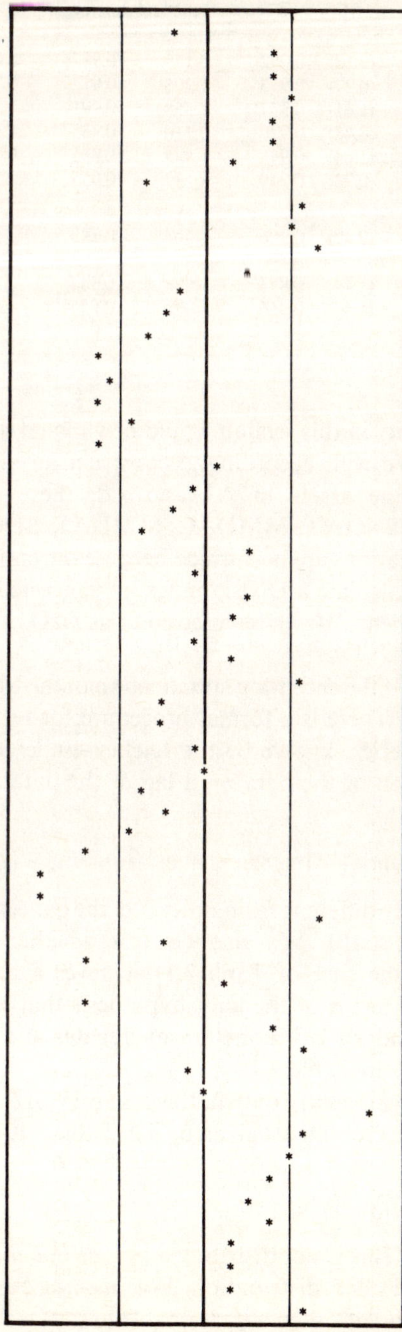

obs	Residual	Actual	Fitted
70.2	−0.004 09	−0.007 29	−0.003 20
70.3	0.008 46	0.005 26	−0.003 20
70.4	0.008 92	0.005 72	−0.003 20
71.1	0.014 42	0.011 22	−0.003 20
71.2	0.009 00	0.005 80	−0.003 20
71.3	0.008 18	0.004 98	−0.003 20
71.4	0.005 56	0.002 36	−0.003 20
72.1	−0.009 70	−0.012 90	−0.003 20
72.2	0.015 58	0.012 38	−0.003 20
72.3	0.014 49	0.011 29	−0.003 20
72.4	0.018 37	0.015 17	−0.003 20
73.1	0.006 99	0.003 78	−0.003 20
73.2	−0.004 32	−0.007 52	−0.003 20
73.3	−0.006 33	−0.009 53	−0.003 20
73.4	−0.008 29	−0.011 49	−0.003 20
74.1	−0.018 70	−0.021 90	−0.003 20
74.2	−0.015 59	−0.018 79	−0.003 20
74.3	−0.019 15	−0.022 35	−0.003 20
74.4	−0.011 98	−0.015 18	−0.003 20
75.1	−0.017 94	−0.021 14	−0.003 20
75.2	0.001 80	−0.001 40	−0.003 20
75.3	−0.002 13	−0.005 33	−0.003 20
75.4	−0.004 79	−0.007 99	−0.003 20
76.1	−0.008 44	−0.011 64	−0.003 20
76.2	0.005 97	0.002 77	−0.003 20
76.3	−0.001 97	−0.005 17	−0.003 20
76.4	0.007 87	0.004 67	−0.003 20
77.1	0.004 98	0.001 78	−0.003 20
77.2	−0.002 35	−0.005 55	−0.003 20
77.3	0.005 20	0.002 00	−0.003 20
77.4	0.014 82	0.011 62	−0.003 20
78.1	−0.006 30	−0.009 50	−0.003 20
78.2	−0.006 87	−0.010 07	−0.003 20
78.3	−0.002 07	−0.005 27	−0.003 20
78.4	−0.000 20	−0.003 40	−0.003 20
79.1	−0.009 51	−0.012 71	−0.003 20
79.2	−0.005 41	−0.008 61	−0.003 20
79.3	−0.010 57	−0.013 77	−0.003 20
79.4	−0.020 20	−0.023 40	−0.003 20
80.1	−0.034 11	−0.037 31	−0.003 20
80.2	−0.033 83	−0.037 03	−0.003 20
80.3	0.019 38	0.016 18	−0.003 20
80.4	−0.005 84	−0.009 04	−0.003 20
81.1	−0.020 05	−0.023 25	−0.003 20
81.2	0.004 40	0.001 20	−0.003 20
81.3	−0.019 59	−0.022 79	−0.003 20
81.4	0.008 07	0.004 87	−0.003 20
82.1	0.018 80	0.015 60	−0.003 20
82.2	−0.005 44	−0.008 64	−0.003 20
82.3	−0.000 66	−0.003 86	−0.003 20
82.4	0.032 51	0.029 31	−0.003 20
83.1	0.016 15	0.012 95	−0.003 20
83.2	0.012 76	0.009 56	−0.003 20
83.3	0.008 19	0.004 99	−0.003 20
83.4	0.006 23	0.003 03	−0.003 20
84.1	0.008 07	0.004 87	−0.003 20
84.2	0.005 14	0.001 94	−0.003 20
84.3	0.003 44	0.000 24	−0.003 20
84.4	0.003 79	0.000 59	−0.003 20
85.1	0.018 89	0.015 69	−0.003 20

Figure 2.3 Real MSI1 – differenced logs.

Table 2.1 Dickey–Fuller tests on US data, logarithms (1970–85)

Variable	μ	(t)	α	(t)	δ	τ	Adjusted R^2	DW
SumM1	0.002	(0.06)	0.0001	(0.18)	0.992	−0.179	0.987	1.074
SumM2	0.120	(0.10)	−0.0000	(0.27)	0.953	−1.205	0.912	0.742
MQ	0.247	(1.60)	−0.0006	(1.61)	0.937	−1.558	0.991	1.157
MSI1	0.016	(0.55)	−0.0001	(0.48)	0.970	−0.710	0.985	1.111
MSI2	0.046	(1.97)	−0.0006	(2.44)	0.946	−1.885	0.985	0.789
A2D	−0.000	(0.04)	−0.0003	(0.73)	0.949	−1.137	0.955	1.135
Non-durable consumption	0.144	(1.55)	0.0000	(0.49)	0.906	−1.562	0.793	1.507
Durable consumption	0.040	(1.99)	0.0006	(1.44)	0.875	−1.922	0.882	1.920
Total consumption	0.205	(1.51)	0.0002	(1.44)	0.916	−1.496	0.955	1.524

maintained assumption of separability in this section would be violated if we were to include its components. We will, accordingly, construct an alternative measure of money from the assets in A1 and A2; these are: CUR+DDCON, OCD, SNOWC, SNOWT, MMDAC, MMDAT, SDCB, and SDSL + SDSB. Here the summations are performed because the entities have identical user costs. We then calculate a Divisia index, as suggested by aggregation theory, of these components. It will be referred to as A2D in the following exercises.

What we have seen, then, is that a differenced-log specification of the MSI1 data appears to induce stationarity. There is a formal procedure for testing for 'unit-roots' in economic time series, known as the Dickey–Fuller test. What one does is to run a regression of the data on a lag of the data and trend, as in

$$\log M_t = \mu + \alpha \text{ trend} + \delta \log M_{t-1} + e_t \tag{2.58}$$

and then test to see if δ is significantly different from unity (i.e. the concern is that the data might have a 'unit-root'). We also test for whether the differencing (of the logarithms in the case of Table 2.1) achieves a result which is unrelated to trend (i.e. the test is of the joint hypothesis that $\alpha = 0$ and $\delta = 1$). The results, for the standard US monetary aggregates and the quarterly consumption data, appear in Table 2.1.

In Table 2.1, then, trend enters significantly only in the case of MSI2. We also perform Dickey–Fuller tests on the statistic given by δ in Table 2.1. The test statistic is calculated as

$$DF = (\delta - 1)/S_\delta$$

where S_δ is the standard error on δ. This is not distributed as t, as one might suspect, but has its own 'Dickey–Fuller' distribution. For an n of 50, for example, if the test statistic exceeds -2.93, then we are unable to say (at the 5 per cent level) that the data series does *not* contain a unit root. Given the

results in the τ column of Table 2.1, it is clear that each of the series quite possibly has a unit root and is, thereby, non-stationary. The solution, of course, is either to difference the data or detrend it by some other method. This is the normal result for both monetary and consumption data.

2.5.3 The identification of a rational expectations model

The discussion to this point suggests that the appropriate monetary variables would be differenced (i.e. 'integrated order one') logarithms of the representative monetary aggregate, with broader measures doing somewhat better than narrower, although only marginally so. The theoretical discussion, in Section 2.5.1 suggests that (accepting the differencing) should we *identify* a model on the data having an

$$\text{ARIMA}(1, 1, 1)$$

we would be supporting the 'adjustment-version' of the rational expectations hypothesis; should we have an

$$\text{ARIMA}(0, 1, 1)$$

we would be supporting instantaneous adjustment in a rational expectations context; and should we find

$$\text{ARIMA}(0, 1, 0)$$

the implication would be that the data are a random walk (which is also certainly consistent with rational expectations).

In order to identify a model for a time series, be it rational or not, the first thing we could do is look at the autocorrelation, partial autocorrelation and inverse autocorrelation functions. Let us do this, for SumM2 (which we might suspect is a flawed measure of moneyness on account of its being simple-sum in construction), MSI1 and A2D. These last two, to repeat, are the official Fisher-ideal indices and the GARPed Divisia-aggregated variable from Chapter 1. We will also present a summary of our results for all of the other variables, but, of course, the plots are too numerous to reproduce here. What we are looking for is explained in the following summary.

	$MA(q)$	$AR(p)$	$ARMA(p, q)$	White noise
Autocorrelation function	$D(q)$	T	T	0
Partial autocorrelation function	T	$D(p)$	T	0
Inverse autocorrelation function	T	$D(p)$	T	0

Here $D(q)$ means that the function drops off after lag q; T means that it tails off exponentially and 0 means that the function is zero at all non-zero lags.

For SumM2, the autocorrelation (ACF) and partial autocorrelation (PACF) functions are exhibited in Figure 2.4 – we will forbear to show the

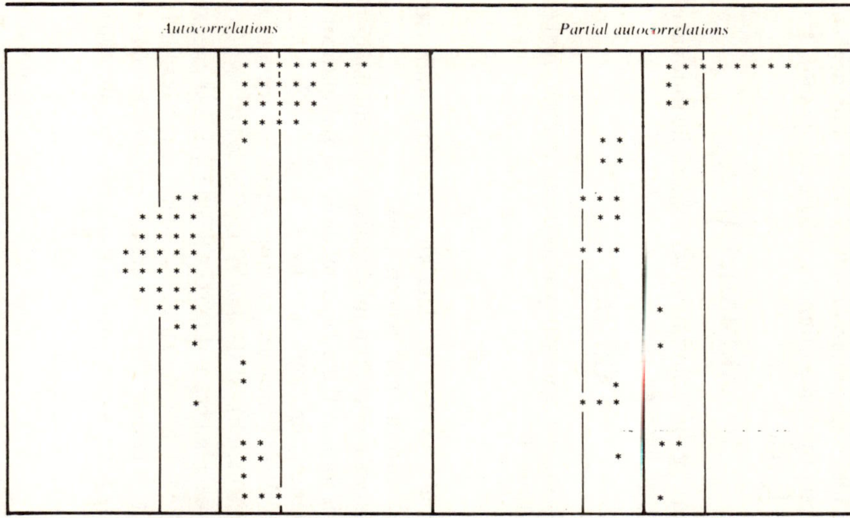

Lag	AC	PAC
1	0.580	0.580
2	0.372	0.052
3	0.352	0.178
4	0.270	−0.012
5	0.098	−0.147
6	−0.024	−0.118
7	−0.030	0.010
8	−0.178	−0.209
9	−0.290	−0.116
10	−0.276	−0.025
11	−0.373	−0.220
12	−0.374	0.002
13	−0.320	−0.011
14	−0.205	0.084
15	−0.156	0.029
16	−0.077	0.078
17	0.044	0.038
18	0.044	−0.066
19	−0.048	−0.243
20	0.038	0.009
21	0.188	0.137
22	0.154	−0.051
23	0.111	0.016
24	0.207	0.112

Notes: *Q*-statistic (24 lags) 87.047; SE of correlations 0.129.
*The actual variable used is the differenced logarithm of SumM2.

Figure 2.4 Graphical identification of SumM2* (1970–1 to 1985–2).

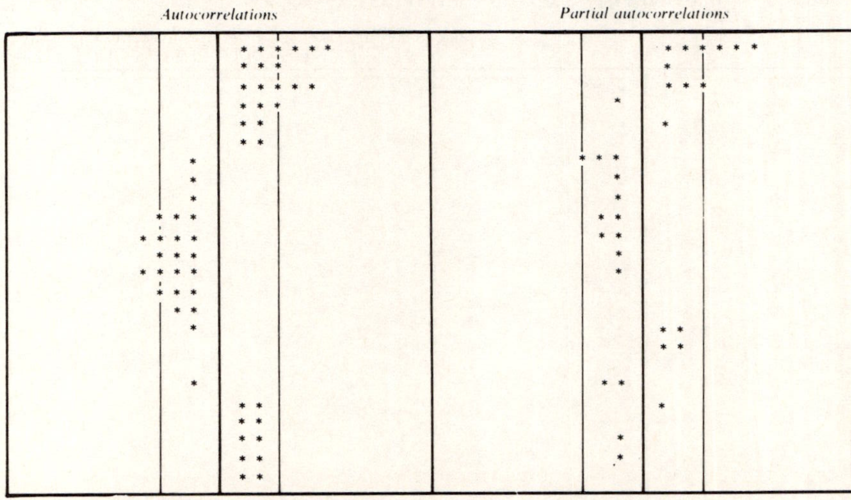

	AC	PAC
1	0.424	0.424
2	0.252	0.088
3	0.351	0.267
4	0.194	−0.057
5	0.167	0.068
6	0.144	−0.030
7	−0.091	−0.234
8	−0.084	−0.044
9	−0.067	−0.056
10	−0.252	−0.177
11	−0.288	−0.132
12	−0.247	−0.049
13	−0.308	−0.070
14	−0.240	0.008
15	−0.184	0.021
16	−0.113	0.155
17	0.022	0.152
18	0.006	−0.006
19	−0.071	−0.120
20	0.118	0.097
21	0.178	0.019
22	0.129	−0.041
23	0.157	−0.056
24	0.149	−0.004

Notes: *Q*-statistic (24 lags) 59.578; SE of correlations 0.129.
*The actual variable used is the differenced logarithm of MSII.

Figure 2.5 Graphical identification of MSII* (1970–1 to 1985–1).

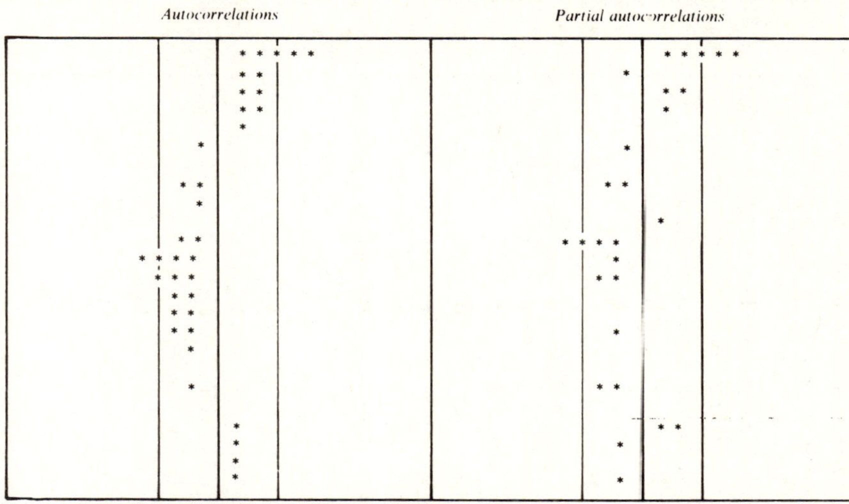

Lag	AC	PAC
1	0.411	0.411
2	0.122	−0.056
3	0.126	0.116
4	0.164	0.091
5	0.079	−0.032
6	−0.060	−0.107
7	−0.027	0.028
8	−0.120	−0.168
9	−0.100	0.018
10	0.026	0.112
11	−0.184	−0.282
12	−0.271	−0.089
13	−0.263	−0.120
14	−0.144	−0.037
15	−0.121	−0.002
16	−0.171	−0.051
17	−0.080	0.002
18	−0.035	0.026
19	−0.061	−0.121
20	−0.024	−0.019
21	0.066	0.116
22	0.059	−0.062
23	0.039	0.034
24	0.058	−0.054

Notes: *Q*-statistic (24 lags) 31.678; SE of correlations 0.129.
*The actual variable used is the differenced logarithm of A2D.

Figure 2.6 Graphical identification of A2D* (1970–1 to 1985–2).

Table 2.2 Identification results, US monetary and consumption data (1970–1 to 1985–1)

Variable	Identification stage		
SumM1	ARIMA (1, 1, 3)	or	ARIMA (3, 1, 3)
SumM2	ARIMA (?, 1, 1)		
MQ	ARIMA (?, 1, 3)		
MSI1	ARIMA (0, 1, 3)	or	ARIMA (3, 1, 3)
MSI2	ARIMA (1, 1, 3)	or	ARIMA (3, 1, 3)
A2D	ARIMA (1, 1, 1)		
Non-durable consumption	ARIMA (?, 1, 3)		
Durable consumption	ARIMA (0, 1, 0)		
Total consumption	ARIMA (3, 1, 3)		

inverse autocorrelations, although they occasionally provide different information, as we shall see. Here the ACF drops off fairly quickly, but certainly not exponentially, and it also cycles; this suggests an ARMA (p, q) representation. The partial autocorrelation function drops off after one lag, suggesting an AR(1) process at work. Combining these insights one might expect an ARIMA(1, 1, ?) with possibly a low-order MA term. This variable would be expected to do well in a rational expectations test.

A second variable which has stood up reasonably well in other tests in this study, MSI1 (the Fisher-ideal index figure produced by the Federal Reserve), in this case appears to be represented by a low-order AR process but possibly higher order MA. In Figure 2.5 we show the ACF and PACF for this variable. Here, again, the autocorrelation function declines too slowly, with a strong cycle. (Note that in both cases the Q-statistic is quite significant (the expected value for Q is 24 for 24 lags) and several autocorrelations are significant, both being findings which indicate an error structure in the data that is highly non-random.) The PACF shows a similar pattern to SumM2, with several shorter lags showing marginal significance (the correlations are out to the vertical lines, which indicate two standard deviations). This data, too, could be modelled as ARIMA(1, 1, ?), with a possibly longer MA term than rational expectations would support.

The graphical identification of the variable we have proposed in this study, the Divisia index of the successfully 'GARPed' cash and savings deposit variables (A2D), is shown in Figure 2.6. Here the ACF drops off quite sharply, while there is only a suggestion of a higher process, at a lag of $t - 11$. We can identify an MA(1) and an AR(1), such that an ARIMA(1, 1, 1) might be appropriate. This pattern, with its non-significant Q-statistic, is much the most likely of the three variables examined to pass the rational expectations test.

Table 2.2 collects the results of an inspection of the data for the eight series which we are examining here. The reader is warned that this is an impressionistic procedure subject to different interpretations by different researchers. We do not plan to leave matters in quite this nebulous a state, however.

Table 2.3 AIC coefficients for SumM2* (ARIMA procedure)

		Moving average lags				
		0	1	2	3	4
Autoregressive lags	0	−325.90	−346.92	−347.80	−346.77	−347.36
	1	−352.00**	−350.03	−349.30	−347.98	−347.21
	2	−343.73	−349.14	−345.52	NC	−349.02
	3	−341.82	−348.22	−346.54	−348.71	−348.60
	4	−348.25	−346.96	−344.65	−349.35	−347.70

* The actual variable used is the differenced logarithms of SumM2.
NC = non-converged after 50 iterations.
**Optimal value.

In Table 2.2 the '?' identifies significant lags of fairly long duration (e.g. 11 quarters), while the appearance of two models indicates the model suggested by the IACF (inverse auto-correlation function) v. the PACF. Of the monetary variables examined in this way, only A2D appears to be highly likely to meet the specifications of the rational expectations hypothesis, although SumM2 has some potential in this direction, depending on how long the lags in the AR process turn out. MSI1 does not do as well here, as indicated in Figure 2.5, in view of the behaviour of the inverse autocorrelation function (not shown there). We note that the consumption variables exhibited similar difficulties, with durable consumption satisfying the informal test (it turns out to be a random walk, in differenced-logarithmic form). These are not unusual results for the aggregate consumption numbers either.

2.5.4 Rational expectations estimations

In the following pages we will consider several sorts of estimations consistent with the rational expectations hypothesis. The first of these will be a series of estimates of the ARIMA(p, d, q) form, over a grid of the likely possibilities, in order to see just what can be determined about the true nature of the model that generates the data; again we are looking for ARIMA(1, 1, 1), (0, 1, 1) and (0, 1, 0) models as consistent with the rational hypothesis. In the first test, to be discussed in a moment, we cover the grid of possibilities employing the ARIMA model, using the Akaike criterion (AIC) in order to choose the best model.[13] A typical set of results for this test appears in Table 2.3 for SumM2; we wish to minimize the AIC.

The procedure illustrated in Table 2.3 selects an ARIMA(1,1,0) representation for SumM2, indicated by the asterisk; this is close to the rational expectations predictions but is not one of our three models. The specification ARIMA(1, 1, 1) is the second best reported here and is a specification consistent with rational expectations.

For the variable A2D we can look at a similar collection of the AIC numbers, again searching for a minimum to the AIC (Table 2.4). This test selects the same model (ARIMA(1, 1, 0)), but in this case an

Table 2.4 AIC coefficients for A2D* (ARIMA procedure)

		Moving average lags				
		0	1	2	3	4
Autoregressive lags	0		−228.33	−226.76	−224.80	−223.20
	1	−228.49**	−226.85	−225.24	−223.32	−221.85
	2	−226.70	−224.94	−221.66	−221.26	−222.36
	3	−225.46	−223.67	−226.64	−223.76	−220.78
	4	−223.92	−221.94	−220.77	−216.90	NC

* The actual variable used is the differenced logarithms of A2D.
NC = non-converged after 50 iterations.
** Optimal value.

Table 2.5 Model selection (ARIMA (*p*, *d*, *q*) specifications)

Variable	AIC model	Most significant*
SumM1	ARIMA (3, 1, 1)	ARIMA (2, 1, 4)
SumM2	ARIMA (1, 1, 0)	ARIMA (1, 1, 0)
MQ	ARIMA (4, 1, 2)	ARIMA (1, 1, 3)
MSI1	ARIMA (3, 1, 3)	ARIMA (3, 1, 0)
MSI2	ARIMA (2, 1, 3)	ARIMA (2, 1, 3)
A2D	ARIMA (1, 1, 0)	ARIMA (1, 1, 0)
Non-durable consumption	ARIMA (1, 1, 4)	ARIMA (0, 1, 3)
Durable consumption	ARIMA (0, 1, 0)	ARIMA (0, 1, 0)
Total consumption	ARIMA (3, 1, 0)	ARIMA (3, 1, 0)

* Models in which the longest lag for *each* process is significant (0.05 level). The standard error of the regression was employed to break ties.

ARIMA(0, 1, 1) is not far behind. The results drop off steadily from this point, as well.

It seems, then, that both SumM2 and the Divisia measure A2D perform well enough in this test to suggest looking further towards other implications of the rational expectations theory. Before doing that, however, Table 2.5 presents the results of following the same procedure for all the variables we have been considering. These appear in the AIC model column of the table. In this column it is quite clear that while none of the data has very long ARIMA footprints, durable consumption alone appears to satisfy the criteria for rationally determined variables, although SumM2 and A2D come close. The other monetary data, perhaps for reasons already provided in this study (mostly referring to crimes of aggregation) appear to have no chance of passing a formal rational expectations test, since the data themselves cannot be described as 'rational'. In a second look, in the last column of the table, an attempt was made to locate the most significant result, picking AR and MA processes which terminated in a significant lag and then choosing among the survivors the one with the lowest residual error. This did not produce any major changes in the results.

The last test we propose to look at here, again following many of MacDonald and Peel's (1986) suggestions, is to see if any variables known to economic agents *at the time they formed their expectations* also influence the results of the agents acting on their own assumptions. This is a 'semi-strong form' test of market efficiency (as defined by Fama, 1970). That is, as this literature puts it, *current* realizations of a rationally determined variable should be independent of (*orthogonal* to) information available in *previous* time periods if this information is correctly incorporated (using a correct model) into the plans of the rational economic agents. In particular, the current values of the variables (SumM2 and A2D here) should be independent of the past values of anything known to agents at the time they set their plans in motion. This means no significant correlation from the lagged values of such entities as interest, income or even the past values of the supposedly rational variables themselves (assuming, as we are, that we are modelling the variables in log-difference form).

Table 2.6 illustrates two sets of what we are arbitrarily calling 'information-orthogonality tests' for SumM2. In the first nine rows of the table we have illustrated three different collections of information variables; these are lagged values of the commercial paper rate (R), SumM2 itself (M), total consumption expenditures (C) and real GNP (Y). Note that R1 indicates the first lag on the interest rate, etc. In this first part of the table, three different model specifications are attempted, each consistent with rational expectations as described above, as indicated by the first column of the table. Employing the AIC to choose the best representation, the model selected is in Line 5 and is an ARIMA(0, 1, 1) representing the long-run rational expectations framework. Because four of the information variables (R1, R2, M1 and M2) are significant, however, we reject the hypothesis of rationality for these data. It is noticeable that none of the nine specifications is free of this problem. This is, indeed, the typical result in the literature.

MacDonald and Peel suggest that economic agents may not actually have known the values of the variables R1, M1, C1 and Y1 at the time they set their plans in motion and that it might be unreasonable to expect these variables not to show an influence on the realization for the money stock, one period later.[14] They propose simply dropping these variables in a second pass at the data. In their case, this does not alter the conclusion of non-rationality, but for SumM2 the test comes down much more strongly in favour of rationality when judged this way, with the model selected by the AIC being in Row 11. This result is again an ARIMA(0, 1, 1), showing only one violation for Y4. This is a somewhat anomalous result which might well be the result of the incorrect deseasonalisation of the data rather than of a failure of the rational hypothesis. All-in-all, this first set of results, unlike those obtained in the British study which is our model, does well for the rational propositions.

Our second strong candidate for rationality is A2D, the GARP-tested Divisia aggregate. In Table 2.7 we put it through the same paces as SumM2,

Table 2.6 Information orthogonality tests: SumM2

Variable	Model	R1	R2	R3	R4	M1	M2	M3	M4	C1	C2	C3	C4	Y1	Y2	Y3	Y4	AIC
log SumM2	(0, 1, 0)	−0.0074*	0.0044*	−0.0001	0.0045*									0.0078*	0.0097*	−0.0018	−0.0244*	−372.085
		(7.55)	(3.59)	(0.09)	(4.55)									(2.17)	(2.16)	(0.40)	(6.43)	
log SumM2	(0, 1, 1)	−0.0072*	0.0041*	−0.0001	0.0046*									0.0058	0.0120	−0.0024	−0.239*	−371.187
		(6.84)	(3.37)	(0.10)	(3.96)									(0.90)	(1.37)	(0.31)	(3.76)	
log SumM2	(1, 1, 1)	−0.0072*	0.0041*	−0.0001	0.0046*									0.0058	0.0124	−0.0028	−0.0238*	−369.215
		(6.76)	(3.25)	(0.08)	(3.90)									(0.88)	(1.36)	(0.34)	(3.70)	
log SumM2	(0, 1, 0)	−0.0071*	0.0037*	−0.0013	0.0036*	0.0076	−0.0218	0.0130	−0.0091					0.0043	0.0125	0.0010	−0.0182*	−370.842
		(6.71)	(2.63)	(0.85)	(2.63)	(0.72)	(1.48)	(0.89)	(1.02)					(0.71)	(1.58)	(0.14)	(2.69)	
log SumM2	(0, 1, 1)	−0.0061*	0.0073*	−0.0024	0.0010	0.0682*	−0.0907*	0.0220	−0.0036					0.0044	0.0030	−0.0040	−0.0049	−381.148
		(7.09)	(4.16)	(1.20)	(0.84)	(4.61)	(3.45)	(0.91)	(0.34)					(0.63)	(0.24)	(0.34)	(0.65)	
log SumM2	(1, 1, 1)	−0.0070*	0.0041*	−0.0020	0.0040*	0.0148	−0.0384	0.0275	−0.0136					0.0048	0.0100	0.0038	−0.0193*	−370.504
		(6.68)	(2.80)	(1.22)	(2.79)	(1.14)	(1.77)	(1.34)	(1.32)					(0.73)	(1.07)	(0.43)	(2.62)	
log SumM2	(0, 1, 0)	−0.0063*	0.0038*	−0.0008	0.0011	0.0073*	−0.0184*	0.0076*	−0.0092*	0.0209*	−0.0095*	0.0069*	−0.0141*					−363.031
		(7.17)	(3.17)	(0.67)	(1.16)	(2.64)	(6.52)	(2.76)	(3.75)	(7.80)	(3.41)	(2.42)	(4.89)					
log SumM2	(0, 1, 1)	−0.0066*	0.0045*	−0.0010	0.0017	0.0127	−0.0199	0.0052	−0.0060	0.0210*	−0.0097	0.0068	−0.0168					−359.577
		(5.50)	(2.60)	(0.61)	(1.28)	(1.08)	(1.89)	(0.49)	(0.77)	(2.14)	(0.90)	(0.90)	(1.55)					
log SumM2	(1, 1, 1)	−0.0061*	0.0088*	−0.0036	0.0010	0.0733*	−0.0911*	0.0140	0.0012	0.0219*	−0.0262*	0.0168	−0.0142					−371.550
		(7.29)	(4.80)	(1.92)	(0.89)	(8.14)	(7.78)	(1.20)	(0.18)	(2.41)	(2.18)	(1.39)	(1.44)					
log SumM2	(0, 1, 0)		−0.0016	0.0034*	0.0010										0.0098	−0.0043	−0.0247*	−333.749
			(1.24)	(2.00)	(0.77)										(1.29)	(0.41)	(3.09)	
log SumM2	(0, 1, 1)		−0.0000	0.0020	0.0009										0.0078	−0.0070	−0.0206*	−336.075
			(0.03)	(1.23)	(0.66)										(0.97)	(0.78)	(2.44)	
log SumM2	(1, 1, 1)		−0.0003	0.0021	0.0010										0.0089	−0.0076	−0.0209*	−334.144
			(0.15)	(1.23)	(0.69)										(1.04)	(0.82)	(2.48)	
log SumM2	(0, 1, 0)		−0.0027	0.0031	−0.0001		−0.0096	0.0217	−0.0222						0.0065	−0.0021	−0.0137	−332.721
			(1.83)	(1.62)	(0.06)		(0.54)	(0.84)	(1.59)						(0.71)	(0.17)	(1.32)	
log SumM2	(0, 1, 1)		−0.0012	0.0023	0.0001		−0.0040	0.0142	−0.0178						0.0055	−0.0040	−0.0132	−332.573
			(0.71)	(1.20)	(0.04)		(0.22)	(0.58)	(1.26)						(0.60)	(0.38)	(1.27)	
log SumM2	(1, 1, 1)		−0.0014	0.0025	−0.0001		0.0002	0.0078	−0.0157						0.0057	−0.0042	−0.0128	−330.736
			(0.69)	(1.09)	(0.05)		(0.01)	(0.15)	(0.65)						(0.61)	(0.40)	(1.21)	
log SumM2	(0, 1, 0)		−0.0038*	0.0026	−0.0007		−0.0208	0.0226	−0.0202		0.0192	0.0103	−0.0298					−331.897
			(2.96)	(1.29)	(0.42)		(1.29)	(1.06)	(1.59)		(1.05)	(0.47)	(1.50)					
log SumM2	(0, 1, 1)		−0.0029	0.0018	−0.0008		−0.0156	0.0162	−0.0189		0.0128	0.0113	−0.0242					−330.576
			(1.75)	(0.82)	(0.43)		(0.75)	(0.59)	(1.23)		(0.55)	(0.43)	(1.00)					
log SumM2	(1, 1, 1)		−0.0030	0.0020	−0.0009		−0.0109	0.0095	−0.0165		0.0136	0.0102	−0.0241					−328.797
			(1.64)	(0.80)	(0.46)		(0.35)	(0.20)	(0.69)		(0.57)	(0.38)	(0.97)					

*Statistically significant results (*t*-values are in parentheses).

Table 2.7 Information orthogonality tests: A2D

Variable	Model	R1	R2	R3	R4	M1	M2	M3	M4	C1	C2	C3	C4	Y1	Y2	Y3	Y4	AIC
log A2D	(0, 1, 0)	−0.0171*	0.0093*	0.0008	0.0094*									0.0075	0.0194	0.0070	−0.0458*	−238.060
		(5.23)	(2.30)	(0.18)	(2.62)									(0.42)	(0.76)	(0.29)	(3.45)	
log A2D	(0, 1, 1)	−0.0169*	0.0090*	0.0004	0.0098*									0.0042	0.0232	0.0086	−0.0479	−237.233
		(5.04)	(2.33)	(0.10)	(2.64)									(0.21)	(0.85)	(0.34)	(2.33)	
log A2D	(1, 1, 1)	−0.0174*	0.0095*	−0.0002	0.0103*									0.0026	0.0274	0.0052	−0.0460*	−236.067
		(5.10)	(2.35)	(0.05)	(2.71)									(0.13)	(0.98)	(0.20)	(2.22)	
log A2D	(0, 1, 0)	−0.0165*	0.0068	−0.0031	0.0062	−0.0677	−0.2524	0.1232	0.0353					−0.0071	0.0203	0.0140	−0.0404*	−234.971
		(5.06)	(1.57)	(0.67)	(1.50)	(0.38)	(1.13)	(0.55)	(0.24)					(0.55)	(1.40)	(0.96)	(3.00)	
log A2D	(0, 1, 1)	−0.0195*	−0.0012	−0.0022	0.0089	−1.0544*	0.6862	−0.0305	0.0976					−0.0051	0.0239	−0.0014	−0.0334	−239.714
		(6.08)	(0.28)	(0.45)	(1.78)	(4.43)	(2.83)	(0.15)	(0.57)					(0.23)	(1.06)	(0.07)	(1.59)	
log A2D	(1, 1, 1)	−0.0196*	0.0022	−0.0019	0.0087	−0.9535*	0.6780*	−0.1139	0.1158					−0.0062	0.0271	−0.0002	−0.0358	−237.757
		(5.87)	(0.03)	(0.38)	(1.72)	(2.05)	(2.65)	(0.29)	(0.58)					(0.28)	(1.13)	(1.01)	(1.68)	
log A2D	(0, 1, 0)	−0.0161*	0.0064	−0.0001	0.0030	−0.0502	−0.2634	0.1284	0.0263	0.0289	0.0146	−0.0172	−0.0374					−232.299
		(4.97)	(1.29)	(0.03)	(0.65)	(0.23)	(0.89)	(0.44)	(0.15)	(0.69)	(0.30)	(0.35)	(0.88)					
log A2D	(0, 1, 1)	−0.0196*	−0.0027	0.0012	0.0056	−1.2695*	0.8914*	−0.0855	0.1284	0.0534	0.0022	−0.0244	−0.0527					−239.457
		(6.18)	(0.66)	(0.25)	(1.27)	(4.10)	(3.01)	(0.45)	(0.75)	(1.14)	(0.05)	(0.59)	(1.21)					
log A2D	(1, 1, 1)	−0.0204*	−0.0057	−0.0010	0.0062	−1.5390*	0.8458*	0.1361	0.1196	0.0543	−0.0031	−0.0289	−0.0474					−238.435
		(6.53)	(0.62)	(0.13)	(1.62)	(2.30)	(2.07)	(0.29)	(0.56)	(1.15)	(0.07)	(0.65)	(1.05)					
log A2D	(0, 1, 0)		−0.0045	0.0098*	0.0005										0.0076	−0.0007	−0.0436	−216.424
			(1.21)	(2.04)	(0.13)										(0.36)	(0.02)	(1.95)	
log A2D	(0, 1, 1)		−0.0020	0.0074	0.0007										0.0049	−0.0004	−0.0428	−216.303
			(0.48)	(1.54)	(0.19)										(0.21)	(0.02)	(1.77)	
log A2D	(1, 1, 1)		−0.0022	0.0072	0.0010										0.0055	−0.0004	−0.0431	−214.346
			(0.48)	(1.46)	(0.26)										(0.24)	(0.01)	(1.78)	
log A2D	(0, 1, 0)		−0.0056	0.0066	−0.0050		−0.2751	0.0727	0.0232						−0.0134	0.0064	−0.0281	−215.013
			(1.49)	(1.25)	(0.97)		(1.08)	(0.21)	(0.11)						(0.56)	(0.22)	(1.15)	
log A2D	(0, 1, 1)		−0.0045	0.0058	−0.0046		−0.2614	0.0569	0.0344						−0.0118	0.0050	−0.0292	−213.351
			(1.05)	(1.06)	(0.83)		(0.97)	(0.16)	(0.16)						(0.44)	(0.16)	(1.08)	
log A2D	(1, 1, 1)		−0.0045	0.0058	−0.0046		−0.2727	0.0672	0.0340						−0.0117	0.0048	−0.0293	−211.354
			(1.04)	(1.03)	(0.82)		(0.46)	(0.11)	(0.15)						(0.43)	(0.15)	(1.02)	
log A2D	(0, 1, 0)		−0.0094*	0.0081	−0.0033		−0.2887	0.1036	−0.0090		0.0405	0.0058	−0.0807					−213.821
			(2.62)	(1.41)	(0.63)		(1.10)	(0.29)	(0.04)		(0.82)	(0.10)	(1.62)					
log A2D	(0, 1, 1)		−0.0088*	0.0076	−0.0033		−0.2816	0.0939	−0.0059		0.0390	0.0051	−0.0789					−210.910
			(2.07)	(1.20)	(0.58)		(1.03)	(0.26)	(0.03)		(0.57)	(0.07)	(1.35)					
log A2D	(1, 1, 1)		−0.0088*	0.0076	−0.0033		−0.2764	0.0885	−0.0048		0.0391	0.0054	−0.0790					−208.911
			(2.04)	(1.16)	(0.55)		(0.43)	(0.11)	(0.02)		(0.65)	(0.07)	(1.33)					

*Statistically significant results (*t*-values are in parentheses).

with slightly different results. Here, for the full information set in the first nine rows, the AIC picks the ARIMA(0, 1, 1) model in Row 5. This test has only R1 and M1 as significant information-bearing data which might appear to affect the (log-differences) of A2D one period later than their determination. This is certainly a stronger result, in the direction of rationality, than that obtained for SumM2. When we come to look at the results without R1, M1 (in this case lags in A2D), C1 and Y1, we find only rare cases (Lines 10, 16, 17 and 18) when a lagged variable has information content. While the AIC selects a model which does contain an information-bearing variable (ARIMA(0, 1, 0), the random walk), a second model (ARIMA(0, 1, 1)) is only marginally inferior and has no violations of the hypothesis. All this is most encouraging for the rational expectations hypothesis, bearing in mind that the SumM2 results in the top of Table 2.6 are the typical results in the literature. One must also note, however, that since there are a lot of other potential information-bearing variables out there, there is clearly no sense in claiming that 'rational money' has been found. Rather, what surely can be asserted is that attention to the preparation of the data does have some payoff and, even more strongly, that some measures appear to be quite defective for such purposes – and dare we say, for any purpose so far proposed for them. SumM1 and the MSI quantities are (unfortunately) among the casualties, although whether these are more than flesh wounds has yet to be established. Indeed, more testing of the data presented here is clearly warranted, but to do so would extend this discussion beyond reason. We note, however, that some interesting matters of simultaneity exist since we are operating under the assumption of separability of money-holding from consumption. That should not make a major difference for A2D (and appears not to on some preliminary tests utilizing the seemingly unrelated regression technique) because that variable has been chosen so that it may be nearly separable from consumption on these particular data (as discussed in Chapter 1).

NOTES

1. It is worth underscoring here that the inventory model can be derived directly from the general transactions model. (See Saving (1976) for a simple proof.)
2. Our separability tests in Chapter 1 which suggest that some forms of money and consumption goods are not separable from certain forms of 'money' should be recalled here. Saving's response, following the line laid down in Pesek and Saving (1967), might well be to argue that to the extent that an asset pays interest, it is not money. If that criterion is used, then the appropriate items of money for a rigorous test of the Saving model would be CUR, DDCON, and OCD. The latter do, however, pay interest, and so the model just described would have to be modified slightly for such a test. These items are appropriate because in our weak separability tests we found a likely separability of these items from a group including savings assets and consumer goods. No such tests exist in the literature.

3. Strictly speaking

$$\frac{\mu_t^{\mathrm{m}} - \mu_{t-1}^{\mathrm{m}}}{\mu_t^{\mathrm{m}}} \leq \frac{1}{1+\theta}(\theta - \pi)$$

at the optimum, where μ is the marginal utility of money and θ is the rate of time preference. Here satiation occurs when the rate of inflation equals the rate of time preference. This is reasonable.
4. He also points out that (provided both bonds and money are actually held)

$$\frac{\lambda_t^{\mathrm{b}} - \lambda_{t-1}^{\mathrm{b}}}{\lambda_t^{\mathrm{m}} - \lambda_{t-1}^{\mathrm{m}}} = \frac{r}{\pi}$$

which he describes as a portfolio diversification condition analogous to the familiar marginal rate of substitution result among commodities.
5. Equation (2.38) is, in effect, a flow constraint for consumers. See Chapter 4 for further discussion of the constraints facing consumers and other agents (in, a dynamic context).
6. We are saying, in effect, that money-holding is consumption-constrained. The recent literature on the aggregate consumption function makes much of the possibility that it is liquidity-constrained. Usually this is taken to suggest that there are imperfections in the lending market (and that is how we will discuss it in Chapters 5 and 6), but actually such a constraint is implicit in the fact that the stock (money) and flow (consumption, money services) constraints must be satisfied jointly in a complete solution of the general consumption-money-holding problem (see D. Fisher, 1970). In Chapter 4, there is more material on these dual constraints in a dynamic context.
7. In contrast to the MA structure, the AR has a direct connection with the stationarity question. This is due to, e.g. Equation (2.44)'s being a difference equation of order one whose single root might be explosive (and therefore non-stationary) in practice.
8. The originator of this line of research is Bomhoff (1980) who also arrives, as we shall see, at an ARIMA(0, 1, 1) model for the (log of) the money-demand function, approximately for the same reasons given here.
9. The long-term interest rate may follow a Martingale process if the market is efficient; often, this seems to be the case. If the short-term market is efficient, then the short rate also may, but need not, follow a random walk (of $i_t = i_{t-1} + u_t$). According to Pesando (1979) and Mishkin (1978*a*), it does not. This does not necessarily mean that the short-term rate is not 'efficient' since (as explained by Mishkin) the *expected* short-term rate may itself be the source of the serial correlation that produces the apparent inefficiency. In the empirical work which follows, a short-term interest rate is used simply because it seems to work better in all tests.
10. An autoregressive integrated moving-average (ARIMA) process is described as being of order (p, d, q), where p is the degree of the AR part, d describes the order of the differencing, and q is the degree of the MA part.
11. That is, transactions theory (Friedman, 1977; Heller and Khan, 1979) suggests that the entire term structure of interest rates might be substituted into the demand for money. One more practical reason to use the difference between the long and the short rate, as suggested in the text, is to avoid collinearity in the two interest rates. This is frequently mentioned when it appears that two or more interest rates might be appropriate for theoretical reasons.
12. The filter used calculates the anticipations as the sum of a permanent, a seasonal and a transitory component. Cuthbertson and Taylor argue that this method of

forecasting is probably closer to what economic agents probably do, in practice. We should also note that Bomhoff (1982) favours the use of a Kalman-filtering technique to arrive at rational forecasts of the price level. In this study, Bomhoff uses an inverted money-demand function to generate the forecasts. The Kalman technique permits modelling structural change endogenously, thus by-passing the effects of so-called 'shifts' in the demand for money.

13. The Akaike information criterion is calculated as

$$-2\log(L)+2k$$

where L is the likelihood function and k is the number of free parameters. This balances goodness of fit with the loss of degrees of freedom. One tries to minimize this number. See Harvey (1981) for a discussion.

14. As we noted above, while the short-term rate may be generated in an efficient market, it may yet not follow a random walk (Pesando, 1979). Speaking somewhat casually, moving the lag back one period would tend to alleviate this problem.

3

THE DEMAND-SYSTEMS APPROACH TO THE ANALYSIS OF MONETARY SUBSTITUTION

3.1 INTRODUCTION

In Chapters 1 and 2 we began our discussion of simultaneous liquid-asset demand systems with a view of money as an asset that either enters the utility function directly or appears there, in the final analysis, as the result of a substitution from some more precisely defined cost-saving constraint. We also discussed a result by Feenstra (1986) who suggests that putting money directly into the utility function is actually equivalent to having it only in the constraints for a broad class of transactions functions. Accepting this point, it is now possible to consider an important line of attack on money-demand problems in which money appears in the utility function in the first instance. This approach makes use of the broad range of economic and econometric tools that have been developed for 'demand-systems analysis' and it will be the general task of this chapter to lay out this material with particular emphasis on recent developments. As we shall see, the methods used – involving primarily the modelling of the indirect utility function and flexible functional forms – provide a firm grip on questions concerning substitution (and complementarity) among the liquid assets in actual situations. This material thus bears on the question of how best to estimate a demand for money function; how, therefore, to define money; and, further, what monetary concept to use to best represent 'moneyness' in both a money-supply and a monetary-policy context. This literature is offered as an alternative to the ideal index approach of Chapter 1, and the results of the major empirical experiments in this literature are compared with those of the index number literature to see what seems to hold up across the two methodologies.

In Section 3.2 we lay some of the groundwork for our later material by running through what is sometimes referred to as the 'characteristics approach' (as in Lancaster, 1966) to the demand for financial assets. This is the mean-variance (portfolio) model, and it is placed here because its clean lines make it an especially useful framework to use in describing the properties of the simultaneous-equations structure. But the analogy most often used these

days is with a consumer-choice problem, and the remainder of the chapter takes up this path, beginning with some of the earlier studies at the end of Section 3.2. The bulk of the chapter, however, is concerned with the flexible functional forms (in a systems context); these are called 'flexible' because they can introduce sufficient parameters to come arbitrarily close to an unknown, but desired, function.

The discussion actually begins with a very general asset-choice problem in which the 'user cost' of a financial asset is derived from an intertemporal, consumption/money-holding/bond-holding paradigm. From here we consider how duality can be employed to convert from financial product space to budget-share space. With these basic theoretical preliminaries in hand, the discussion turns (in Section 3.4) to a specific example, the Translog expenditure system. Here we begin from first principles and derive the exact equations to estimate for financial assets. At this point we return to the empirical results of Chapter 1, where a set of four financial assets (including total consumption) is proposed. These are estimated as a set of budget-share equations via the Translog model on recent US data. In view of known problems with the Translog model, and on account of some difficulties apparent with the estimations reported here, we continue in Section 3.5 with a recently proposed flexible form known as the Fourier on the same data set. This flexible form is termed semi-non-parametric (there are arbitrary parameters whose number can be increased almost without limit) and has several advantages over the Translog method. In any event this model appears to work very well on US data and, more importantly, appears to provide some guidance on questions of the appropriate definition of money and, even, on the famous 'case of the missing money' in the post-1973 US monetary data.

3.2 EARLY APPROACHES TO THE DEMAND ANALYSIS OF MONETARY CHOICE

We begin our discussion in this section with a model – the mean-variance model – which has actually not been used extensively on monetary problems, primarily because it is an especially clear framework as well as one specifically designed to deal with financial asset choice under uncertainty. What we will get from this is a precise statement of what advantages demand theory can bring to the study of monetary substitution, and possibly a useful model, at least for pedagogical purposes. We also have several uses for the model for specific problems in later chapters. By revealed preference, the disadvantages of this model seem to have been too great to have generated much of an empirical literature, but the pedagogical value – all we wish to extract at this point – seems considerable.

To get down to specifics, the wealth-holder is assumed to be attempting to combine various assets into potential portfolios and then to pick the best of

these portfolios, the best being the one which maximizes his expected utility. What we have said amounts to the assumption that the representative wealth-holder will maximize a utility function such as Equation (3.1); this, of course, is just a repetition of Equation (1.7):

$$u = U(E, V) \qquad (U_1 > 0, U_2 < 0) \tag{3.1}$$

The next step in the process of defining the role of money in this literature is generally that of setting down some utility function – preferably a quadratic – which is, at the same time, consistent with assets whose returns are normally distributed (and hence can be described completely by the first two moments of their statistical distributions). Such a utility function, utilizing π for the expected return, is

$$u = a - c\exp(-b\pi) \tag{3.2}$$

where a, b and c are positive constants. We note that the derivatives of Equation (3.2) are alternating positive and negative in sign.

The variable π in the above expression refers to expected returns, as noted, and so it is inherently stochastic. In this context the optimization problem before us is that of maximizing the expression in an *expected utility* framework. Rephrased, then, the problem is that of maximizing Equation (3.3):

$$E(u) = a - cE[\exp(-b\pi)] \tag{3.3}$$

If, as noted, we assume that π is distributed normally, with mean μ_π and variance σ_π^2, then the probability derived from the normal distribution can replace the expectation on the right-hand side of Equation (3.3). This provides the expression

$$E(u) = a - c\exp\left[-b\left(\mu_\pi - \frac{b}{2}\sigma_\pi^2\right)\right] \tag{3.4}$$

It turns out that by maximizing the expression in parentheses in Equation (3.4) we also maximize $E(u)$, so the problem becomes that of maximizing the spread between the mean and the (weighted) variance. Equation (3.5) conveys this idea:

$$W = \mu_\pi - \frac{b}{2}\sigma_\pi^2 \tag{3.5}$$

Here the mean and the variance refer to the expected values of these concepts for the *entire* portfolio of financial assets. The expected signs here are, of course, positive for μ_π and negative for σ_π^2, with the latter representing a form of risk aversion.[1] The problem we have, then, is that of finding expressions for the terms μ_π and σ_π^2 from the available market information on the expected returns and expected variances of the individual assets which make up the portfolio. In this sense μ_π and σ_π^2 are clearly aggregates, and what we will propose here are, in effect, methods for computing these aggregates.

Let us now switch to matrix notation for ease of exposition. Let $\tilde{\mathbf{v}}$ be a vector $(n \times 1)$ of sums invested in financial assets and let $\tilde{\mathbf{m}}$ be an associated vector of the actual yields of these assets, however these may be computed. Thus the actual yield (π) of the portfolio is given by the following inner product:

$$\pi = \tilde{\mathbf{m}}'\tilde{\mathbf{v}} \tag{3.6}$$

When an individual constructs a portfolio, he naturally does so not with the actual yields of Equation (3.6) but with expected yields. We are not going to propose anything novel about how to measure such expectations here, but we must, in any case, phrase our problem in a stochastic form. That is, let us write actual yields as the sum of expected returns $(\tilde{\mathbf{m}}^*)$ plus an error term $(\tilde{\mathbf{e}})$, where the error term represents a vector of forecasting errors. This results in Equation (3.7) in which, to anticipate, the expected value of the forecasting errors will be assumed to be zero.

$$\tilde{\mathbf{m}} = \tilde{\mathbf{m}}^* + \tilde{\mathbf{e}} \tag{3.7}$$

We may now combine Equations (3.6) and (3.7) to obtain

$$\pi = (\tilde{\mathbf{m}}^* + \tilde{\mathbf{e}})'\tilde{\mathbf{v}} = \tilde{\mathbf{m}}^{*\prime}\tilde{\mathbf{v}} + \tilde{\mathbf{e}}'\tilde{\mathbf{v}} \tag{3.8}$$

This expression relates the actual return of the portfolio to the expected return plus the forecasting error. Taking expectations of both sides of Equation (3.8) and making use of the already stated assumption that the mean forecasting error is zero, we obtain

$$\mu_\pi = E(\pi) = \tilde{\mathbf{m}}^{*\prime}\tilde{\mathbf{v}} \tag{3.9}$$

This gives us μ_π for use in Equation (3.5). Needless to say, $\tilde{\mathbf{m}}^*$ is a vector of expected yields and will not be directly observable. In empirical work, that is to say, an assumption about how expectations are actually formed would be needed before the data could be brought in.

The variance of the yield is the other parameter required for Equation (3.5). One way of defining this variance is

$$\sigma_\pi^2 = E[(\pi - E(\pi))^2] \tag{3.10}$$

We may rewrite the term within the square brackets in Equation (3.10) directly in terms of Equations (3.8) and (3.9) to produce

$$\sigma_\pi^2 = E\{[(\tilde{\mathbf{m}}^{*\prime}\tilde{\mathbf{v}} + \tilde{\mathbf{e}}'\tilde{\mathbf{v}}) - \tilde{\mathbf{m}}^{*\prime}\tilde{\mathbf{v}}]^2\} = E[(\tilde{\mathbf{e}}'\tilde{\mathbf{v}})^2] \tag{3.11}$$

We are therefore seen to be asserting the reasonable proposition that actual variations in earnings come entirely from forecasting errors. Since the term $\tilde{\mathbf{e}}'\tilde{\mathbf{v}}$ is a scalar,[2] we may write it out as the equivalent scalar, $\tilde{\mathbf{v}}'\tilde{\mathbf{e}}\tilde{\mathbf{e}}'\tilde{\mathbf{v}}$. When we take expectations, we get yet another form for Equation (3.11):

$$\sigma_\pi^2 = \tilde{\mathbf{v}}'E(\tilde{\mathbf{e}}\tilde{\mathbf{e}}')\tilde{\mathbf{v}} = \tilde{\mathbf{v}}'S\tilde{\mathbf{v}} \tag{3.12}$$

Thus the variance of the portfolio appears as a set of 'weights' (really,

amounts invested) bordering the variance–covariance matrix constructed from the forecasting errors.

Let us now assume that the representative wealth-holder in question is restricted to holding only a certain set of types of assets and holds positive quantities of each. In particular, we could be looking at the wealth-holder's collections of cash, savings balances and other liquid assets. In any event, regardless of what we put into the defined collection, the representative wealth-holder will face a budget constraint of the general form of

$$\tilde{\mathbf{v}}'\tilde{\mathbf{i}} + W = 0 \tag{3.13}$$

Here W suggests an overall wealth (or income) constraint (here with an implicit negative sign) and $\tilde{\mathbf{i}}$ is the unit vector of suitable length, introduced here merely to perform the summation required. Subject to this constraint the wealth-holder will maximize Equation (3.5), with the definitions for the mean and the variance provided by Equations (3.9) and (3.12). Explicitly, this is

$$\theta = \tilde{\mathbf{m}}^{*\prime}\tilde{\mathbf{v}} - \frac{b}{2}\tilde{\mathbf{v}}' S \tilde{\mathbf{v}} \tag{3.14}$$

The maximization problem set here is, given $\tilde{\mathbf{m}}^*$, S and W, to choose $\tilde{\mathbf{v}}$ such that Equation (3.14) is maximized subject to Equation (3.13). To solve the problem we form the following Lagrangean expression, noting that it is a stochastic formulation:

$$L = \tilde{\mathbf{m}}^{*\prime}\tilde{\mathbf{v}} - \frac{b}{2}\tilde{\mathbf{v}}' S \tilde{\mathbf{v}} + \lambda(\tilde{\mathbf{v}}'\tilde{\mathbf{i}} + W) \tag{3.15}$$

We can then calculate the first-order conditions for the maximum as Equations (3.16):

$$\left.\begin{aligned} \frac{\partial L}{\partial \tilde{\mathbf{v}}} &= \tilde{\mathbf{m}}^* - bS\tilde{\mathbf{v}} + \lambda\tilde{\mathbf{i}} = 0 \\ \frac{\partial L}{\partial \lambda} &= \tilde{\mathbf{v}}'\tilde{\mathbf{i}} + W = 0 \end{aligned}\right\} \tag{3.16}$$

Assuming that the second-order conditions are also met, we can write our stable solution vector for the monetary quantities and the Lagrangean multiplier as Equation (3.17):

$$\begin{bmatrix} \tilde{\mathbf{v}} \\ \lambda \end{bmatrix} = \begin{bmatrix} bS & -\tilde{\mathbf{i}} \\ -\tilde{\mathbf{i}}' & 0 \end{bmatrix}^{-1} \begin{bmatrix} \tilde{\mathbf{m}}^* \\ W \end{bmatrix} \tag{3.17}$$

The coefficient matrix in this expression may then be inverted – using the method of partitioned matrices – to yield the demand functions for financial assets as in Equation (3.18):

$$\tilde{\mathbf{v}} = \frac{1}{b}\left[S^{-1} - \frac{S^{-1}\tilde{\mathbf{i}}\tilde{\mathbf{i}}'S^{-1}}{\tilde{\mathbf{i}}'S^{-1}\tilde{\mathbf{i}}}\right]\tilde{\mathbf{m}}^* - \left[\frac{S^{-1}\tilde{\mathbf{i}}}{\tilde{\mathbf{i}}'S^{-1}\tilde{\mathbf{i}}}\right]W \tag{3.18}$$

It is these functions which would be estimated by simultaneous-equations methods.

The power of demand-systems analysis does not come from the form of the equation in Equation (3.18) for, after all, what we have is (expected) interest rates and wealth (or income) as independent influences on (say) the demand for money, and these are the standard variables. Rather, the power comes from several sets of restrictions that are implied by the theory – restrictions which current econometric technique permits us to apply (and test) across these equations when they are estimated. For one thing, S is a symmetric matrix, clearly, and so is S^{-1}. This being the case, since

$$\frac{S^{-1}\tilde{\mathbf{i}}\tilde{\mathbf{i}}'S^{-1}}{\tilde{\mathbf{i}}'S^{-1}\tilde{\mathbf{i}}}$$

is symmetric, so is the entire first matrix in the brackets in Equation (3.18). This result is similar to the condition in consumer demand theory which requires that the matrix of substitution effects among commodities be symmetric. For a second set of restrictions, we find that the row sums of the matrix just described are zero. To calculate a row sum, we simply post-multiply a matrix by the unit vector. This calculation produces

$$S^{-1}\tilde{\mathbf{i}} - \frac{S^{-1}\tilde{\mathbf{i}}\tilde{\mathbf{i}}'S^{-1}\tilde{\mathbf{i}}}{\tilde{\mathbf{i}}'S^{-1}\tilde{\mathbf{i}}} = S^{-1}\tilde{\mathbf{i}} - S^{-1}\tilde{\mathbf{i}}\left[\frac{\tilde{\mathbf{i}}'S^{-1}\tilde{\mathbf{i}}}{\tilde{\mathbf{i}}'S^{-1}\tilde{\mathbf{i}}}\right] = 0 \qquad (3.19)$$

For a third set of restrictions we note that the first matrix has non-negative diagonal terms, again a result that corresponds with one in consumer demand theory. Finally, we can show that the column sums of the second matrix in Equation (3.18) are unity. This property, which corresponds to 'Engle aggregation' in consumer demand theory, is easily established by premultiplying that term by $\tilde{\mathbf{i}}'$.

The value of this presentation is that it is absolutely clear how a well-conditioned economic theory can produce very specific advice as to how to conduct empirical tests. The restrictions appearing in the specializations of the simultaneous-equations framework, which we will employ later in this chapter, are different only in detail from those just outlined. The ability to work in a well-structured microanalytical framework is the principal reason why this approach to financial studies is taken. But the reader should be aware that any specialization carries explicit costs with it. These are all too well-known in the case of the mean-variance model and have pretty much limited its usefulness to that of participating in pedagogical displays. However, not only are there further techniques in the microeconomic literature which can be used on the asset problem, but there are also functional forms that are considerably less restrictive than the quadratic. Chief among the former is the use of duality theory to justify a calculation of the accessible 'budget-share equations', and prominent among the latter are the Translog and Fourier flexible functional forms. These methods will be described (and illustrated) in the remainder of this chapter.

There are not many studies in the literature which utilize the mean-variance model in a money-demand context and so as our next step, we will move on to more general (but early) demand-system approaches.[3] Of these, there is a study on US data by Gramlich and Hulett (1972) who are concerned with both the supply and the demand for savings deposits. Their procedure is almost exactly the same as that outlined in the theoretical discussion of the mean-variance model, and they estimate a set of equations similar to (3.18), with numerous restrictions (and adjustments) and with some attempt to bring in the supply side (in the form of, for example, interest-rate ceilings). They generally find low substitution, somewhat to their surprise. A system of demand equations can, of course, be fitted directly to the data, even without the full set of restrictions of consumer theory, and that is how demand-system studies of money demand actually began. Thus, Feige (1964) uses a demand-system approach to estimate monetary-components' cross-elasticities directly. His results, under the symmetry restrictions, suggest that demand deposits may well be the complements of savings and loan deposits, and in later work (1974) he regards weak substitution among the liquid assets as the most likely result (see also Feige and Pearce, 1977, for a survey of this work). But, and this is not a point of criticism, these results generally are not obtained with the full set of cross-equation constraints or with an appropriate method of estimation (such as that of 'seemingly unrelated regressions').

Weak substitutes – or, frequently, failure to establish statistically significant relationships – might suggest that single-equation methods would be adequate after all, but the low substitution coefficients seem to contradict common sense. After all, an individual can usually switch between savings and demands deposits at will, although whether he does so or not is what is really tested in these studies – and it is what we ought to test. In any case, Lee (1966, 1972) adjusts Feige's data and arrives at the opposite conclusion on substitutability. Indeed, there was a certain amount of discussion on this level in the 1970s which came to something of a standoff on the question of what magnitudes of substitutability are appropriate among the monetary assets.

In 1969, a new sort of study was conducted when Chetty formulated an explicit direct utility of money model from which he derives the demand functions for liquid assets. His approach is to maximize the following generalized constant elasticity of substitution (CES) utility function

$$u = (\beta_0 x_0^{-\rho_0} + \beta_1 x_1^{-\rho_1} + \beta_2 x_2^{-\rho_2} + \ldots + \beta_n x_n^{-\rho_n})^{-\frac{1}{\rho_0}} \qquad (3.20)$$

subject to a wealth constraint of the form

$$W = \frac{x_0}{1 + r_0} + \frac{x_1}{1 + r_1} + \ldots + \frac{x_n}{1 + r_n} \qquad (3.21)$$

where the r_j are nominal rates of interest (i.e. own rates) on the various assets and x_0 is (arbitrarily) money. This is actually a two-period problem, and

$X_j (j = 1, \ldots, n)$ here is the value of the jth alternative asset next period. Thus it is discounted (by its own interest rate in this period) back to the initial value of financial wealth. The sequence $\{r_0, r_1, \ldots, r_n\}$ could be thought of as a kind of term structure of interest rates.

The first-order conditions for this problem are

$$\frac{\partial U}{\partial x_i} - \frac{\lambda}{1 + r_i} = 0 \qquad (i = 0, \ldots, n) \qquad (3.22)$$

$$W = \sum_{i=0}^{n} \frac{x_i}{1 + r_i} \qquad (3.23)$$

Since we have put down an explicit (CES) utility function we may calculate the partial derivatives needed for Equation (3.22) directly. Then, using these derivatives, combining Equations (3.22) and (3.23), and taking logs, we produce

$$\log x_i = \frac{-1}{\rho_i + 1} \log \frac{\beta_0 \rho_0}{\beta_i \rho_i} - \frac{1}{\rho_i + 1} \log \frac{1}{1 + r_i} + \frac{\rho_0 + 1}{\rho_i + 1} \log x_0 \qquad (3.24)$$

This can be solved for $\log x_0$ and then estimated directly. Chetty (1969) does this by single-equation methods (OLS and 2SLS yield identical results). He concludes that time deposits, savings and loan deposits and mutual savings bank deposits 'are all good substitutes for money. Thus, we have provided empirical evidence for Gurley and Shaw's hypothesis' (p. 278). The ranking of closeness of substitution with money is

$$T > MS > SL$$

and the data are US annual, 1945–66. A follow-up paper by Moroney and Wilbratte (1976) also estimates the CES directly but includes income and other interest-rate variables to deal with a potential problem of omitted variables. They appeal to duality theory to justify their version of Equation (3.24) and find relatively close substitution among the short-term assets. They also find long-term assets to be close substitutes for money as *MS*, *SL*, etc. Again, however, the tests are single-equation in form.

There are some immediate problems with the procedure just laid out, as detailed by Donovan (1978) and others. For one thing, Equation (3.24) is used to produce demand functions for financial estimation without the benefit of Equation (3.23), the budget (wealth) constraint. As pointed out by Brainard and Tobin (1968) in their famous 'pitfalls' paper, the demand systems approach permits the imposition of an overall constraint of the form

$$\sum_{i=1}^{n} M_{it}^{d} = W_t$$

This enables us to avoid the problem that single-equation estimates (when summed) may produce inconsistent results if unconstrained (a pitfall!).[4] Then, too, by using the simple interest rates described above, Chetty and

others do not actually measure the values of the service flows provided by each asset. What they need, says Donovan, are the (rigorously derived) rental prices (i.e. the user costs) of these assets. Indeed, the budget constraint itself should be expressed in terms of these user costs. Furthermore, the CES utility function is less than general in some respects, most notably in that the assets themselves are assumed to be strongly separable from each other. In this event the marginal rate of substitution between asset i and asset j is independent of the level of any other asset k. Weak separability among the competing assets is certainly a less restrictive posture but, even so, may itself not be appropriate for many collections of financial assets (*within* the group), as was shown in various ways in Chapter 1.

The Chetty approach has been pursued in recent years by Boughton (1981) and by Rossiter and Lee (1984). The latter in particular use an appropriate simultaneous-equations estimation technique (of Zellner, 1962) in order to arrive at estimates of the partial elasticities of substitution among assets. Among their findings we find that the different periods (1952–60 and 1961–75) are significantly different, the utility function is not homothetic in income (nor separable in the monetary assets) and elasticities of substitution, while apparently higher than most studies, are lower in the second data period than in the first. Incidentally, Boughton finds low substitutability among the monetary assets.

3.3 BASIC THEORETICAL ISSUES IN THE DEMAND-SYSTEMS APPROACH

Basically, what we are going to do now is derive a set of demand functions for liquid assets from a more general framework in which the representative household maximizes an intertemporal utility function defined over commodities, money, leisure and financial assets, subject to an appropriate intertemporal budget constraint. We will state the general problem first and then show the steps which lead us to a manageable subset of this more general problem. The subset involves demand functions for the financial assets alone. Thus, Section 3.3.1 will consider the theory, explicitly deriving the appropriate user cost of money. Then, Section 3.3.2 will show why and how duality theory might be employed explicitly in the rationalization of estimable functions from which elasticities of substitution can be derived. These methods will be described formally from first principles. Finally, Sections 3.4 and 3.5 will consider the traits and track-records of the various flexible functional forms that have been suggested in the simultaneous-equations framework described in Section 3.3. Primary here will be discussion, comparison and demonstration of the Translog (TL) and Fourier flexible functional forms for providing estimates of the indirect utility function.

3.3.1 The demand-systems approach to asset demand functions

Following Barnett (1981, 1987), we will assume continuous replanning at each t and also that the representative household maximizes the following intertemporal utility function, where

$\tilde{\mathbf{x}}_s$ = vector of planned *per capita* real consumption of goods and services during period s,
$\tilde{\mathbf{m}}_s$ = vector of planned *per capita* real monetary assets held during period s,
B_s = quantity of a benchmark asset (see below) held during period s (in real, *per capita* form) and

$$u_t = U_t(\tilde{\mathbf{m}}_t, \ldots, \tilde{\mathbf{m}}_{t+T}, \tilde{\mathbf{x}}_t, \ldots, \tilde{\mathbf{x}}_{t+T}; B_{t+T}) \tag{3.25}$$

The household also supplies labour in period s ($= L_s$) and this figures in its overall utility function. Equation (3.25) is a subutility function assumed to be a weakly separable part of the more general function.[5] The benchmark asset (B) is included here to represent, in effect, an important element in the opportunity cost of holding money. In particular, B_s will be assumed to perform the role of facilitating the transfer of wealth between periods while at the same time providing (by assumption) no liquidity characteristics. It is, thus, a non-money alternative store of value in this scheme.

Let us, then, assume that Equation (3.25) can be written as the following, which is weakly separable in each period's consumption of goods and monetary services:

$$u_t = U_t[v_t(\tilde{\mathbf{m}}_t), \ldots, v_{t+T}(\tilde{\mathbf{m}}_{t+T}); c_t(\tilde{\mathbf{x}}_{t+T}), \ldots, c_{t+T}(\tilde{\mathbf{x}}_{t+T}); B_{t+T}] \tag{3.26}$$

Weak separability, in this instance, implies that the marginal rate of substitution between financial assets (e.g. two monies) in period t is independent of the components in the other aggregates. Monies at time t may interact fully, however, when studied separately. Two things are involved here – the separation of the various entities from money and, e.g. the separation of assets in time period $t+j$ from time period $t+j+1$. The former was discussed at some length in Chapter 1 and need not be gone into further here. With regard to the intertemporal separability, we employ this assumption because we wish to work with a one-period utility function in what follows. As a matter of convenience, though, it turns out that if we assume continuous replanning (at each t) along with separability, then there exists a two-stage procedure, proved by Green (1964), which produces a one-period utility function and an associated single (collapsed) budget constraint which can be used to derive the demand functions for current period assets, consumption and bond demands. As Barnett puts it:

> In the first stage the consumer selects aggregate monetary asset expenditure . . . and aggregate consumer goods expenditure for each period within his planning horizon and his terminal bond . . . holdings, B_{t+T}. The chosen

> bond holdings are to be carried forward to the start of his next planning horizon. In the second stage he allocates current monetary asset expenditure and current aggregate consumer goods expenditure over individual current assets and consumer goods. (1981, p. 199)

The consumer faces a series of (intertemporal) budget constraints for each of s periods between the present (t) and the end of his planning horizon $(t + T)$. These are (for each s)

$$\tilde{\mathbf{p}}_s'\tilde{\mathbf{x}}_s = w_s L_s + \sum_{i=1}^{n} [(1 + r_{i,s-1})\bar{p}_{s-1}^* m_{i,s-1} - \bar{p}_s^* m_{is}] + [(1 + R_{s-1})\bar{p}_{s-1}^* B_{s-1} - \bar{p}_s^* B_s] \tag{3.27}$$

where the $\bar{p}^*$ expected $(*)$ price indices (not, of course, for period t). In Equation (3.27), then, each of the expressions in square brackets represents planned changes in asset holdings; r_i and R are one-period nominal yields on the i monetary assets and the benchmark asset respectively (and are paid at the beginning of the next period, for simplicity). Thus, the dimension of the problem is that of a series of flows of consumer services financed by labour income and changes in the stocks of financial assets over the same period.[6] Define

$$\rho_s = (1 + r_t)(1 + R_{t+1}) \ldots (1 + R_{s-1})$$

as the discounting factor for future periods, again noting that R_s is not paid in the period between s and $s + 1$, but at the start of $s + 1$.

We may collapse the series of constraints in Equations (3.27) into a single constraint by progressively eliminating ρ_s between B_{t+T} and initial bond-holdings (B_{t-1}), starting with B_{t+T-1} and working down to B_t. The values in the constraints referring to future periods must of course be discounted by the appropriate ρ_s in this process. The result (Barnett, 1981, p. 196) is a single constraint of

$$\sum_{s=1}^{t+T}\left(\frac{\tilde{\mathbf{p}}'}{\rho_s}\right)\tilde{\mathbf{x}}_s + \sum_{s=t}^{t+T}\sum_{i=1}^{n}\left[\frac{\bar{p}^*}{\rho_s} - \frac{\bar{p}_s^*(1 + r_{is})}{\rho_{s+1}}\right]m_{is} + \sum_{i=1}^{n}\frac{\bar{p}_{t+T}^*(1 + r_{i,t+T})}{\rho_{t+T+1}}m_{i,t+T} + \frac{\bar{p}_{t+T}^*}{\rho_{t+T}}B_{t+T} = \sum_{s=t}^{t+T}\left(\frac{W_s}{\rho_s}\right)L_s + \sum_{i=1}^{n}(1 + r_{i,t-1})\bar{p}_{t-1}^* m_{i,t-1} + (1 + R_{t-1})B_{t-1}\bar{p}_{t-1}^* \tag{3.28}$$

The point of this exercise is not to tax the reader's patience but to show explicitly, in the proper theoretical context, just where the notions in this literature arise. In Equation (3.28), for example, the discounted value of consumption, changes in money asset balances and final balances (and bonds) are equated to the revenues from work, and from monetary assets and bonds. In consequences of this interpretation, the term in square brackets represents the user cost of using monetary balances for transactions in

period s. We can write out this important concept as

$$\pi_s = \frac{\bar{p}_s^*}{\rho_s} - \frac{\bar{p}_s^*(1 + r_{is})}{\rho_{s+1}} \tag{3.29}$$

and it is immediately apparent that the current period user cost (π_{it}) is then

$$\pi_{it} = \frac{\bar{p}_t^*(R_t - r_{it})}{1 + R_t} \tag{3.30}$$

recalling the definition of ρ given above (i.e. since $\rho = 1$ for the first period). This is the monetary analogue of Jorgenson's (1963) user cost for durable goods (see Donovan, 1978, and Barnett, 1981). Here r_{it} is the current period own yield and R_t is the yield on the (non-monetary) benchmark asset. Note that when this expression is used to calculate the user costs of financial assets:

> User costs commonly are viewed as the prices of the services of durables rather than of their stocks (see Donovan, 1978). In that interpretation services are assumed to be proportional to stocks, and units of quantities and prices are assumed to have been chosen such that the proportionality constants are one. Hence user-cost evaluated stocks (stocks multiplied by corresponding user costs) are expenditures *on the services* of the stocks. (Barnett, 1981, p. 197)

Notice that the interest rates appearing in these expressions are nominal interest rates.

We are in possession of the weakly separable utility function in Equation (3.26) and the collapsed budget constraint, Equation (3.28). The next step is to employ the 'multistage maximization procedure' in order to collapse the problem to one involving only the user costs and quantities of monetary assets. The key condition here is the weak separability already employed for Equation (3.26). In the first of two stages, the consumer selects aggregate monetary-asset expenditure, aggregate consumer goods expenditure for each period and his terminal bond-holdings (B_{t+T}). The second stage, then, is to maximize

$$U(m_{it}, \ldots, m_{nt}) \tag{3.31}$$

subject to

$$\sum_{i=1}^{n} \pi_{it} m_{it} - W_t = 0 \tag{3.32}$$

Thus, as we did with the mean-variance model, we could derive demand functions for the m_i assets directly from these relations, although that is not our intention here.

As Barnett (1981) points out, what we have here is a utility tree – a nested tree – which we can estimate from the bottom up (Equations (3.31) and (3.32) being the bottom). We should note that the optimal consumer price level appears in Equation (3.32) in the definition of π, and so the solution is conditional on already having the correct optimal price index. But because of separability we do not need optimal quantities of consumer goods in the asset

demand functions, and while we need them for the correct solution of p_t, it is expedient – and general practice – to use an already available price index (preferably an ideal statistical price index, as discussed in Chapter 1) for the purpose of deflating the financial assets. This procedure is cost-effective even if it is not, strictly speaking, correct.

3.3.2 Duality theory in the study of monetary asset demands

Let us follow the standard outline of duality theory for demand analysis, but translate it into the notation of the asset-demand framework to economize on space. The asset problem just described postulates a utility function of $U(m_1, \ldots, m_n)$ subject to a budget constraint of $\tilde{\boldsymbol{\pi}}'\tilde{\mathbf{m}} = W$, recalling that W is defined as expenditures on this class of assets alone. The direct solution of this system produces a set of demand functions for assets of the general form of

$$m_i^* = \theta_i(\tilde{\mathbf{p}}, W) = \theta_i(\tilde{\mathbf{v}}) \qquad (i = 1, \ldots, n) \tag{3.33}$$

where $v_i = p_i/W$ is a set of 'normalized' prices. The second equality in Equation (3.33) is possible under the assumption that $\phi_i(\cdot)$ is homogeneous in $\tilde{\mathbf{p}}$ and W.

The utility function $U(m_1, \ldots, m_n)$ is defined as the *direct utility function*; substituting the m_i^* into that function we obtain an alternative function $u^* = U(\tilde{\mathbf{m}}^*)$. This function can be written as

$$u = U[\theta(\tilde{\mathbf{p}}, W)] = U[\theta(\tilde{\mathbf{v}})] \equiv g(\tilde{\mathbf{v}}) \tag{3.34}$$

That is, we can substitute the demand functions into the utility function (for the optimal quantities of financial assets) and then switch to the normalized form, again imposing the homogeneity condition on $\theta(\cdot)$. The direct utility function has quantities as arguments, while the *indirect utility function* – like the demand functions – has normalized prices as arguments. There are situations – mainly involving ease of calculation – when we might prefer to work with the normalized prices of Equation (3.34), which is why we do this (see Diewert, 1974*b*).

We have hinted at the main reason for wanting to work with the indirect utility function, and it is now time to be more explicit about that. In fact, in this study we will be using specific, and sometimes complex, functional forms for the indirect utility function – in particular the Translog and the Fourier flexible functional forms – for which the direct calculations are especially difficult or even intractable. In any case, assuming that we have the indirect utility function in hand – say, a Translog indirect utility function – the next problem is to acquire demand functions for the various assets. The rule which enables us to do this is known as Roy's identity and, in the context of the asset-demand formulation we are interested in, this is

$$M_i(\tilde{\mathbf{v}}^*) \equiv \frac{\partial g(\tilde{\mathbf{v}}^*)/\partial v_i}{\sum_{j=1}^{n} v_j \partial g(\tilde{\mathbf{v}}^*)/\partial v_j} \qquad \text{(for all } i\text{)} \tag{3.35}$$

That is, given knowledge of the normalized prices and the indirect utility function, we can derive the parameters of the asset-demand functions (in the normalized prices) from knowledge of the partial derivatives of the indirect utility function, arranged as in Equation (3.35). The conditions under which Roy's identity holds are exactly those regularity conditions which establish duality. Rather than pursue the proof of this important proposition here, we will turn to a consideration of two special cases, the Translog and the Fourier, as illustrations of the methods. We will offer some contemporary illustrations on US data, as well.

3.4 THE TRANSLOG UTILITY FUNCTION IN STUDIES OF MONEY DEMAND[7]

The problem considered here is the maximization of a second-stage utility function subject to a second-stage monetary expenditure constraint. That is, in the second stage of a two-stage maximization problem, with the assumption of weak separability between monetary assets and consumer goods, we postulate a direct utility function of the general form of

$$U(x_{1t}, x_{2t}, \ldots, x_{mt})$$

subject to

$$\sum_{i=1}^{n} \pi_{it} x_{it} - M_t = 0$$

where

$$\pi_i = \frac{p_i^*(R_t - r_{it})}{1 + R_t}$$

and an indirect utility function of

$$g(v_1, v_2, \ldots, v_n)$$

where

$$v_i = \frac{\pi_i}{m}$$

Then, by application of Roy's identity, we will be able to move from estimates of the indirect function to estimates of the elasticities of substitution among the assets.

The demand-systems approach provides both a set of neoclassical restrictions on individual behaviour which can be tested against particular bodies of data and a rich supply of alternative functional forms for demand systems which can serve as 'specification hypotheses' for actual estimation. Since demand theory actually says nothing about the functional form that must be used, many functional forms have been examined in the literature in an attempt to represent consumer preferences. These alternative forms

transform the behavioural postulates of the theory into restrictions on parameters and differ, one to the other, in their initial parameterization. In many cases, the restrictions are implicit, e.g. use of the functional form requires certain homothetic combinations of the independent variables, but because the theory is often not well-structured, it is frequently difficult to impose and test these restrictions (as to their statistical significance). A properly executed simultaneous-equations demand system is an effective answer to the problem in that the restrictions can then be derived directly. It is an effective answer because the restrictions become explicit in the context of a particular functional form. Flexible functional forms, which permit a wide range of interactions among the commodities being tested, are especially useful in this respect. More to the point, a non-flexible functional form will not provide a suitable framework for estimating complementarity and substitutability.[8]

The major property of flexible functional forms is that they impose fewer undesirable *a priori* restrictions on the structure of preferences. Basically, these functions are designed to approximate a utility function by some specific functional form that itself has enough parameters to provide a second-order approximation to the unknown function (see Diewert, 1974*b*). Mainly, as we shall see, they differ in the specific way in which they carry out this approximation and in how general the approximation method is (how well it retains the character of the unknown function).

Considering a specific example, then, the Translog version of the problem can be set up as follows, starting with the indirect utility function in order to avoid certain well-known problems.[9] The logarithm of the indirect utility function can be approximated by a function that is quadratic in the logarithms of the ratios of prices to the value of monetary expenditures, as in Equation (3.36):

$$\log v = \log \alpha_0 + \sum_i \alpha_i (\log v_i) + \frac{1}{2} \sum_i \sum_j \gamma_{ij} (\log v_i)(\log v_j) \qquad (3.36)$$

In fact, the function just exhibited can be derived as a second-order Taylor-series expansion to an arbitrary utility function at (or near) a particular point. At that point the Translog is, indeed, a reasonably good approximation for many practical exercises. We will thus go through this process because it provides an insight into the estimation procedure.

Starting with the implicit utility function of

$$\log v = \log v(v_1, v_2, \ldots, v_n) \qquad (3.37)$$

where the variables are as defined earlier, the expansion of log v around an arbitrary point log v^* yields the expression

$$\log v = \log v^* - \sum_i \alpha_i \log v_i^* + \frac{1}{2} \sum_i \sum_j \gamma_{ij} \log v_i^* \log v_j^*$$

$$+ \sum_i \left(\alpha_i + \frac{1}{2} \sum_j \gamma_{ij} \log v_i^* \right) \log v_i + \frac{1}{2} \sum_i \sum_j \gamma_{ij} \log v_i \log v_j \qquad (3.38)$$

where

$$\alpha_i = \frac{\partial \log v}{\partial \log v_i} \quad \text{and} \quad \gamma_{ij} = \frac{\partial^2 \log v}{\partial \log v_i \, \partial \log v_j}$$

This is a general indirect Translog utility function which has been expanded around an arbitrary point v^*.[10]

Using Roy's identity in the logarithmic form appropriate for the Translog and recalling that $v_j = \pi_j / M$, we have

$$\frac{\pi_j x_j}{M} = \frac{(\partial \log v)/(\partial \log \pi_j)}{[-(\partial \log v)/(\partial \log M)]} \qquad (j = 1, \ldots, n) \qquad (3.39)$$

We can then directly calculate the budget share for the jth asset as

$$S_j = \frac{\alpha_j + \sum_i \gamma_{ij} \log v_i}{\alpha_m + \sum_i \gamma_{im} \log v_i} \qquad (i, j = 1, \ldots, n) \qquad (3.40)$$

where, for simplicity, $S_j = \pi_j x_j / M$, $\alpha_m = \Sigma_j \alpha_j$ and $\gamma_{im} = \Sigma_j \gamma_{ij}$. Note also that the last named is a set of n parameters that have the interpretation of 'income' elasticities. They are n in number and are estimated directly in the empirical tests of this function. If the parameters are estimated in this form, we need to recognize that the equations for budget shares are homogeneous of degree zero in the parameters. To avoid the simultaneity that would result, we can adopt the normalization common in this literature that $\alpha_m = -1$.[11] In this form, then, Equation (3.40) represents the final result of our theoretical exercise. It is the function that embodies the use of duality and the Translog indirect utility function. As a set of simultaneous budget-share equations with normalized prices as arguments, it carries the additional restriction that the shares must sum to unity. In general, then, only $n - 1$ of the n share equations will be estimated, using the definitions of the parameters to recover the parameters of the redundant equation.

3.4.1 The econometrics of the Translog specification

Rather than specifying and testing the question of existence, i.e. testing the integrability conditions of economic theory, most studies in the Translog literature assume the existence of a representative consumer and represent his preferences with a community utility function in which the assumption of linear homogeneity is essential (as a means of imposing functional regularity on the demand system). Integrability conditions actually imply the existence of underlying utility functions. That is to say, if the system of demand functions can be generated by utility maximization, subject to a budget constraint, the system is integrable. The importance of this is clear: if the integrability conditions are valid, then the theory of individual consumer behaviour is applicable to the analysis of aggregate consumer demand functions in *per capita* form (see Jorgenson and Lau, 1979). In particular, we can test to see whether the system of *per capita* consumer demand equations

is integrable by testing the conditions for integrability. These conditions are homogeneity, summability, symmetry, non-negativity and monotonicity. We will refer to these as the 'theoretical restrictions' to distinguish them from the 'functional form' restrictions that will be discussed below.

To begin with, in the presentation here the equality restrictions are to be taken as maintained hypotheses.[12] For symmetry, if the equations are generated by utility maximization, then symmetry of the Slutsky matrix is represented by a set of restrictions relating the parameters of the cross-partial derivatives as in $\gamma_{ij} = \gamma_{ji}$ (for $i \neq j$ and $i, j = 1, \ldots, n$).[13] Homogeneity, if it applies, really implies the absence of money illusion, and this can be accepted in general, on the basis of a considerable macroeconomic literature to that effect; it is maintained by calculating the variables in real terms. Furthermore, summability (adding up) is easily valid, since by the maximization process $\Sigma_i S_i = 1$, so that, given equality, $\Sigma_j \gamma_{ij} = \gamma_{im}$. We will also take this as a maintained hypothesis; in this event, the parameters of the deleted equation can be obtained from the parameters of the other $n-1$ equations. The non-negativity conditions imply that the values of the fitted demand functions are non-negative (i.e. $S_j \geq 0, j = 1, \ldots, n$). The usual neoclassical monotonicity requirement is

$$\frac{\partial U}{\partial \pi_i} < 0$$

which implies in the case of the indirect utility function

$$\frac{(\partial \log v)/(\partial \log v_i)}{(\partial \log v)/(\partial \log M)} > 0 \qquad (i = 1, \ldots, n)$$

Finally, the quasiconvexity conditions, or, rather, the curvature conditions, require that for the Hessian matrix

$$\left\{ \frac{\partial^2 \mathbf{v}}{\partial v_i \, \partial v_j} \right\} \qquad \text{(for all } i, j\text{)}$$

at most one eigenvalue be negative with the rest being positive or zero. Equivalently, this requirement implies that the well-known Allen–Uzawa elasticities of substitution provide a negative semidefinite matrix of rank equal to, at most, $n - 1$. A necessary, but not sufficient, requirement of the curvature conditions is that the own-elasticities of substitution must all be non-positive.

The foregoing are handed down to us by the general theory of consumer demand and apply, in principle, to any simultaneous-equations demand study. This is not so, though, for the functional form restrictions, which depend on the particular functional form adopted. In the case of the Translog, we consider only linear homogeneity, a set of restrictions which is often employed in Translog (and Cobb–Douglas) studies. In fact, these are restrictions that may well not apply, and thus it is often desirable to test for linear homogeneity. Linear homogeneity, to be precise, implies the set of

restrictions.

$$\sum_j \gamma_{ij} = \sum_i \gamma_{ij} = 0$$

When we consider the actual estimation of a system of non-linear regression equations in which the disturbances are contemporaneously correlated across equations, an appropriate estimation technique is that of seemingly unrelated regressions (SUR). In the case under consideration, however, serial correlation clearly exists in the residuals so that an extension of SUR known as the iterative non-linear seemingly unrelated regression (INSUR) method is adopted. To test the validity of the restrictions, whether they are theoretical (e.g. symmetry) or functional form (e.g. linear homogeneity, neutrality) restrictions on the indirect utility function, we could use a test such as the likelihood-ratio test.[14]

The parameters of interest to us in our monetary analysis are not necessarily those of the demand functions, but, rather, the estimates of the elasticities of substitution among the assets. The way to get at these at the estimation stage is to derive income and price elasticities and then to use the Slutsky equation to derive the elasticities of substitution (as in Chetty, 1969). We will exhibit these formulae below, in the course of our discussion of some sample results for the US monetary data of recent vintage.

3.4.2 An example of the Translog specification: US data

The following results are not meant to be definitive in any sense, although they do work out reasonably well, but are meant to demonstrate the method described in the discussion thus far. We also want to add some basic econometric material to the discussion, with reference to the Translog model. The discussion in Chapter 1 arrived at a 'like-assets' configuration of the monetary quantities in which some doubts were expressed about the separability of the consumption decision from the asset-holding decision, at least on this particular set of monetary assets. In the following exercise we will concentrate on the short-term financial sector – looking at a system of demand equations for the following sets of assets, divided into two groups as suggested by the GARP tests in Chapter 1.

Set	Variables
A1	Currency, DDCON, OCD
A2	SDCB, SDSL, SDSB, SNOWC, SNOWT, MMDAC, MMDAT
A3	STDCB, STDTH
A4	DURABLE, NONDURABLE, SERVICE (CONSUMPTION)

Look back to Table 1.2 for slightly more detail on these variables and recall both that these are simple sums within each category and that the full set (of

four conglomerate assets) pass the GARP test in Chapter 1 – with zero violations.

We will begin with a basic and unrestricted test of the Translog model on the complete collection. As already noted, what we do is to deflate the monetary quantities by population and the price level, a process which imposes homogeneity in those respects, and then calculate monetary shares by means of, e.g. the following calculations:

$$S_1 = \frac{\pi_1(Currency + DDCON + OCD)}{MM}$$

where MM is total expenditures on the entire set of assets considered in the problem. To construct the independent variables, the prices are normalized by means of

$$v_i = \frac{\pi_i}{MM}$$

and are then normalized again by dividing by the mean of each set in order to place the Taylor's expansion around the point $V^* = 1$. The final transformation, then, involves taking the log of each of the normalized shares. These variables are referred to as LA1, LA2, LA3 and LCON in what follows.

There are four shares and four normalized log-price shares in this first problem, but, as already noted, one equation must be dropped. Thus only three equations are estimated, with the parameters of the fourth being recovered from the adding-up conditions of the model. In addition, the serial correlation in the residuals must be constrained in order to be the same across equations, or the final results will depend on which equation is deleted. The result is a set of six equations, three representing the structure and three modelling the common AR(1) process we are assuming holds across all equations. The method of estimation is that of iterative seemingly unrelated regressions, and the serial correlation is handled by means of a conditional least squares method.[15] The first of the equations estimated, in terms of the variables defined above, is

$$S1 = \frac{\alpha_1 + \gamma_{11}LA1 + \gamma_{12}LA2 + \gamma_{13}LA3 + \gamma_{14}LCON + W_1LT}{MM}$$

where $MM = -1 + M1(LM1) + M2(LOCD) + M3(LMMDAC) + M4(LSDCB) + M5(LSTDCB) + WM(LT)$.[16] There are, as noted, two other sets of equations. Note that the W_i measure the influence of (the log of) trend on each equation, and the M_i are analogous to 'income' responses (with MM, as defined above, not income as such, but total real *per capita* expenditure on this class of assets).

The results of the estimate of a *non-symmetrical* version of this set of equations appear in Table 3.1. The parameters of Table 3.1 are reasonably well determined, as it turns out, with 14 of the 24 estimated parameters

Table 3.1 The Translog demand for US liquid assets and consumption, non-symmetric version. Quarterly data, 1970–85–2 (t-values in parentheses)

Dependent variable share	Constant	Normalized user cost of A1	A2	A3	CON	W	R^2
A1	−0.061	−0.066	0.008	0.033	0.099	0.012	0.985
	(21.26)	(2.83)	(0.67)	(12.62)	(3.49)	(5.12)	
A2	−0.050	0.018	−0.032	0.038	0.327	0.030	0.835
	(3.82)	(0.43)	(1.50)	(4.90)	(5.50)	(6.00)	
A3	−0.048	−0.005	0.002	−0.022	0.038	−0.001	0.988
	(12.53)	(0.26)	(0.17)	(8.27)	(1.42)	(0.72)	
CON	−0.841	0.081	0.094	0.436	0.664	0.144	...
		(0.27)	(0.63)	(16.97)	(1.93)		

Notes: 'ρ' = 0.970 (38.86) and WM = 0.185 (4.92).

achieving t-values of two or better and with each equation producing at least two significant parameters. It is thus instructive for comparative purposes to construct a table of elasticities (own-, cross-, income and substitution) for this formulation, even though a non-symmetric formulation is economic nonsense (it is being done to establish a comparison). The formula for the income elasticities for this model is

$$E_i = 1 + \frac{\left(-\sum_i \gamma_{ij} \Big/ S_i\right) + \sum_i \sum_j \gamma_{ij}}{-1} \tag{3.41}$$

while the own-price elasticities are

$$\eta_{ii} = -1 + \frac{(\gamma_{ii}/S_i) - \sum_i \gamma_{ij}}{-1} \tag{3.42}$$

and the cross-price elasticities are

$$\eta_{ij} = \frac{(\gamma_{ij}/S_i) - \sum_i \gamma_{ij}}{-1} \tag{3.43}$$

It can then be shown that the cross-elasticities, using the Slutsky equation, are

$$\eta_{ij} = S_j(\sigma_{ij} + E_i)$$

From this last expression, as explained by Diewert (1974*b*), the elasticities of substitution can be derived as

$$\sigma_{ij} = \frac{\eta_{ij}}{S_j} - E_i \tag{3.44}$$

Note, in particular, how the elasticity of substitution is related to the income

Table 3.2 Elasticities and cross-elasticities, Translog model, non-symmetric version

Good	Income elasticity	Cross-elasticities with respect to other good			
		A1	A2	A3	CON
A1	−0.254	0.110	−0.059	−0.056	−0.495
A2	0.727	−0.332	−0.288	−0.275	−5.412
A3	9.391	0.132	−0.030	−0.057	0.336
CON	0.628	−6.831	−0.040	−0.033	−0.662
		Elasticities of substitution			
A1		1.549			
A2		−4.716	−5.033		
A3		11.558	9.998	8.211	
CON		−0.492	−0.167	−0.068	−0.158

Table 3.3 The Translog demand for US liquid assets and consumption, symmetric version (t-values in parentheses)

Dependent variable share	Constant	Normalized user cost of					
		A1	A2	A3	CON	W	R^2
A1	−0.062	−0.063	0.016	0.009	0.071	0.004	0.989
	(39.55)	(8.03)	(2.91)	(3.33)	(2.58)	(1.29)	
A2	−0.065	0.016	−0.033	0.012	0.176	0.013	0.833
	(9.06)		(3.73)	(3.54)	(3.80)	(2.35)	
A3	−0.045	0.009	0.014	−0.028	0.137	−0.001	0.945
	(9.29)			(9.65)	(4.15)	(0.43)	
CON	−0.828	0.071	0.206	0.137	0.536	0.079	...
					(1.21)		

Notes: 'ρ' = 0.929 (30.79) and WM = 0.051 (1.02).

elasticity (this has a bearing on the interpretation of the following results, in a few cases).

A table of the elasticities calculated from Table 3.1 appears as Table 3.2, the results of which show some complementarity among the assets (negative off-diagonal signs for the elasticity of substitution). Equally problematic is one case when the own-elasticity of substitution shows a significant non-negative result (for A3) so that satisfaction of the second-order conditions for a maximum does not appear to hold. In sum, while a lot of complementarity can be explained away, these results are not really all that appealing.

The theory of consumer choice actually requires that the coefficient matrix behind Table 3.1 be symmetric. This set of conditions can be imposed directly in the Translog model, by assuming $G(i,j) = G(j,i)$. Indeed, as will be explained, the set of restrictions itself can be tested for significance, although we rarely get satisfactory results from this sort of procedure. Table 3.3

Table 3.4 Elasticities and cross-elasticities, Translog model, symmetric version

Good	Income	Cross-elasticities with alternative good			
		A1	A2	A3	CON
A1	0.542	0.106	−0.063	−0.103	0.574
A2	3.669	−0.255	−0.967	−0.359	−2.376
A3	2.741	−0.148	−0.034	−0.262	−1.920
CON	0.737	−0.054	0.004	−0.015	−0.672
		Elasticities of substitution			
A1		2.269			
A2		−0.490	−12.060		
A3		0.323	2.192	−2.814	
CON		−0.150	0.805	0.428	−0.073

Table 3.5 The Translog demand for US liquid assets, symmetric version (t-values, in parentheses)

Dependent variables share	Constant	Normalized user cost of				
		A1	A2	A3	W	R^2
A1	−0.361	−0.338	0.218	0.084	0.033	0.980
	(45.28)	(8.53)	(6.92)	(3.20)	(1.68)	
A2	−0.369	0.218	−0.009	0.159	0.084	0.858
	(15.83)		(0.21)	(7.45)	(2.87)	
A3	−0.270	0.084	0.159	−0.130	−0.019	. . .
				(6.88)		

Notes: 'ρ' = 0.919 (22.83) and WM = 0.098 (1.66).

presents results for the same US data, in this case under the assumption of symmetry. Here the model fits much better, with 13 of the 17 parameters being reasonably well determined.

To see the effect of the restrictions on the estimates of the elasticities and thus to get a rough idea of the effect of the restrictions, we may compare Table 3.4 with Table 3.2. These results make more sense, particularly in the negative diagonals of the cross-elasticity matrix (and in all but one of the substitution matrix diagonal terms). In most cases assets are substitutes for each other, but for A1 (currency, etc.) there is a complementarity relation with both A2 (savings deposits) and the consumption aggregate. This is the sort of result we often find with these models, and, at least in this case, there appear to be few obvious violations to consumer theory (and the results appear to be reasonably well determined). Note, however, the positive 'own'-elasticity of substitution on A1.

Of particular interest, of course, is the separability of the financial decision from the consumption decision. In Chapter 1, the GARP procedure which

was used implied that we might have some difficulty in this respect, and so it is instructive to repeat the experiment of Table 3.3 for a three-asset collection (Table 3.5). Note, however, that a direct test is also possible, although it is not performed in this example (see the discussion in Section 3.6 below).

The results shown in Table 3.5 are again well determined with nine of the 12 parameters being significant. (We were unable to get a three-asset, non-symmetrical version to converge.) As the following tabulation suggests, the assets appear to be weak substitutes or even complements for each other.

	A1	A2	A3	Income elasticity
A1	0.179			0.455
A2	−0.184	−0.094		1.552
A3	0.012	0.375	−0.528	0.974

Unfortunately, while the coefficients in Table 3.5 appear to be reasonably well defined, this does not carry over to the elasticities. The reason for this will become apparent when we look at an alternative *global* estimating technique.

3.5 THE FOURIER FLEXIBLE FORM AND MONEY DEMAND

Another way to employ flexibility – and gain some generality at the same time – is to estimate the elasticities of substitution among monetary assets by employing the classical Fourier sine/cosine series expansion of the indirect utility function. This method will produce an expenditure system (and estimates of the elasticities of substitution) with the property that the average prediction bias may be made arbitrarily small by increasing the number of terms in the expansion. Furthermore, we retain the ability to test the important integrability conditions – with special emphasis on the symmetry conditions that often fail in the Translog tests. We can do this, as implied above, because the validity of the integrability conditions implies that the theory of individual consumer behaviour is applicable to the analysis of aggregate consumer demand functions in *per capita* form.[17]

Demand-for-money studies generally use CES or Translog functions, and so there are a number of general properties to consider before proceeding with the particulars. Since we are proposing to demonstrate yet another flexible functional form and others are readily available (the minflex Laurent, Barnett, 1983; the generalized Translog, Serletis, 1988*a*, etc.), a little salesmanship is in order. The CES function satisfies certain regularity conditions globally but places unnecessarily stringent conditions on the possible values of the Allen elasticities of substitution (the AES). Flexible functional forms – a Taylor expansion such as the Translog – usually possess flexibility and impose no undesirable restrictions; Taylor's theorem, however, only

applies locally. Of course, the local applicability of the approximation suffices to transform propositions from the theory of demand into restrictions on the parameters of the approximating expenditure system. There is a further drawback with the Translog, and that is that Taylor's theorem fails to provide a satisfactory means of understanding the statistical behaviour of the parameter estimates and the test statistics. In contrast, the Fourier series expansion used in this section permits a natural transition from demand theory to statistical theory in the special sense of providing direct estimates of the standard errors for purposes of statistical inference. All this is available as long as we assume that the Fourier flexible form is actually tracking the true indirect utility function (El Badawi, *et al.* 1982). The approach is often called 'semi-non-parametric' in that standard demand theory is invoked up to the level of the indirect utility function before non-parametric techniques take over.

3.5.1 The Fourier model

Once again, the framework laid out in Section 3.3.2, involving the indirect utility function and the normalized user-cost expressions, is adopted. Following Gallant (1981), the Fourier flexible form approximation of an indirect utility function $g(\mathbf{v})$ may be written as

$$g_k(\mathbf{v}) = a_0 + \mathbf{b}'\mathbf{v} + \frac{1}{2}\mathbf{v}'C\mathbf{v} + \sum_{\alpha=1}^{A} \sum_{j=-J}^{J} a_{j\alpha} \exp(ij\mathbf{k}'_\alpha \mathbf{v}) \qquad (3.45)$$

Here

$$C = -\sum_{\alpha=1}^{A} a_{0\alpha} \mathbf{k}_\alpha \mathbf{k}'_\alpha \quad \text{and} \quad a_{j\alpha} = \bar{a}_{-j\alpha}$$

In an empirical investigation it is actually more convenient to work with a sine/cosine representation than the exponential just written and so we can use the following equivalent formulation. Note that the Fourier requires a normalization of the data (so that they lie on $0 \leq \mathbf{v} \leq 2\pi$:[18]

$$g_k(\mathbf{v}) = u_0 + \mathbf{b}'\mathbf{v} + \frac{1}{2}\mathbf{v}'C\mathbf{v} + \sum_{\alpha=1}^{A} \left\{ u_{0\alpha} + 2\sum_{j=1}^{J} [u_{j\alpha} \cos(j\mathbf{k}'_\alpha \mathbf{v}) - w_{j\alpha} \sin(j\mathbf{k}'_\alpha \mathbf{v})] \right\} \qquad (3.46)$$

in which

$$C = -\sum_{\alpha=1}^{A} u_{0\alpha} \mathbf{k}_\alpha \mathbf{k}'_\alpha$$

The empirical problem faced is to choose A (the number of terms) and J (the degree of the approximation). In general, these two parameters may be chosen according to either a deterministic procedure – using, for example,

some fixed rule – or an adaptive rule – such as increasing A when a significance test rejects the model being used. In the latter case the procedure is very much like that employed with the Almon lag, where both degree and lag length are chosen for the approximating function with one eye on the fit of the equation. In practice, low numbers of J are chosen primarily in order to permit a sufficient number of terms in A (because higher values of J result in a large loss of degrees of freedom). Furthermore, while a $J = 1$ has the easy intuition that it allows the capture of the influence of changes in relative prices, values of J greater than that have no obvious intuition. In turn, A has to be increased by the number of assets each time, another choice that is expensive in degrees of freedom. These distinctions may seem hard to grasp here but will be a lot clearer when we illustrate these choices below.

After differentiating Equation (3.46) and then applying Roy's identity, we arrive at the following Fourier expenditure system:

$$f_i(\mathbf{v}, \theta) = \frac{v_i b_i - \sum_{\alpha=1}^{A} \left\{ u_{0\alpha}\mathbf{v}'\mathbf{k}_\alpha + 2\sum_{j=1}^{J} j[u_{j\alpha}\sin(j\,\mathbf{k}'_\alpha\mathbf{v}) + w_{j\alpha}\cos(j\,\mathbf{k}'_\alpha\mathbf{v})] \right\} k_{i\alpha} v_i}{\mathbf{b}'\mathbf{v} - \sum_{\alpha=1}^{A} \left\{ u_{0\alpha}\mathbf{v}'\mathbf{k}_\alpha + 2\sum_{j=1}^{J} j\,[u_{j\alpha}\sin(j\mathbf{k}'_\alpha\mathbf{v}) + w_{j\alpha}\cos(j\mathbf{k}'_\alpha\mathbf{v})] \right\} \mathbf{k}'_\alpha\mathbf{v}} \tag{3.47}$$

These expressions are expenditure shares for the monetary assets. We could, at this point, go on to recover the parameters of the original equations, but, as before, our interest is primarily in the calculation of the elasticities of substitution. This statistic is again calculated using Diewert's method (1974*a*). That is, the Allen partial elasticity of substitution (AES) between two liquid assets i and j, σ_{ij}, can be derived from the estimates of the indirect utility function by use of the following formula:

$$\sigma_{ij} = \frac{\left(\sum_k v_k g_k\right) g_{ij}}{g_i g_j} - \frac{\sum_k v_k g_{jk}}{g_j} - \frac{\sum_k v_k g_{ik}}{g_i} + \frac{\sum_m \sum_k v_k g_{km} v_m}{\sum_n v_n g_n} \tag{3.48}$$

Here g_i and g_{ij} denote elements of

$$\frac{\partial}{\partial v_i} g(\mathbf{v}) \quad \text{and} \quad \frac{\partial^2}{\partial v_i \partial v_j} g(\mathbf{v}) \tag{3.49}$$

respectively.

Given that the AES is of primary concern, two points must be emphasized. First, as Gallant argues: 'global approximation to within arbitrary accuracy of the elasticities of substitution appears to us to be a far more appealing property than equality at (or near) a single point' (1981, p. 221). That is, if we let $\sigma_{ij}(\mathbf{v})$ correspond to the true indirect utility function and let $\sigma_{ijk}(\mathbf{v})$ correspond to the Fourier flexible form, then Gallant shows that for $\delta > 0$

there is a k with

$$|\sigma^*_{ij}(\mathbf{v}) - \sigma_{ijk}(\mathbf{v})| < \delta \tag{3.50}$$

for all $\mathbf{v} \in \mathbf{V}$. Second, El-Badawi, Gallant and Souza (1982) show that if the Fourier flexible form is used with an estimation procedure that satisfies the identification condition, then consistent estimation of price, income and substitution elasticities is possible. They conclude that if $\sigma_n(\mathbf{v})$ is an elasticity of substitution computed from $g_{kn}(x|\theta_n)$, if $\sigma^*(\mathbf{v})$ is computed from $g(\mathbf{v})$, and if $\lim_{n\to\infty} k_n = \infty$, then

$$\lim \mathrm{Sup}_{x\in X} |\sigma_n(\mathbf{v}) - \sigma^*(\mathbf{v})| = 0 \tag{3.51}$$

A similar result holds for the other elasticities.

When it comes to estimating the asymptotic standard errors in order to provide economic inferences of the AES, the INSUR procedure used by Gallant (1981) is employed. We are also interested in using the parameter estimates obtained from the Fourier indirect utility function to verify the restrictions on the form of the indirect utility function; the restrictions are for non-negativity, monotonicity and curvature (quasiconvexity). The positivity and monotonicity restrictions are checked by direct computation of the values of both the fitted demand functions and the gradient vector of the estimated indirect utility function, respectively. The curvature conditions are tested by examining the computed (σ_{ij}) matrix. A necessary, but not sufficient, requirement of the curvature condition is that the own elasticities of substitution must all be non-positive. As we will see, occasionally they are not in these tests.

3.5.2 An example of the Fourier specification on US data

This section will repeat the test of Section 3.4.2 in which two different configurations, a three-financial asset, and a three-asset + consumption configuration, are compared for the quality of the fit. In the Fourier, as we shall see, symmetry must be imposed (which is just as well), and, with the present version of the model (in the SAS system) an adjustment cannot be made for serial correlation. The former is required by consumer theory anyway, and the latter is possibly redundant in a system flexible enough to capture the underlying aggregator function to any degree of precision.

The first requirement is a return to Equation (3.47), the Fourier expenditure system. These are the equations to be estimated, and what is in the control of the researcher here, is the choice of the number (A) and the degree of the approximation (J); this is done by selecting what are known as 'multi-indices'. Usually, one chooses $J = 1$ in consumer-demand studies, since this can be interpreted as capturing the influence of relative prices on the budgetary shares. For the multi-indices themselves (we are approximating the unknown function by constructing weighted indices of the user costs), a reasonable procedure is to use all the 'basic indices' for the size of the

problem at hand. For a three-asset problem, for example, the Fourier system, Equation (3.46) for $J = 1$ and $A = 6$ would look like

$$\begin{aligned} g(\mathbf{x}) = u_0 + [b_1 b_2 b_3]\begin{bmatrix} x_1 \\ x_2 \\ x_3 \end{bmatrix} + [x_1 x_2 x_3] C \begin{bmatrix} x_1 \\ x_2 \\ x_3 \end{bmatrix} \\ + u_{01} + 2[u_{11}\cos(x_1) - v_{11}\sin(x_1)] + u_{02} \\ + 2[u_{12}\cos(x_2) - v_{12}\sin(x_2)] + u_{03} + 2[u_{13}\cos(x_3) \\ - v_{13}\sin(x_3)] + u_{04} + 2[u_{14}\cos(x_1 + x_2) \\ - v_{14}\sin(x_1 + x_2)] + u_{05} + 2[u_{15}\cos(x_1 + x_3) \\ - v_{15}\sin(x_1 + x_3)] + u_{06} + 2[u_{16}\cos(x_2 + x_3) \\ - v_{16}\sin(x_2 + x_3)] \end{aligned} \tag{3.52}$$

In this set-up, C is as defined immediately below Equation (3.46). Note that the vectors $\mathbf{k}_\alpha$ in this exercise consist of[19]

$$\mathbf{k}_\alpha = \begin{bmatrix} 1 \\ 0 \\ 0 \end{bmatrix} \cdot \begin{bmatrix} 0 \\ 1 \\ 0 \end{bmatrix} \cdot \begin{bmatrix} 0 \\ 0 \\ 1 \end{bmatrix} \cdot \begin{bmatrix} 1 \\ 1 \\ 0 \end{bmatrix} \cdot \begin{bmatrix} 1 \\ 0 \\ 1 \end{bmatrix} \cdot \begin{bmatrix} 0 \\ 1 \\ 1 \end{bmatrix}$$

At this point we must be aware of a problem of possible over-fitting in the attempt to drive the fit of the equation to a very precise level. This will occur, for example, if too many of the potential **k**-vectors are selected (there are many more available in the software). What could happen is that the elasticities of substitution could oscillate wildly – and quite unbelievably (see El Badawi, *et al.* 1982). Below we will note sharply oscillating elasticities in the US case, so we must be quite precise about this point. Indeed, note that only a minimal set of multi-indices is employed here.

To see how all of this works in practice, consider again the three composite assets (A1, A2, A3) studied with the Translog model. The result of the estimation stage of this problem is not particularly revealing, but it does provide information on the goodness of fit of the model. Accordingly, in Table 3.6 we present the parameters just described and their standard errors. In any case, not very many of these parameters are significant (8 out of 22), a result that does not compare particularly well with the Translog, in the three-asset case. Of course with an approximating technique such as the Fourier, non-significant parameters pose no particular problem.

The Fourier procedure provides estimates of price and income elasticities, cross-elasticities and their standard errors, and it also provides estimates of the Allen elasticities of substitution with similar statistical detail. Table 3.7 lists the complete set of cross-substitution elasticities and the income elasticities – along with the standard errors – and in Figures 3.1 and 3.2, we

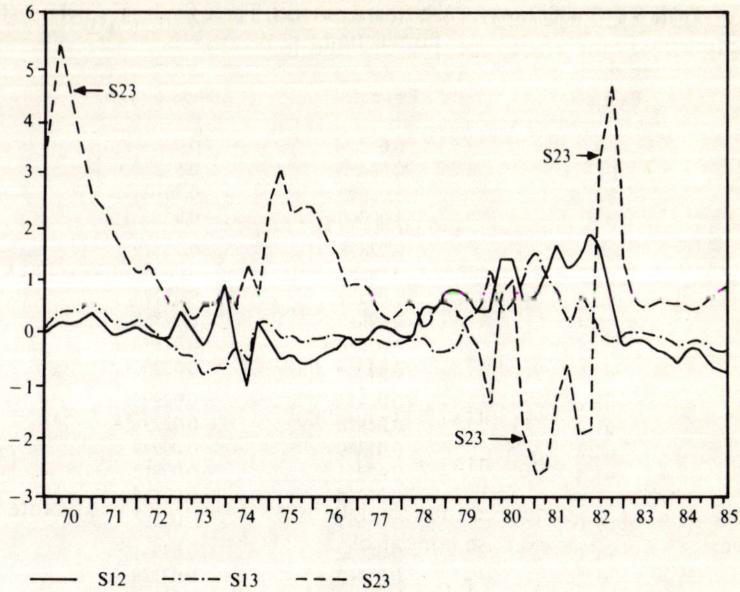

Figure 3.1 Three-asset elasticities of substitution.

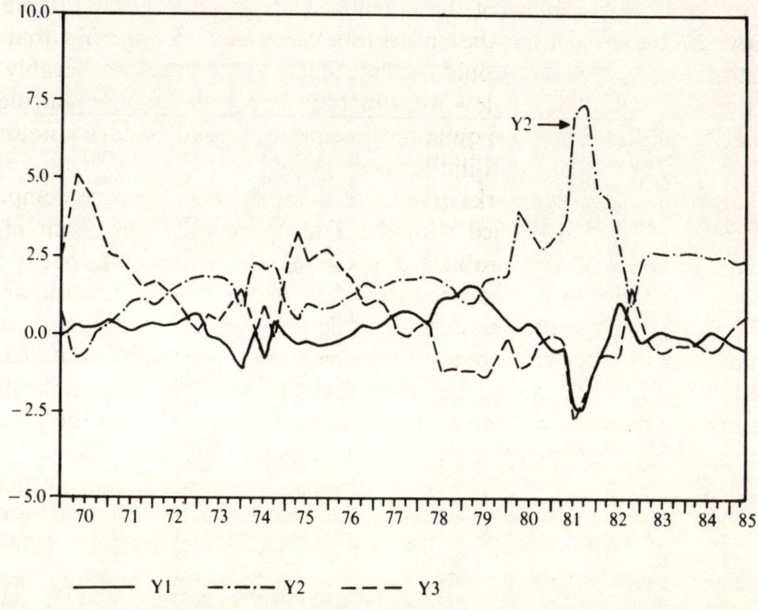

Figure 3.2 Three-asset income elasticities.

Table 3.6 Coefficients for the Fourier model. Three financial asset formulation

Parameter	Estimate	Standard error
u0, 0	0.0	0.0
B1	−0.58450	0.51274
B2	−2.08095	0.80108
B3	−1.00000	0.0
u0, 1	0.23818	0.13729
u0, 2	−0.08657	0.04263
u0, 3	0.05530	0.02776
u0, 4	−0.09918	0.04568
u0, 5	−0.07746	0.01870
u0, 6	−0.04466	0.02356
u1, 1	−0.06953	0.02992
u1, 2	0.04846	0.02291
u1, 3	−0.01360	0.00949
u1, 4	−0.00251	0.00813
u1, 5	−0.01048	0.02154
u1, 6	0.00677	0.00580
v1, 1	−0.08632	0.07351
v1, 2	0.04962	0.03128
v1, 3	0.00161	0.01027
v1, 4	0.02465	0.00920
v1, 5	−0.03152	0.01247
v1, 6	0.01754	0.01312

Table 3.7 Income and substitution elasticities, three-asset case – Fourier model

	σ_{12}	σ_{13}	σ_{23}	Y_1	Y_2	Y_3
1970.1	−0.009 (0.37)	0.183 (0.61)	3.431 (0.75)	0.031	0.528	2.898*
.2	0.180 (0.55)	0.408 (1.11)	5.548 (2.23)*	0.311	−0.782	5.215*
.3	0.133 (0.49)	0.406 (0.94)	4.855 (1.78)*	0.252	−0.466	4.585*
.4	0.189 (0.39)	0.446 (0.61)	3.608 (0.98)*	0.272	0.124	3.363*
1971.1	0.386 (0.34)	0.568 (0.42)	2.614 (0.63)*	0.538	0.379	2.544*
.2	0.098 (0.27)	0.365 (0.38)	2.336 (0.44)*	0.286	0.670	2.407*
.3	−0.073 (0.23)	0.178 (0.31)	1.865 (0.27)*	0.143	1.089	1.938*
.4	0.008 (0.20)	0.156 (0.25)	1.422 (0.22)*	0.314	1.257	1.510*
1972.1	0.105 (0.21)	0.268 (0.29)	1.160 (0.27)*	0.396	1.001	1.777*
.2	−0.026 (0.19)	0.096 (0.24)	1.288 (0.21)*	0.336	1.276	1.457*
.3	−0.130 (0.19)	−0.079 (0.21)	0.941 (0.20)*	0.312	1.541*	1.110
.4	−0.082 (0.17)	−0.219 (0.20)	0.542 (0.22)*	0.498	1.736*	0.594
1973.1	−0.391 (0.26)	−0.418 (0.22)	0.600 (0.20)*	0.142	1.890*	0.727
.2	−0.016 (0.18)	−0.412 (0.19)*	0.235 (0.19)	0.675	1.903*	−0.127
.3	−0.270 (0.31)	−0.820 (0.37)*	0.517 (0.44)	0.449	1.909*	−0.075
.4	0.140 (0.38)	−0.655 (0.36)	0.465 (0.48)	0.885	1.717*	−0.546
1974.1	0.914 (0.72)	−0.656 (0.82)	0.863 (0.96)	1.579	0.903	−1.083
.2	−0.304 (0.26)	−0.253 (0.20)	0.480 (0.20)*	0.149	2.326*	−0.118
.3	−1.065 (0.60)	−0.499 (0.49)	1.295 (0.29)*	−0.721	2.183	0.979
.4	0.213 (0.26)	0.184 (0.23)	0.684 (0.25)*	0.435	2.253	−0.082
1975.1	−0.104 (0.29)	0.168 (0.40)	2.426 (0.38)*	0.018	0.992	2.226*
.2	−0.518 (0.41)	−0.131 (0.73)	3.130 (0.66)*	−0.293	0.483	3.316*
.3	−0.427 (0.33)	−0.067 (0.45)	2.244 (0.34)*	−0.225	1.043	2.349*
.4	−0.588 (0.40)	−0.198 (0.57)	2.438 (0.40)*	−0.357	0.885	2.678*

Table 3.7 Continued

	σ_{12}	σ_{13}	σ_{23}	Y_1	Y_2	Y_3
1976.1	−0.534 (0.37)	−0.139 (0.53)	2.370 (0.39)*	−0.301	0.860	2.672*
.2	−0.439 (0.31)	−0.096 (0.38)	1.864 (0.27)*	−0.180	1.120	2.174*
.3	−0.324 (0.26)	−0.061 (0.29)	1.515 (0.22)*	−0.024	1.297	1.785*
.4	−0.100 (0.19)	−0.080 (0.21)	0.839 (0.21)*	0.348	1.649*	0.912
1977.1	−0.241 (0.21)	−0.154 (0.22)	0.980 (0.20)*	0.201	1.528*	1.242
.2	−0.141 (0.19)	−0.133 (0.20)	0.830 (0.21)*	0.343	1.593*	1.002
.3	0.120 (0.24)	−0.141 (0.21)	0.358 (0.24)	0.754	1.772*	0.154
.4	0.088 (0.18)	−0.249 (0.20)	0.248 (0.22)	0.764	1.838*	−0.042
1978.1	−0.048 (0.18)	−0.204 (0.20)	0.461 (0.22)*	0.520	1.860*	0.340
.2	0.068 (0.19)	−0.143 (0.20)	0.368 (0.22)*	0.432	1.880*	0.434
.3	0.472 (0.35)	−0.087 (0.20)	0.056 (0.22)*	1.178	1.800*	−1.103
.4	0.454 (0.61)	−0.407 (0.44)	0.485 (0.58)	1.182	1.567	−1.010
1979.1	0.782 (0.89)	−0.358 (0.68)	0.583 (0.79)	1.556	1.108	−1.117
.2	0.791 (0.97)	−0.262 (0.73)	0.446 (0.76)	1.584	1.050	−1.107
.3	0.666 (0.74)	0.255 (0.29)	−0.012 (0.32)	1.229	1.801*	−1.419
.4	0.401 (1.06)	0.520 (0.44)	−0.320 (0.44)	0.837	1.908*	−0.764
1980.1	0.390 (1.31)	1.193 (0.55)*	−1.382 (0.50)*	0.484	1.893*	−0.002
.2	1.407 (1.15)	0.404 (0.32)	0.728 (0.44)	0.129	4.030*	−0.973
.3	1.436 (0.89)	0.505 (0.36)	1.016 (0.41)*	0.439	3.389*	−0.883
.4	0.644 (1.40)	1.180 (0.53)*	−1.883 (0.58)*	−0.121	2.824*	−0.130
1981.1	0.689 (1.70)	1.568 (0.76)	−2.656 (0.86)*	−0.490	3.059*	0.046
.2	1.088 (1.81)	1.186 (0.63)	−2.603 (0.86)*	−0.461	3.488*	−0.180
.3	1.658 (3.87)	0.695 (1.16)	−1.262 (1.89)	−2.261	7.164*	−2.720*
.4	1.211 (3.35)	0.091 (1.32)	−0.567 (1.90)	−2.329	7.434*	−2.024
1982.1	1.393 (2.42)	0.677 (0.66)	−1.974 (1.04)	−0.878	4.716*	−0.749
.2	1.867 (2.35)	0.431 (0.43)	−1.780 (0.84)*	−0.306	4.348*	−0.583
.3	1.590 (1.98)	−0.085 (0.44)	3.347 (1.01)*	1.168	3.138*	−0.731
.4	0.547 (0.89)	−0.191 (0.84)	4.723 (1.11)*	0.661	0.756	1.708
1983.1	−0.240 (0.33)	−0.007 (0.24)	1.465 (0.24)*	−0.207	2.520*	0.385
.2	−0.141 (0.33)	0.033 (0.26)	0.596 (0.21)*	0.064	2.676*	−0.363
.3	−0.146 (0.37)	−0.008 (0.18)	0.434 (0.20)*	0.164	2.626*	−0.580
.4	−0.321 (0.32)	−0.078 (0.21)	0.597 (0.21)*	−0.041	2.638*	−0.264
1984.1	−0.364 (0.32)	−0.118 (0.22)	0.567 (0.21)*	−0.044	2.617*	−0.278
.2	−0.567 (0.36)	−0.234 (0.28)	0.570 (0.25)*	−0.166	2.622*	−0.258
.3	−0.299 (0.45)	−0.166 (0.27)	0.419 (0.32)	0.168	2.492*	−0.597
.4	−0.334 (0.32)	−0.137 (0.21)	0.514 (0.21)*	0.027	2.566	−0.334
1985.1	−0.636 (0.36)	−0.320 (0.28)	0.688 (0.29)*	−0.250	2.422*	0.207
.2	−0.716 (0.40)	−0.352 (0.31)	0.838 (0.24)*	−0.364	2.304*	0.533

*Significant results (standard error in parentheses).

graph the same information. Here the statistically significant results are marked with asterisks, and, transparently, they involve the income elasticities of A2 (savings deposits), A3 (small savings deposits), and the elasticity of substitution between the two collections. Equally transparent is that the currency plus deposits (A1) aggregate is not very precisely defined in this test.[20]

One thing we might do, although it is a little casual, is to compare the Translog, three-asset, symmetric elasticities with those obtained by averaging the columns in Table 3.7. These figures are as follows, with the own rates (not exhibited in the table) also summed:

	Translog				Fourier			
	Income	A1	A2	A3	Income	A1	A2	A3
*A*1	0.455	0.179			0.197	−0.106		
*A*2	1.552	−0.184	−0.094		1.987	0.180	−0.932	
*A*3	0.974	0.012	0.375	−0.528	0.565	0.057	0.946	−1.497

These are pretty similar results on the whole. Again, the evidence from the Fourier is that there is (on average) low substitution among the financial assets.

But the Fourier is at its strongest when the details are on the line, and here, both in the table and in the two figures that follow, we begin to see why, specifically, the US demand for money has been so hard to estimate with conventional methods of aggregation in recent years. In Table 3.7 and Figures 3.1 and 3.2, there are large swings in both the income and substitution elasticities, with the sharpest movements coming in the *significant* σ_{23} numbers.[21] Indeed, and again it is obvious, the large swings occur in a recession. The recession years are, *of course*,

1970–1

1974–5

1980–2

to ignore the precise (quarterly) timing. What happens, possibly, is that strong income pressures on savers force the liquidation of savings accounts (and produce the estimates of significantly positive income elasticities) and sharp changes in interest rates. Both events slide consumer-savers along their utility surfaces producing sharp changes in the estimates of (marginal) elasticities. It is clear that any aggregation procedure which fails to internalize these swings is not going to produce a stable aggregate. The simple-sum measures do not, while the Divisia will (being tied to the same consumer theory that produced the Fourier model), at least if no other problems emerge (such as inaccurate user-costs). Note, however, that the asset group here is fairly broad and involves the elimination of a lot of the non-consumer assets in the M2 index components.

Unfortunately, the model just discussed does not fit all that well, and it is reasonable to ask how the results fare with a four-asset structure that includes the non-separable (see Chapter 1) consumption goods. Recall, in regard to this contention, that if time deposits (A3) are included in the problem, then consumption goods must also be included because the two are not separable from each other. Passing over the uninteresting Fourier coefficients this time (in this case there were 18 multi-indices and 20 of the 37 parameters estimated were significant), we exhibit the full set of elasticities of substitution and the income elasticities in Table 3.8. Here the results are

much better-determined (the statistics in parentheses are t-values), and the improvement in performance includes the cash assets (A1) in this case.[22] All the substitution relations show significance here, with σ_{23} – the elasticity of substitution between savings deposits and time deposits – exhibiting a particularly firm relation. The elasticities also are often well in excess of unity, showing relatively strong substitution. This is the sort of result we really expect. The income elasticities (asterisks indicate significance at the 0.05 level) are not as impressive.

Before considering the time pattern of the results just provided, we need to look at a summary of the table, compared in this case with the four-asset Translog. The Fourier numbers, again, are averaged for purposes of this comparison.

	Translog					Fourier				
	Income	A1	A2	A3	A4	Income	A1	A2	A3	A4
*A*1	0.542	0.106				0.879	−3.851			
*A*2	3.669	−0.490	−0.967			2.714	1.258	−8.104		
*A*3	2.741	0.323	2.192	−0.262		2.803	1.119	2.876	−1.590	
*A*4	0.737	−0.150	0.805	0.428	−0.672	0.898	0.171	0.412	−0.224	−0.042

A strong substitution between the savings assets, as is visible in the table, exists for the Fourier, and all the elasticities but σ_{34} show a substitution relation. The results do differ somewhat from the Translog, but the strongest results and the income elasticities are comparable, and all results appear to be roughly equivalent across the two parts of the table. Note that the averages of the own-elasticities are all negative for the Fourier, as required by the theory.

The detailed results from the Fourier tell a very dramatic story, as it turns out, and pin down more precisely the relation between time deposits and consumption. Figure 3.3 shows the substitution elasticities among cash (A1) and the other three entities. Not only are the relations (especially σ_{12}) not constant over time, but also there are sharp breaks (in σ_{12}) during periods of financial disturbance (1970–3, 1974–5, 1980–2) with the first two recessions driving the elasticity of substitution toward stronger complementarity and the last toward relatively strong substitutability. Any method of aggregation which does not internalize the substitution/complementarity relation between cash and savings assets would surely tend to come unglued during recessions, transparently.

As Figure 3.4 suggests, the (strong) substitution relation between savings deposits and time deposits is also subject to a measure of cyclical uncertainty, with the close substitution at the beginning approaching zero as the period ends. The cash/time deposit substitution elasticity was included in the picture mainly to guide the eye, but what is notable is that one set of figures is again a virtual mirror image of the other especially during the cyclical disturbances.

Table 3.8 Income and substitution elasticities, four-asset case (*t*-values in parentheses)

	σ_{12}	σ_{13}	σ_{14}	σ_{23}	σ_{24}	σ_{34}	Y_1	Y_2	Y_3	Y_4
70.1	−4.053 (1.19)	1.568 (0.60)	0.977 (3.59)	10.650 (4.14)	0.673 (2.80)	−0.676 (2.37)	1.774	2.669*	15.848*	0.251
.2	−6.155 (1.77)	4.574 (1.65)	0.374 (1.95)	10.343 (3.85)	0.858 (3.31)	−0.817 (2.31)	0.573	2.878*	16.668*	0.267
.3	−6.782 (2.17)	4.634 (2.01)	0.156 (0.92)	8.403 (4.37)	0.951 (4.05)	−0.802 (2.74)	0.106	2.699*	12.818*	0.398
.4	−9.522 (2.81)	5.328 (2.15)	−0.104 (0.51)	9.539 (4.28)	1.202 (4.38)	−1.026 (3.09)	−0.232	3.705	13.756*	0.330
71.1	7.364 (2.40)	−1.398 (0.56)	0.205 (0.69)	10.047 (4.12)	−0.497 (2.30)	−0.737 (2.32)	0.638	0.338	11.878*	0.692
.2	9.896 (3.45)	−0.014 (0.01)	0.512 (1.47)	8.380 (4.33)	−0.659 (3.08)	−0.735 (2.64)	1.322	−0.106	9.707*	0.729
.3	7.524 (3.03)	−0.825 (0.43)	0.598 (2.18)	7.259 (5.01)	−0.450 (2.48)	−0.625 (2.91)	1.139	−0.178	8.245*	0.777
.4	5.345 (2.56)	−2.000 (1.26)	0.309 (1.80)	5.889 (5.48)	−0.259 (1.78)	−0.448 (2.71)	0.493	−0.211	6.428*	0.882
72.1	7.649 (3.10)	−1.265 (0.66)	0.258 (1.07)	6.740 (4.82)	−0.462 (2.64)	−0.547 (2.55)	0.728	−0.237	7.580*	0.834
.2	9.286 (4.05)	0.508 (0.36)	0.510 (2.06)	4.849 (4.44)	−0.528 (3.12)	−0.508 (2.95)	1.404	−0.511	5.359*	0.888
.3	11.063 (4.64)	3.485 (2.65)	0.764 (2.63)	3.605 (3.25)	−0.612 (3.29)	−0.573 (3.51)	2.201*	−0.463	4.183*	0.887
.4	8.881 (4.32)	3.438 (3.02)	0.680 (3.15)	2.000 (2.19)	−0.319 (2.65)	−0.415 (3.43)	1.886*	−0.522	2.718*	0.968
73.1	6.405 (3.93)	1.202 (1.32)	0.885 (5.42)	1.754 (2.63)	−0.196 (1.77)	−0.291 (3.22)	1.654	−0.743	1.922*	1.033
.2	6.969 (4.14)	4.241 (3.51)	0.474 (2.62)	1.161 (1.26)	−0.193 (1.59)	−0.370 (3.45)	1.212	−0.292	2.262*	1.025
.3	−0.392 (0.35)	−0.302 (0.44)	0.439 (4.13)	2.276 (4.54)	0.430 (5.79)	−0.181 (2.55)	0.670	0.644	1.444	1.034
.4	−1.577 (1.36)	1.055 (1.23)	0.004 (0.04)	2.474 (3.65)	0.542 (6.55)	−0.240 (3.06)	−0.063	1.228	1.897*	1.025
74.1	−6.658 (3.51)	4.819 (3.48)	−0.704 (2.77)	3.101 (2.72)	1.193 (7.07)	−0.480 (4.18)	−0.804	4.222*	2.796*	0.878
.2	−8.573 (3.16)	1.638 (2.09)	−0.459 (2.49)	4.898 (7.10)	1.407 (9.02)	−0.549 (4.68)	0.199	5.250*	0.514	0.727
.3	−7.968 (3.02)	7.554 (4.63)	−1.218 (3.86)	1.313 (1.11)	1.847 (8.10)	−0.327 (1.36)	−1.668	6.031*	−0.125	0.868
.4	−10.140 (3.82)	−2.108 (1.96)	0.120 (0.75)	7.156 (8.26)	1.327 (7.87)	−0.480 (3.84)	0.746	4.172*	3.854*	0.620
75.1	−9.540 (3.49)	6.722 (4.58)	−0.804 (3.61)	3.977 (4.26)	1.506 (7.15)	−0.772 (4.00)	−1.421	3.668*	8.895*	0.766
.2	−4.288 (2.38)	6.527 (4.52)	−0.658 (3.31)	1.450 (1.83)	1.026 (7.58)	−0.282 (1.34)	−1.693	1.252	3.243*	1.014
.3	−4.547 (2.59)	4.391 (4.00)	−0.609 (3.59)	1.652 (2.52)	1.000 (8.21)	−0.261 (1.67)	−1.432	1.361	2.482*	1.041
.4	−3.106 (1.98)	4.896 (4.32)	−0.619 (3.63)	0.825 (1.24)	0.907 (8.07)	−0.132 (0.75)	−1.520	0.878	2.224*	1.106
76.1	−1.381 (1.01)	2.560 (2.63)	−0.244 (1.60)	0.993 (1.57)	0.668 (6.76)	−0.030 (0.20)	−0.941	0.192	2.432*	1.104
.2	−0.462 (0.37)	0.029 (0.03)	−0.012 (0.09)	1.384 (2.25)	0.499 (5.46)	0.007 (0.06)	−0.564	−0.136	2.350*	1.112
.3	0.329 (0.28)	−1.720 (2.13)	0.149 (1.14)	1.607 (2.67)	0.370 (4.30)	0.037 (0.42)	−0.273	−0.343	2.176*	1.120
.4	3.129 (2.50)	−2.214 (2.87)	0.462 (3.75)	1.936 (3.32)	0.056 (0.66)	−0.047 (0.62)	0.516	−0.635	2.092	1.094
77.1	4.460 (3.01)	−1.349 (1.72)	0.748 (5.08)	1.385 (2.27)	−0.031 (0.33)	−0.045 (0.57)	1.207	−0.870	1.651	1.082
.2	4.048 (2.88)	−1.546 (2.05)	0.595 (4.17)	1.442 (2.37)	−0.008 (0.09)	−0.042 (0.53)	0.908	−0.787	1.706*	1.094
.3	3.303 (2.65)	−0.738 (1.09)	0.232 (1.53)	1.130 (1.68)	0.056 (0.68)	−0.047 (0.58)	0.272	−0.501	1.647	1.122
.4	3.458 (2.67)	0.183 (0.26)	0.298 (1.88)	0.679 (0.96)	0.068 (0.82)	−0.065 (0.78)	0.453	−0.473	1.325	1.124

78.1	1.619 (1.44)	−2.537 (4.08)	0.242 (1.64)	1.436 (2.51)	0.196 (2.52)	0.050 (0.69)	0.050	−0.386	1.584	1.140
.2	2.101 (1.66)	−2.163 (3.61)	0.427 (2.85)	1.025 (1.79)	0.182 (2.24)	0.065 (0.89)	0.465	−0.469	1.232	1.138
.3	0.898 (0.90)	0.966 (1.21)	−0.174 (1.10)	0.472 (0.64)	0.317 (4.08)	−0.053 (0.64)	−0.491	0.210	1.203	1.157
.4	−1.705 (1.45)	1.078 (1.22)	−0.160 (1.15)	0.984 (1.43)	0.583 (6.51)	−0.101 (1.16)	−0.152	1.174	0.598	1.084
79.1	−2.678 (2.17)	2.722 (2.38)	−0.380 (2.44)	0.681 (0.92)	0.711 (7.67)	−0.188 (2.12)	−0.382	1.686*	0.470	1.056
.2	−3.260 (2.51)	3.230 (2.67)	−0.469 (2.88)	0.745 (1.04)	0.779 (8.15)	−0.230 (2.64)	−0.510	1.956*	0.549	1.040
.3	−4.390 (3.24)	−0.313 (0.46)	−0.194 (1.27)	2.289 (3.56)	0.863 (8.22)	−0.078 (1.05)	−0.141	2.379*	0.506	0.987
.4	−5.963 (2.95)	−1.066 (1.43)	0.225 (1.02)	4.334 (6.25)	1.018 (5.57)	−0.208 (2.36)	0.596	3.988*	−0.366	0.797
80.1	−2.078 (0.62)	−1.655 (1.45)	0.286 (0.89)	5.153 (5.62)	−0.719 (2.54)	−0.166 (1.22)	−0.127	5.356*	−0.443	0.780
.2	−3.182 (0.87)	2.332 (3.15)	−0.376 (1.07)	3.380 (3.90)	1.339 (4.70)	−0.385 (3.42)	−0.711	8.036*	−0.592	0.680
.3	−6.609 (2.60)	1.264 (1.62)	−0.229 (0.91)	4.685 (6.38)	1.270 (7.23)	−0.466 (4.13)	0.310	5.687*	−0.216	0.722
.4	1.958 (0.45)	−1.710 (1.36)	0.052 (0.14)	3.769 (3.67)	0.565 (1.66)	−0.005 (0.09)	−1.146	6.085*	−0.212	0.820
81.1	15.698 (2.13)	−0.471 (0.39)	1.510 (1.94)	1.103 (0.53)	−0.589 (0.98)	0.161 (0.76)	−0.384	5.771*	0.029	0.846
.2	16.832 (2.11)	0.161 (0.14)	1.587 (1.91)	−1.631 (0.74)	−0.212 (2.07)	0.322 (1.42)	−1.427	6.585*	0.258	0.834
.3	22.826 (2.32)	0.880 (0.55)	2.786 (2.39)	−0.500 (0.17)	−0.889 (0.99)	0.197 (0.65)	0.094	6.198*	0.015	0.728
.4	25.661 (2.46)	−0.028 (0.02)	1.287 (1.43)	3.986 (1.42)	−1.873 (2.36)	−0.077 (0.30)	−0.526	9.302*	−0.030	0.646
82.1	19.562 (2.26)	−0.220 (0.18)	0.825 (1.15)	2.071 (0.94)	−0.981 (1.50)	0.051 (0.23)	−1.458	8.601	0.072	0.747
.2	14.225 (1.87)	−0.265 (0.24)	0.032 (0.06)	2.573 (1.47)	−0.295 (0.55)	−0.006 (0.03)	−2.013*	9.791*	0.015	0.720
.3	−0.724 (0.14)	4.178 (3.12)	−0.069 (1.37)	−0.831 (0.45)	2.200 (3.92)	−0.163 (0.72)	−3.317*	12.119*	−0.936	0.760
.4	−7.364 (2.90)	5.609 (3.88)	−0.737 (2.08)	0.818 (0.65)	2.016 (6.63)	−0.219 (0.95)	−1.928*	7.046*	−0.734	0.893
83.1	−5.101 (2.72)	3.907 (5.20)	−0.594 (2.56)	0.854 (1.38)	1.255 (6.46)	−0.146 (1.24)	−0.532	3.516*	−0.206	0.976
.2	−3.757 (2.39)	0.199 (0.31)	−0.115 (0.57)	2.023 (3.73)	0.844 (6.28)	−0.102 (1.06)	0.573	2.350*	0.034	0.979
.3	−3.580 (2.33)	−0.464 (0.69)	0.054 (0.25)	2.235 (4.00)	0.787 (5.66)	−0.083 (0.88)	0.632	2.249*	−0.003	0.964
.4	−2.014 (1.50)	−0.251 (0.41)	−0.006 (0.03)	1.381 (2.57)	0.641 (4.90)	0.014 (0.14)	0.671	1.576	0.156	1.022
84.1	−2.067 (1.54)	0.053 (0.09)	0.026 (0.11)	1.250 (2.17)	0.660 (4.46)	0.009 (0.08)	0.667	1.656*	0.074	1.020
.2	−1.714 (1.28)	0.372 (0.61)	0.155 (0.54)	0.958 (1.53)	0.652 (3.88)	0.037 (0.30)	0.980	1.621	0.040	0.998
.3	−2.593 (1.82)	−0.432 (0.69)	0.275 (1.00)	1.754 (2.99)	0.675 (4.31)	−0.040 (0.41)	1.075	1.828*	−0.076	0.966
.4	−1.120 (0.92)	−0.409 (0.68)	0.092 (0.38)	1.091 (1.93)	0.523 (3.55)	0.044 (0.42)	0.769	1.274	0.138	1.046
85.1	0.912 (0.72)	0.004 (0.01)	0.008 (0.03)	0.203 (0.33)	0.354 (2.26)	0.160 (1.27)	0.719	0.676	0.345	1.104
.2	1.648 (1.20)	0.530 (0.90)	−0.085 (0.35)	−0.239 (0.35)	0.308 (1.84)	0.212 (1.43)	0.550	0.497	0.429	1.133

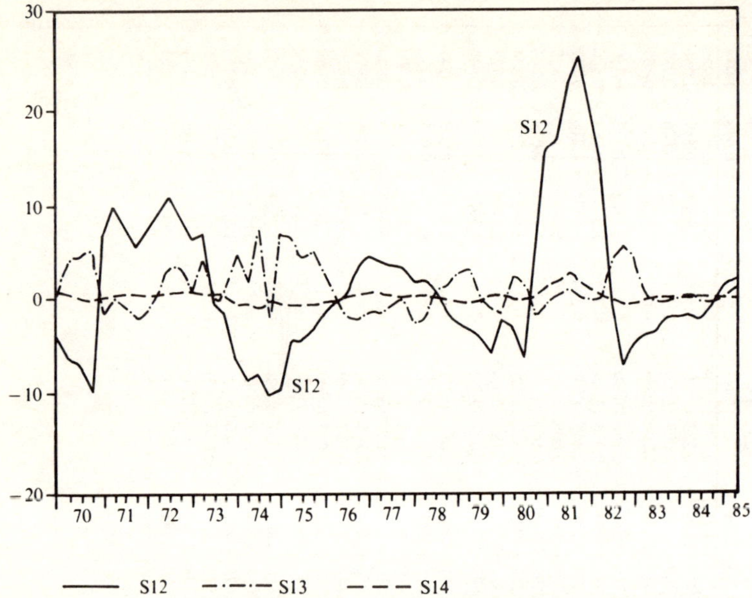

Figure 3.3 Elasticities of substitution with cash.

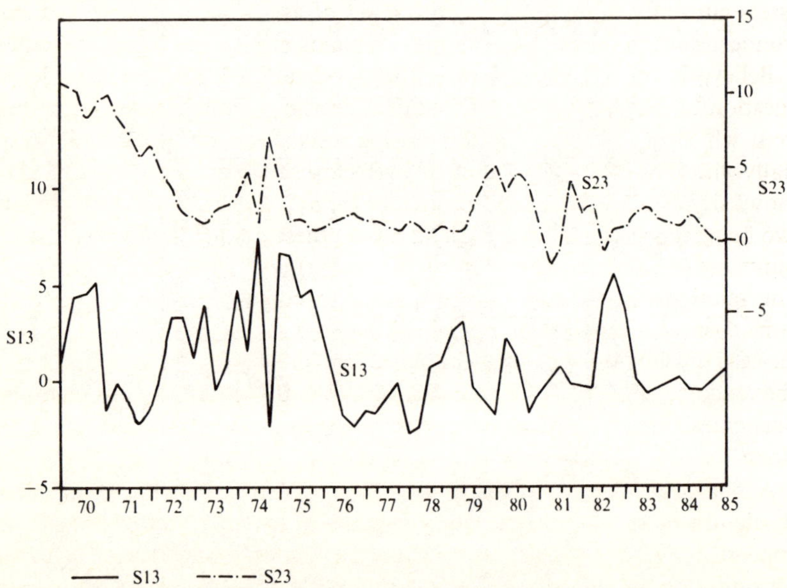

Figure 3.4 Substitution elasticities, financial assets.

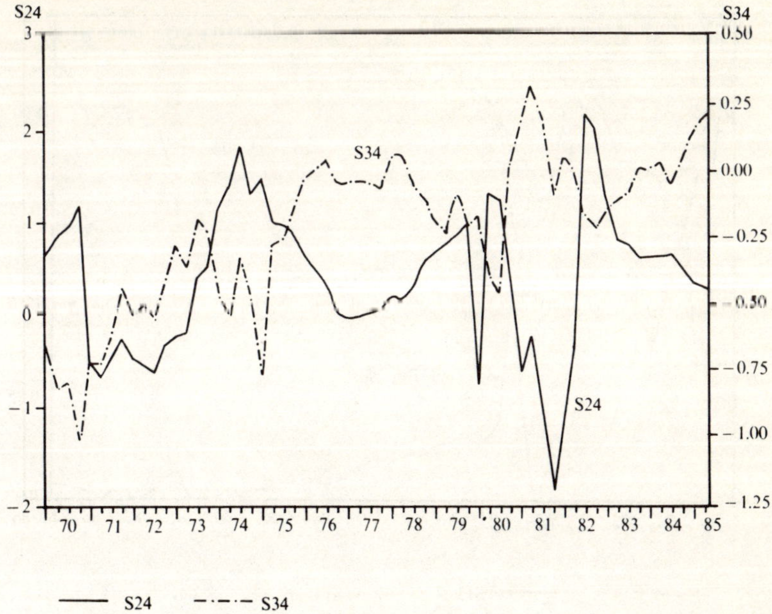

Figure 3.5 Substitution elasticities, savings assets and consumption.

It seems that financial aggregation would need to include time deposits in order to internalize the variations spotted here. No measure of financial assets currently in use does so with a set of assets such as this. It is small wonder that the demand for 'money' remains elusive in empirical studies.

Believe it or not, the above is the good news. When we consider the question of the separability of financial decisions from consumption decisions, which in our GARP and Translog tests show non-separability (especially with time deposits), we find an even closer relationship. Table 3.8 above shows significant substitution elasticities for σ_{14}, σ_{24} and σ_{34}, with the latter two being especially significant. The reason these do not show up well on the summary (the comparison with the Translog) is apparent from Figure 3.5. The relation varies from substitutability to complementarity. Indeed, the same cyclical sensitivity is apparent in the two series, and what is worse for the case for separability is that the elasticities show the reversed images noted above (correlation = −0.74). Internalizing all the variability in substitution elasticities appears to involve an aggregate that goes beyond financial assets alone.

A final way to look at this is in terms of the behaviour of the income elasticities of the four commodity bundles. The most striking result here appears in Figure 3.6, where the income elasticities of time deposits (A3) and consumption are compared. Here, from 1970 to 1978 at least, the two are very strong mirror images (correlation = −0.67). After that there appears to

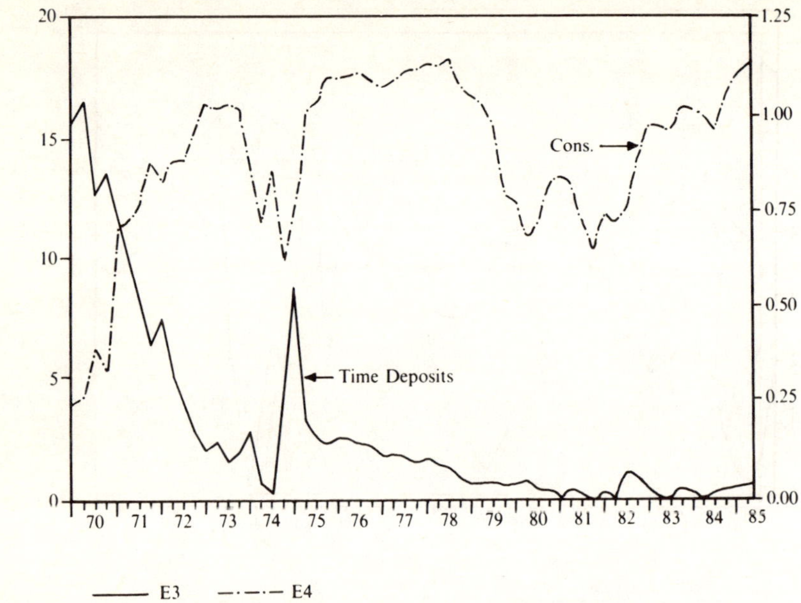

Figure 3.6 Income elasticities: A3 and consumption.

be little relation, with the income elasticity of time deposits near zero in the 1980s.

A final look at the income elasticities shows the cyclical sensitivity of this statistic once more as seen in Figure 3.7. Here a cyclically dominated association of savings deposits and cash assets seems to appear, with the sharp spikes in the savings assets matched particularly well with those in the income elasticity of cash (A1).

It would seem, in summary, that there is considerable volatility in all the basic substitution and income elasticities and that the cyclical sensitivities of the relationships are particularly obvious. Since the values of the elasticities of substitution vary from firm substitutes to complements, a simple-sum aggregation technique is likely to produce 'missing money', apart from any other ways this can be done (such as fitting a log-linear, single-equation money-demand function). Divisia numbers of the entire set of financial assets used here would internalize much of the diversity. One further problem is particularly worrying: the assumption of the separability of financial assets from consumer goods might not hold. Even the Divisia is vulnerable to this problem, of course, since it does not solve the problem of an incorrect selection of assets. These results, taken together, provide an explanation, at the least, of the stability-missing money puzzles that have dominated the money-demand literature for the past dozen or so years. There are, of course, many other possible explanations.

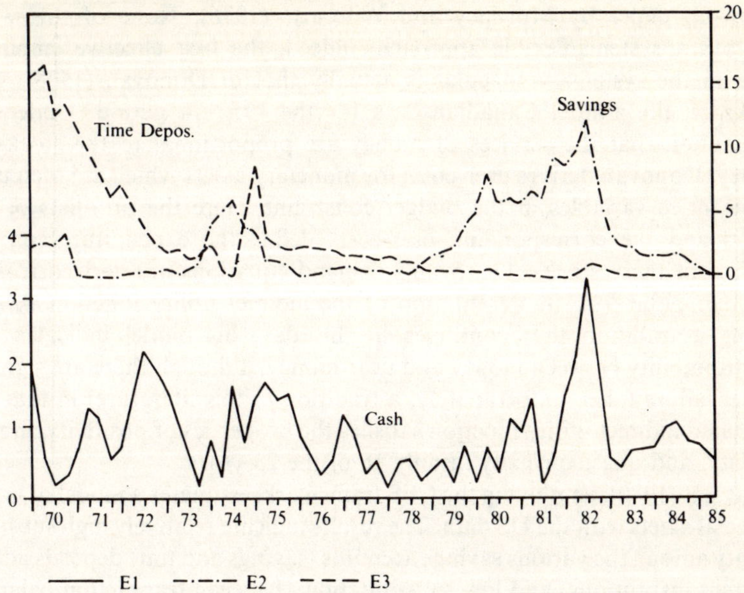

Figure 3.7 Income elasticities among financial assets.

3.6 OTHER EMPIRICAL RESULTS FOR DEMAND SYSTEMS: A SURVEY

The demand-system approach is designed to pay particular attention to the income elasticities and the elasticities of substitution among monetary assets. The underlying question for the income elasticities concerns whether or not 'economies of scale' exist. As we will see, the answer is often 'yes'. With respect to the elasticities of substitution, one of the most curious – *and consistent* – results in all of monetary economics is the evidence of very low substitution or even (sometimes) complementarity among the liquid financial assets. Indeed, in several instances it is suggested that currency might be a closer substitute for time deposits than it is for demand deposits. These sorts of results are robust across definitions of the money stock and across *flexible* functional forms, but not across all possible functional representations of the aggregate consumer's utility function. The reason for referring to this as a 'curious result' is the tradition in the money-and-banking literature that for technical reasons most of these assets are very close substitutes. What might resolve the issue, however it goes, is effective work on the supply side of the financial services industry. This topic is pursued in Chapter 5 and, especially, Chapter 6.

As discussed above, Chetty's (1969) paper utilizing the CES function finds high substitutability among financial assets and this result is continued in a

follow-up paper by Moroney and Wilbratte (1976). None of this work employs a systems/flexible approach; indeed, the first effective empirical work in the systems vernacular is actually that of Donovan (1978), who works on the annual Canadian data for the 1952–74 period. Under the assumption that the services of money are proportional to the stocks of money, Donovan derives user-costs for monetary assets which are then used as the price variables in the budget constraint. Here the products of the stocks and the corresponding user-costs define the expenditures on the services of these stocks. Donovan's demand equations are derived from a Gorman–polar-form representation of the indirect utility function. Establishing a tradition that continues to this day, his model indicates low substitutability between money and near money, although there are signs of model failure (also, unfortunately, a tradition in this literature) in that the estimated indirect utility function satisfies the properties of positivity, monotonicity, and quasiconvexity in only 16 of the 23 years.

Barnett (1980), employing the CES framework, estimates a model of liquid financial assets with the US data. The results indicate relatively high substitutability among the various savings accounts (savings and time deposits across different institutions) and low substitutability between transaction balances and a pass-book account aggregate. While the savings aggregate chosen was arbitrary, Barnett also applies aggregation and index number theory to the construction of the monetary aggregates. This is one of the early empirical tests of the Divisia v. the simple-sum techniques of aggregation; the principal result is that a simple-sum index appears to fail to internalize the actual long-run substitution effects that have occurred in the money markets during the 1970s, while either a Divisia index or the Fisher ideal index does.

Offenbacher's (1979) work is similar to Barnett's on both theoretical and empirical grounds and is the first to employ a flexible functional form (in this case the Translog). Offenbacher also breaks new ground in using an implicit rate of return on bank deposits; this is to be compared with Barnett's use of the regulated own-rates of return on monetary assets. Offenbacher's procedure permits him to study the currency/deposit decision and, in particular, allows the estimation of substitution elasticities between these (and other) assets. Using the linear logarithmic expenditure system (a homogeneous of degree minus one indirect Translog utility function), Offenbacher estimates the elasticities of substitution among currency, demand deposits and time deposits. His main finding is of low substitutability over M2 components in general; he also finds that the substitutability between currency and time deposits is larger – in magnitude – than that between currency and demand deposits. Offenbacher, in his tests, imposes symmetry and linear homogeneity but does not test these restrictions.

Ewis and Fisher (1984) employ the basic Translog functional form to estimate the degree of substitutability among monetary assets. In that paper, instead of making assumptions (such as symmetry and linear homogeneity), they test for the existence of the representative utility function. In so doing,

they avoid the bias that could result from imposing possibly inappropriate restrictions. In the empirical results, this paper shows a role for foreign assets in the US demand for liquid assets (including SumM1), as well as evidence of low substitutability or even complementarity among the monetary assets. However, there are signs of model failure, notably in the rejection of the symmetry restrictions in seven of the nine asset bundles examined.[23]

In a follow-up paper, Ewis and Fisher (1985), employing in the same quarterly US data, re-estimate the elasticities of substitution among the monetary assets by employing Gallant's (1981) Fourier flexible functional form. Their results again indicate low substitutability (and complementarity) among the liquid assets (thus confirming most of the previous work on this topic). With respect to the fit of the model, however, while positivity and monotonicity hold globally, the curvature conditions do not always hold on their data set, although the number of violations is generally not considerable. They do, however, appear to involve the calculation of the user-cost of the cash assets.[24]

Serletis and Robb (1986), using quarterly Canadian data for the period 1968–1 to 1982–4, estimate the degree of substitutability among the services of money and checkable savings and time deposits (over institution types) in a quasihomothetic Translog utility function framework. They compare both summation and Divisia aggregation of the monetary assets in these tests. The quasihomotheticity assumption provides a generalization over the homotheticity assumption.[25] In addition, quasihomotheticity, like homotheticity, is a sufficient condition when combined with weak separability in the theory of consistent multistage optimization. The results of this study lie in three areas. First, with Divisia aggregates the 'performance' statistics are generally better than with the simple-sum indices. Second, with respect to income elasticities, while all assets are normal goods, using the Divisia aggregates economies of scale appear with time deposits, while using simple-sum aggregates this occurs with currency and checkable. Finally, the estimated elasticities of substitution suggest low substitutability among assets, whatever the technique of aggregation. Indeed, there is some evidence here that the 'like-assets' approach to aggregation suggested by Barnett does not hold on this particular data set.

In another test with yet another functional form, Fayaad (1986) uses the variable-parameter Rotterdam model to study the demands for five assets: food, non-durables, services, M1 and 'All-but-M1' financial assets (included in the Federal Reserve's collection of 27 assets). The Divisia procedure is employed to calculate the indices, based on the user-cost approach, and the results 'show that it is possible to specify a model of money demand that closely tracks the flow of M1's monetary services despite its considerable variability over this period' (p. 31). The period is 1969 through 1984. Note, as does Fayaad, that this result presents a potential solution to the money-demand stability problem, where a set of related goods is employed to help locate the 'missing' money.

Serletis (1987*a*), using the Serletis–Robb data, tests further for the appropriateness of the weak separability (aggregation) conditions using the quasi-homothetic Translog functional form. The tests carried out for the separability conditions are based on the assumption that the Translog functional form is an effective second-order approximation to an arbitrary aggregator function. This approach, as already mentioned, has been suggested by Denny and Fuss (1977) and provides a less restrictive test for separability than the Berndt–Christensen (1973) framework. The results, although far from conclusive, suggest that a narrow definition of money could be employed.

In another paper, Serletis (1987*c*) analyses the demand for broad money measures and estimates the degree of substitution among US Divisia money, defined from narrow to broad. This paper makes explicit use of the Strotz–Gorman multistage optimization framework and tests for the appropriateness of the weak separability conditions at various levels of aggregation. The results indicate that Divisia M1 is a net complement to 'near monies', Divisia M2 is a net substitute to 'near monies' and Divisia M3 is a net substitute to 'near monies'. The results also provide strong empirical support for the construction of monetary aggregates broader than M1, since M1, when treated as an elementary asset, can always be grouped together with other assets to form a broader money measure.

NOTES

1. Our analysis is based on quadratic utility; this is a frequently maligned assumption. The basic problem is that the portfolio model turns out to be only (exactly) applicable for a two-parameter statistical model or for the quadratic utility function. Thus

   > In only a limited number of cases will the central limit law be applicable so that an approximation to normality of distribution becomes tenable; and it is well known that quadratic utility has anomalous properties in the large – such as reduced absolute and relative risk-taking as wealth increases, to say nothing of ultimate satiation. (Samuelson, 1970, p. 537)

   By absolute and relative risk aversion we mean (Arrow, 1971)

   $$R_A(Y) = -U''(Y)/U'(Y) = \text{absolute risk aversion}$$

   $$R_R(Y) = -YU''(Y)/U'(Y) = \text{relative risk aversion}$$

   where, e.g., $U' = \mathrm{d}U(Y)/\mathrm{d}Y$. Thus, for the quadratic $U(Y) = a + bY + cY^2$, absolute risk aversion is $1/(-b/2c - Y)$. This expression grows larger as income rises, and this result is considered counter-intuitive since the rich provide us with our stereotypes of risk-takers. Whether this is true is certainly debatable.
2. This is the case since $\tilde{\mathbf{v}}$ is $(n \times 1)$ and $\tilde{\mathbf{e}}'$ is $(1 \times n)$, so that the expression defines an inner product (a scalar).
3. A study utilizing British data on capital-certain assets is by Townend (1972); this was updated by Bhattacharyya (1979).
4. Brainard and Tobin are also concerned that the wealth constraint be applied out of equilibrium (in dynamic problems), and so they specify a simultaneous stock adjustment model with differences between desired and actual stocks depending

on all (other) asset stock disequilibria. The imposition of the overall wealth constraint then affects the estimates of the stock adjustment coefficients, again suggesting a way in which single-equation studies may go wrong. But this framework separates the portfolio allocation decision from the savings–consumption decision and thus is not completely general (another pitfall!).

5. It is not at all obvious that this separability is the case (*it is not* in the GARP tests on the US data described in Chapter 1). Our discussion of the 'value of time' hypothesis in Chapter 2 should also be recalled, at this point.
6. Note that the representative consumer begins period t with the following initial wealth:

$$\sum_{i=1}^{n} (1 + r_{i,t-1})p_{t-1}m_{i,t-1} + (1 + R_{t-1})p_{t-1}B_{t-1}$$

7. Most of the theoretical work reported in Section 3.4 is drawn from Ewis (1982) and Ewis and Fisher (1984).
8. For a discussion of the inappropriateness of these functional forms, see Christensen, Jorgenson and Lau (1975) and Deaton and Muellbauer (1980).
9. If the direct utility function is flexible, then the indirect (if derived from it) loses that property. Furthermore, separability of the direct utility does not imply (nor is implied by) the separability of the indirect function. See Blackorby, *et al.* (1978).
10. If we choose the point $\mathbf{v}^* = 1$, so that $\log \mathbf{v}^* = 0$, then Equation (3.38) directly reduces to Equation (3.36). Taking the expansion around the point of unity is theoretically important because, by doing so, the parameters in Equation (3.36) can be interpreted as the first- and second-order partial derivatives of the indirect utility function. To achieve the expansion empirically, the normalized prices (the v_i) have to be normalized yet again (before the logarithmic transformation) by dividing each v_i by its mean. This step in the estimation ensures that the expansion is around $\mathbf{v}^* = 1$.
11. If the γ_{ij} were all zero (too strong a condition), then Equation (3.36) would be a Cobb–Douglas utility function and the coefficients α_i would be interpreted as the shares of each of the normalized prices. α_m is, as mentioned, the sum of these 'shares'.
12. If the equations are generated by utility maximization, the parameters γ_{im} (for $j = 1, \ldots, n$) appearing in each equation must be the same. This produces a set of restrictions relating the n parameters in the $n-1$ equations, providing a total of $m(m-2)$ restrictions.
13. There are $\frac{1}{2}(n-2)(n-1)$ restrictions of this type among the parameters of the $n-1$ equations estimated directly and $n-1$ such restrictions among the parameters of the equation we estimate indirectly using the adding-up properties of the model.
14. A more appropriate test when the INSUR method of estimation is employed is the Souza–Gallant (1979) test statistic.
15. Each of the basic share equations in the text is supplemented by the following:

$$\text{SM1} = \text{S1} + \text{rho} * \text{Zlag1}(\text{Sm1} - \text{S1})$$

An alternative, not employed in the tests reported here, is the maximum-likelihood procedure, described by the following four equations for each variable estimated:

$$\text{Sm1} = \text{S1} + \text{rho} * \text{Z lag1 (Sm1} - \text{S1)}$$

$$\text{W} = (1 - \text{rho} ** 2) ** (-1/(2 * \_\text{Nused}\_))$$

```
IF_obs_ = 1   THEN   W = W * SQRT (1 - rho ** 2)

Resid.Sm1 = W * Resid.Sm1
```

This is SAS code, of course, but is not completely impenetrable; note that in either method *rho* measures the common serial correlation across the model and is the reason for all this fancy footwork.

16. Note, again, that there is a second equation to deal with the serial correlation, and note that the log of a normalized linear trend (LT) has been included in each regression (the coefficient here is W_i).
17. Jorgenson and Lau (1979, p. 118).
18. The notation of the two forms of the model are connected by

$$a_{0\alpha} = u_{0\alpha} \qquad \alpha = 1, \ldots, A$$

$$a_{j\alpha} = u_{j\alpha} + iw_{j\alpha} \quad \text{and} \quad a_{-j\alpha} = u_{j\alpha} - iw_{j\alpha}$$

the latter for $\alpha = 1, \ldots, A$ and $j = 1, \ldots, J$.

19. The researcher is not limited to this set of K vectors, of course; indeed, the SAS program used to generate these results contains a procedure for generating (and then picking) a very large variety of multi-indices.
20. There is only one instance of significant model failure here, in 1973 (3 observations). The tests used are for monotonicity and necessary conditions for curvature are that the own-elasticities of substitution for the goods not be (significantly) positive. It is the latter condition which fails. The lack of failure in this respect is not really a reason for a celebration, however, because it is obviously partly a result of the rather poorly-fitting equations. This is even clearer in comparison with the four-asset formulation described above.
21. Recall from our discussion above that we do not attribute this phenomenon to overfitting in view of the relatively small number of parameters actually estimated.
22. Fourteen of the 186 own-elasticities of substitution, all for the cash aggregate (A1), were significantly positive. These were for the recession years of 1970, 1974 and 1975 and for 1979 (3 observations) and 1983 (2 observations).
23. Swofford and Whitney (1986), in a comment on this paper, point out that none of the sets tested by Ewis and Fisher pass the non-parametric GARP test. This, too, is evidence of model failure.
24. This was calculated using the Klein (1974) measure of the implicit interest rate on M1, based on Offenbacher's (1979) method. It is worth pointing out that a 'zero interest rate' assumption for this own rate does not really improve the situation.
25. Quasihomotheticity is homotheticity with respect to a point which is not necessarily the origin. It therefore provides linear Engle curves which do not have to pass through the origin. Another paper by Serletis (1988*a*) argues that both homotheticity and quasihomotheticity are rejected (on US data) in a similar setting where *four* versions of the Translog model are compared. The Generalized Translog is the winner in a head-to-head competition to determine which functional form is consistent with the hypothesis of utility maximization.

4

THE NEUTRALITY DEBATE: BASIC ISSUES

4.1 INTRODUCTION

The main part of the literature dealing with the role of money in the macroeconomy is actually concerned with the *neutrality* of money. With respect to the classical-based discussion this concerns the quantity theory of money (a neutrality proposition); during the continuing Keynesian–monetarist debate, neutrality switched sides (i.e. money did not 'matter' to the Keynesians), while in recent years there has been a good deal of discussion about the possible monetary causes of real business cycles. The full discussion of neutrality clearly involves both money supply and money demand, if only because the money stock is determined by their interaction, although it is the custom in this literature to offer up a very sketchy money-supply theory; we will be faithful to this tradition in this chapter. To support the concentration on money demand, we have but to reflect on Friedman's (1956) argument that the quantity theory of money is essentially a theory of the demand for money to see a typical example of this approach. What this chapter will do is take the money supply as exogenously (or, really, arbitrarily) determined. The remainder of the book, however, will consider variations of the money-supply hypothesis, ending up with a framework into which an aggregate banking sector is fit. As the supply structure is broadened, however, the simple neutrality results become less likely and we will become increasingly involved with the role of the authorities in macrostabilization and financial regulation.

Section 4.2 begins the story with a set of classical propositions designed to illustrate (but not necessarily to be precisely faithful to) the long-running controversy over Say's law. We are not going to dig into the work of Say, James Mill, Malthus, Ricardo, and Sismondi that produced the first round of discussions in the early nineteenth century but, instead, will present a view of the debate that has been widely accepted since Patinkin's (1965) explanation of the problem.[1] This basic literature raises the question of how, in the classical approach, money actually affects the system. The standard answer is that it does so by means of a *real balance effect* (a kind of short-run,

non-neutrality proposition), and this is the main topic of Section 4.3.1. Some of the problems with the basic modelling of this effect are also considered at this point. In Section 4.3.2 the discussion is extended to a brief review of a parallel literature on the *net wealth effect* emphasized by Pesek and Saving (1967). This hypothesis also provides reasons why real spending might respond to a monetary stimulus. In this case, though, the debate is a very bitter one.

The results of Sections 4.2 and 4.3 involve the short-run, primarily. Furthermore, most of the discussion in these sections involves monetary *neutrality* – meaning the (null) effect of a change in the stock of money – rather than monetary *super-neutrality*. The latter involves the (null) effect (in a growing economy) of a change in the *growth rate* of the money stock. These concepts are defined in Section 4.4, and two dynamic literatures are considered. One of these involves the basic Sidrauski money-growth model that is the basis of so much recent work on these topics. Here we will look at both long-run neutral, Section 4.4.1, and a long-run non-neutral, Section 4.4.2, versions. Finally, Section 4.5 looks at Lucas's (1980) 'two illustrations' of the quantity theory. These are drawn out from the Sidrauski framework described earlier in the chapter. In this case we will show some results (from Lucas and Dwyer and Hafer, 1988) and then undertake some experiments of our own on the quarterly US data used elsewhere in this study. The tests are not especially favourable to the neutrality idea.

4.2 CLASSICAL NEUTRALITY: GENERAL EQUILIBRIUM AND MICROTHEORETIC RESULTS

Let us assume that there are n goods in an exchange economy with fixed supplies of these goods; it is an exchange economy by virtue of its lack of production. Let us further assume that the nth good is *outside* money, i.e. money supplied by a central banking agency. While all of the n goods in this economy are assumed to be in fixed supply to the m consumers and are equivalent in the sense of providing services, there is a difference between commodities (goods $1, \ldots, n-1$) and money (the nth good) because the former are usually entered directly into the consumer's utility function, while money frequently is not. At the level of the demand function, this choice is moot, but, as we shall see, in some instances we will have to take a stand, since the utility function is manipulated directly. For the first model of this section, however, this issue does not arise.

Continuing with the model, let us next assume that there are $n-1$ *money* prices in the system, with the money price of money being conveniently fixed at unity. We will, as just remarked, assume that all goods are in fixed supply, so that

$$S_i = \bar{S}_i \qquad (i = 1, \ldots, n) \tag{4.1}$$

for commodities and money (S_n). To face these supply functions, suppose

that there are n demand equations, each function of the $n-1$ money prices in the system (the money price of money being unity). These are described by the following:

$$D_i = D_i(P_1, \ldots, P_{n-1}) \qquad (i = 1, \ldots, n) \tag{4.2}$$

Equilibrium, then, which we assume to be unique and stable, is characterized by the following n equations:

$$\bar{S}_i = D_i(P_1, \ldots, P_{n-1}) \qquad (i = 1, \ldots, n) \tag{4.3}$$

What follows now depends on a little slight of hand with the budget constraint. Note, though, that in this system money is spent on goods (we assume that there is no barter) and that one acquires money *only* by parting with goods. That is, any purchase (i.e. demand) of goods must be matched by an equal value of money spent. Money spent is money supplied, in effect, so what we are asserting is expressible as Equation (4.4):

$$\bar{S}_n \equiv P_1 D_1 + \ldots + P_{n-1} D_{n-1} \equiv \sum_{j=1}^{n-1} P_j D_j \tag{4.4}$$

Symmetrically, in this system, an economic agent generates increased money-holdings only by giving up consumption, i.e. by supplying commodities, so that Equation (4.5) is also valid as a parallel description of the budget constraint:

$$D_n \equiv \sum_{j=1}^{n-1} P_j \bar{S}_j \tag{4.5}$$

These relations state the requirement (of a money economy) that *only* money buys goods (and, conversely, only goods buy money). Notice, in either form, that the velocity of money is unity in this model.[2]

We can now move directly to statements of the total demand and supply situation and Walras's law. *Total demand* for all goods consists of the demand for money (Equation (4.5)) plus the demand for all commodities (Equation (4.4)). This produces Equation (4.6):

$$\sum_{i=1}^{n} P_i D_i \equiv \sum_{j=1}^{n-1} P_j D_j + D_n \equiv \bar{S}_n + D_n \tag{4.6}$$

Similarly, *total supply*, taken from the same relations, is given by Equation (4.7):

$$\sum_{i=1}^{n} P_i \bar{S}_i \equiv \sum_{j=1}^{n-1} P_j \bar{S}_j + \bar{S}_n \equiv D_n + \bar{S}_n \tag{4.7}$$

Since things that are identical to the same thing are identical to each other, we may deduce Equation (4.8):

$$\sum_{i=1}^{n} P_i D_i \equiv \sum_{i=1}^{n} P_i \bar{S}_i \qquad (P_n \equiv 1) \tag{4.8}$$

We will refer to this equation as Walras's law; as it appears here, it is the direct result of the statement that all planned or actual spending of funds (in or out of equilibrium) must equal all expected or actual receipts. Taken as a statement of an overall identity between demand and supply at all points, not just at equilibrium, it is the reason why the identity appears in Equation (4.8). Notice that individual product markets are not assumed to be cleared, by application of this overall constraint.

Walras's law was derived in the preceding paragraph and not just assumed (we assumed that only money buys goods), but it is, actually, a theoretical *restriction* that might be applied. Indeed, the n equilibrium equations described as Equation (4.3), along with the Walrasian condition that all things must add up (Equation (4.8)), permit a solution for (at most) the $n-1$ money prices in the system. These, it should be noted, are the only unknowns in the model since the supplies of the quantities are fixed by assumption. There are, further, $n-1$ independent equations in the system since the application of Walras's law has made one of the relationships specified in Equation (4.3) redundant. Should there actually be a solution for the $n-1$ *money* prices, we would be able to calculate an equilibrium price level; it would consist of the unique values of the money prices weighted by the budget shares for each of the commodities, with the whole business calculated at equilibrium. We may refer to this concept as P_m.

$$P_m = f(P_1, \ldots, P_{n-1}) \qquad (\partial P/\partial P_j > 0 \quad \text{for} \quad j = 1, \ldots, n-1) \quad (4.9)$$

Here the weighting scheme just described is not specified and only the property that an increase in a single price will increase the price level is exhibited. The price level is, of course, the opportunity cost of money (i.e. its price) in this exchange (transactions) economy. As noted, the existence of this price is guaranteed by the fact that it is composed of the variable money prices, themselves determinate in this framework.

This exercise, then, defines a general equilibrium system with money in the problem, and provides us with an equilibrium quantity and price (P_m) of money. This is a sufficient framework to deduce a demand function for money (and for each of the other goods if so desired). However, the demand function for money is not an interesting one unless further restrictions are imposed on the system; that is, the model basically has no empirical implications, as we shall see. It is also a non-neutral system by virtue of that fact that money is just like any other commodity (and, presumably, as things stand, could be thought of as having been placed in the utility function where it is forced to have a real effect).

4.2.1 Microeconomic perspectives on monetary neutrality

The essential classical monetary proposition refers to the conditions under which a doubled price level will follow a doubled money stock. This is the theoretical problem of neutrality tackled by Patinkin (1965) and many

others, and at a theoretical level it sometimes boils down to the evaluation of the minimum set of assumptions necessary to generate this result in a general equilibrium system. Let us consider the most frequently used approach, that involving proportionality – or 'money requirements' constraints that essentially force money into the problem.[3]

We will begin with a generic demand for money. Let us define the excess demand for each of the $n-1$ commodities as:

$$D_j(P_1, \ldots, P_{n-1}) - \bar{S}_j \equiv X_j(P_1, \ldots, P_{n-1}) \qquad (j = 1, \ldots, n-1) \tag{4.10}$$

Then, leaving the excess demand for money undefined for the moment, we can illustrate the $n-1$ independent equilibrium conditions for the excess demand problem by Equations (4.11) and Walras's law by Equation (4.12):

$$X_j(P_1, \ldots, P_{n-1}) = 0 \qquad (j = 1, \ldots, n-1) \tag{4.11}$$

$$X_n(P_1, \ldots, P_{n-1}) + \sum_{j=1}^{n-1} P_j X_j(P_1, \ldots, P_{n-1}) \equiv 0 \tag{4.12}$$

X_n, here, is the, as yet, unspecified excess demand for money. For a specification, let us adopt Equation (4.13) as the demand for money:

$$D_n \equiv k \sum_{j=1}^{n-1} P_j \bar{S}_j \tag{4.13}$$

This relation states that consumers desire to hold a proportion (k) of the money value of their initial commodity holdings in the form of money balances (presumably because their money balances are expected to facilitate transactions). Then, since

$$X_n \equiv D_n - \bar{S}_n$$

we can write Equation (4.14), the specialized demand for money as:

$$X_n \equiv k \sum_{j=1}^{n-1} P_j \bar{S}_j - \bar{S}_n \equiv X_n(P_1, \ldots, P_{n-1}; k, \bar{S}_i) \qquad (i = 1, \ldots, n) \tag{4.14}$$

The excess demand for money is, as noted, a function of the $n-1$ money prices, the n initial quantities and the parameter k. Note that k is the inverse of velocity (is, indeed, the famous Marshallian or Cambridge k) so that what we are doing is assuming that velocity is constant. This is a neoclassical–classical framework.

Equation (4.14) is the excess demand-for-money function we are after, and with it we can illustrate the essential classical result. That is, if we double all money prices and the quantity of money in Equation (4.14) we get an excess demand for money function that is, in effect, homogeneous of degree zero in these entities.[4] This is clearly one way in which we can show a link between the standard neutrality proposition and the role of the demand for money in

the construction of the neutrality result. Indeed, it is the restriction on the demand for money in the form of the parameter k that essentially provides this neutrality. Let us now dig behind the demand function in an attempt to provide more structure.

As our next entry, let us consider a basic neoclassical model in which neutrality holds – and for which the full set of neoclassical restrictions (symmetry, etc.) applies; this appears in a paper by Lloyd (1968). In this particular general equilibrium exercise we will assume that individuals *must* hold money; thus it is not necessary to place money in the utility function in order to have an interesting monetary economy. The utility function of the consumer is

$$u = U(X_1, \ldots, X_{n-1}) \tag{4.15}$$

and his budget constraint, written in nominal terms, is

$$\sum_{i=1}^{n-1} P_i X_i + M = Y + \bar{M} \tag{4.16}$$

Note that the X_i here refer to quantities and not the excess demands of the previous model. The additional constraint, which forces money into the problem, is then

$$M = k \sum_{i=1}^{n-1} P_i X_i \tag{4.17}$$

where k is an individual proportionality (i.e. Equation (4.17) is an individual 'quantity theory' restriction for the representative consumer).

In this set-up the individual maximizes Equation (4.15) subject to Equations (4.16) and (4.17) by picking $X_1, \ldots, X_{n-1}$ and M. We can combine Equations (4.16) and (4.17) and form a Lagrangean as follows:

$$L = U(X_1, \ldots, X_{n-1}) - \lambda \left[(1+k) \sum_{i=1}^{n-1} P_i X_i - Y - \bar{M} \right] \tag{4.18}$$

The first-order conditions, then, are

$$U_i - \lambda(1+k)P_i = 0 \tag{4.19}$$

$$-(1+k) \sum_{i=1}^{n-1} P_i X_i + Y + \bar{M} = 0 \tag{4.20}$$

The latter is, of course, the combined constraint. This system can then be solved for the equilibrium values of the X_i (and λ) and then we can substitute into Equation (4.17) to determine the quantity of money demanded. The demand functions that result are, in general form,

$$X_i = h_i(P_1, \ldots, P_{n-1}, Y, \bar{M}) \qquad (i = 1, \ldots, n-1) \tag{4.21}$$

$$M = k \sum_{j=1}^{n-1} P_j h_j(P_1, \ldots, P_{n-1}, Y, \bar{M}) = h_m(P_1, \ldots, P_{n-1}, Y, \bar{M}) \tag{4.22}$$

To see the neutrality result in this basic classical system we first note that a doubling of money and all money prices will not affect the utility function since these entities are not represented there. For β being the change involved, the new combined budget constraint is

$$\beta(1+k)\sum_{i=1}^{n-1} P_i X_i = \beta(Y+M) \tag{4.23}$$

recalling that Y is nominal income and so must also be scaled by β. These observations establish that Equations (4.21) are homogeneous of degree zero in M and $P_1, \ldots, P_{n-1}$ and that the demand for money (in Equation (4.22)) is homogeneous of degree one. This last holds because the right-hand side of Equation (4.17) is now $\beta k \Sigma P_i X_i$, and thus the new demand for money is $\beta M = \beta h_m(\cdot)$. Thus the neutrality propositions go through solely in terms of operations on the budget constraint. We note that this system actually has the full set of neoclassical restrictions (see Bernstein, 1978*a*), in anticipation of some other standard results in which neutrality occurs, but the (other) restrictions do not.

The alternative to having money's role defined by means of an arbitrary budget constraint is to put money directly into the utility function. This is widely done, of course, but the best-known examples of this occur in Samuelson (1947) and Patinkin (1965). Samuelson, it is true, has stressed that money cannot properly be treated just like any other commodity and, in particular, that not only money balances but also the full set of money prices should be included in the utility function. Indeed, if money were not distinguished in some such fashion, we would have results here comparable to our first general equilibrium case, in which money was economically indistinguishable from commodities. Inserting the list of money prices into the function is an arbitrary way of adjusting the *nominal* quantity of money (which is already in the function) so that in effect it appears in real terms. A more usual method is just to include M/P, but, of course, this alternative assumes the existence of a satisfactory price index number (in the sense of Chapter 1). The Samuelson utility function, to be more specific, is

$$u = U(X_1, \ldots, X_{n-1}, M, P_1, \ldots, P_{n-1}) \qquad (P_n \equiv 1) \tag{4.24}$$

This function, then, is assumed to be homogeneous of degree zero in both money prices and the quantity of money.[5] This is an exact statement of the assumption of the absence of 'money illusion' (in this model). Again, it should be emphasized that an important special case of this function is that of $u = U(X_1, \ldots, X_{n-1}, M, P)$ where P is the (ideal?) index number constructed from the individual prices. In this second version, with the same homogeneity condition assumed, we would then obtain $u = U(X_1, \ldots, X_{n-1}, M/P)$. This means that, for the most part, Patinkin and Samuelson can be taken together in this discussion.

Following Bernstein's (1978*a*) discussion we can form a variation on the Samuelson–Patinkin model, using Equation (4.24) and the following budget

constraint:

$$\sum_{i=1}^{n-1} P_i(X_i - \bar{X}_i) + M - \bar{M} = 0 \tag{4.25}$$

The barred variables are initial values, and so this equation merely imposes the condition that the aggregate value of all of the excess demands for goods (commodities plus money) equals zero. The first-order conditions for this system are

$$U_i - \lambda P_i = 0 \qquad (i = 1, \ldots, n-1) \tag{4.26}$$

$$U_m - \lambda = 0 \tag{4.27}$$

$$\sum_{i=1}^{n-1} P_i(X_i - \bar{X}_i) + M - \bar{M} = 0 \tag{4.28}$$

From these equations we can derive a set of n demand equations which take the following forms:

$$X_i = h_i(P_1, \ldots, P_{n-1}, \bar{X}_1, \ldots, \bar{X}_{n-1}, \bar{M}) \quad (i = 1, \ldots, n-1) \tag{4.29}$$

$$M = h_m(P_1, \ldots, P_{n-1}, \bar{X}_1, \ldots, \bar{X}_{n-1}, \bar{M}) \tag{4.30}$$

These are, of course, written in terms of money prices and initial commodity and money endowments.

For this model it cannot be established that the matrix of substitution effects is symmetrical and this same matrix is also not negative semi-definite (because the own-substitution effects are not negative).[6] This is discouraging in view of the importance attached to these concepts in consumer demand theory (and in recent studies of the demand for money). On the other hand, a neutrality result for this system can be demonstrated, and, of course, this is what we would want to do if we are to operate in the neoclassical tradition. In particular, the fact that the utility function is homogeneous of degree zero in money and (all) money prices implies that *if* the demand for money is homogeneous of degree one in the same variables, then the demands for commodities are homogeneous of degree zero. Clearly, then, money is neutral. That is, the assumption of homogeneity of the utility function in M and the P_i is sufficient to establish neutrality in this Samuelson–Patinkin model. This is certainly not surprising.

Basically, then, this section has considered two choices for the role of money in the classical monetary economy. The first of these is the Lloyd–classical model, which uses Equation (4.15) as its utility function, and the second is the Samuelson–Patinkin model, which uses Equation (4.24). In Equation (4.24) both the nominal quantity of money and the list of money prices are in the equation – the latter to represent the idea that money is demanded not for itself, but only for what it will buy – while in Equation (4.15) only real commodities enter. The Lloyd–classical model has the limiting feature that the role of money is entirely arbitrary, while the

Patinkin–Samuelson model, as based on Equation (4.24), actually treats money like all other goods. In particular, the consumer reacts directly to changes in any of the quantities and prices in the domain of U according to his preferences. This reaction initiates changes in the quantities of every commodity demanded, which in turn alters the absolute and relative contribution of the variables to the level of preference satisfaction.

It is certainly more realistic to argue that consumers do not react in such a complete manner and that they actually lump together commodities exhibiting similar characteristics; this, one might argue, can be effected by means of the assumption of a weakly separable utility function. In this respect, an important addendum to this theoretical literature has been generated by Kalman, Dusansky and Wickstrom (1974) who use the utility functions listed as Equations (4.31) and (4.32):

$$u = k\left(\sum_{i=1}^{n-1} P_i X_i + M\right) + \beta(X_1, \ldots, X_{n-1}, M) + \delta(P_1, \ldots, P_{n-1}) \tag{4.31}$$

$$u = k\left(\sum_{i=1}^{n-1} P_i X_i + M + m\right) + \beta(X_1, \ldots, X_{n-1}, M, m) + \delta(P_1, \ldots, P_{n-1}) \tag{4.32}$$

Here k is a positive constant and β and δ are functions. These functions do, indeed, permit the relevant neoclassical restrictions. Further, the second function, coupled with the dual budget constraint of the Clower (1967) model, provides a useful model of the choice problem in the monetary context. Note that m represents *transactions* balances and M *reservations* balances, as in our discussion of the Clower model in Chapter 2.[7] We know of no empirical work on this formulation, however, in spite of its theoretical attractiveness.

4.3 NON-NEUTRALITY: REAL-BALANCE AND NET WEALTH EFFECTS

The issues in this section were once the most controversial of all macroeconomics, but activity in this area has decreased considerably in recent years. The two topics, which are related in some contexts, are:

(a) the real-balance (Pigou) effect of Patinkin (1965);
(b) the net wealth effect (of Metzler, 1951, and Pesek and Saving, 1967),

and the following discussions consider the basic theoretical positions taken. Section 4.3.1 deals with the mainstream 'real-balance effect' while Section 4.3.2 considers the wealth effect. We will employ this material primarily as a bridge between money demand and money supply, although it definitely

stands alone as suggesting the classical/neoclassical approach to the way money affects the real variables of an (admittedly artificial) economic system.

4.3.1 The real-balance effect

Let us assume, following Lloyd (1964), that the consumer maximizes a utility function in which the quantity of money balances is one of the arguments. Equation (4.33) is this function with, as before, S_n denoting real-money balances:

$$u = U(S_1, \ldots, S_n) \tag{4.33}$$

Note that an easy justification of this expression, as indeed seen in Patinkin (1965), is to think of real-money balances as an argument in the utility functions of representative money-holders. This method of proceeding makes it possible to generate an effect (a *real-balance effect*) on real spending decisions, at least in the short-run. The consumer is assumed to be constrained by his nominal income (Y) and his nominal money balances (M_0). This amount is spent at the set of money prices $\{P_i\}$, as described in Equation (4.34):

$$Y + M_0 = \sum_{i=1}^{n} S_i P_i \tag{4.34}$$

Let the price of money P_n be the price level, itself a function of the $n-1$ money prices. That is, let us not follow the convention that $P_n \equiv 1$, but, rather, allow that the decision to hold money is part of the budget constraint.

The first-order conditions for a maximum for this system can be written out as in Equations (4.35), where U_i is a marginal utility:

$$\left.\begin{aligned} U_i + aP_i &= 0 \qquad (i = 1, \ldots, n) \\ Y + M_0 &= \sum_{i=1}^{n} S_i P_i \end{aligned}\right\} \tag{4.35}$$

From these results and from the second-order conditions, not written out here, the usual comparative-statics results can be derived. In the case of the demand for a commodity, we often find further analysis considering the topics of the income effect, the own-price effect on demand and the cross-price effects on demand, but in the case of the Patinkin analysis, because one of the components of wealth is involved, our attack is different. Instead of the list just given, we will discuss the following:

(a) the income effect of a change in Y;
(b) the real-balance effect of a change in M_0 or in P, the price level; and
(c) the real-balance effect generated by a change in the price of any commodity other than money.

These effects will all be measured on the demand for the sth commodity.

We proceed, as is usual with comparative statics, by totally differentiating Equations (4.35); the result is Equations (4.36) for the n marginal conditions and Equation (4.37) for the budget constraint. The U_{ij} are second derivatives of the utility functions:

$$\left.\begin{aligned} &\overline{a\,\mathrm{d}P_1} + P_1\,\mathrm{d}a + U_{11}\,\mathrm{d}S_1 + U_{12}\,\mathrm{d}S_2 + \ldots + U_{1n}\,\mathrm{d}S_n = 0 \\ &\vdots \\ &\overline{a\,\mathrm{d}P_n} + P_n\,\mathrm{d}a + U_{n1}\,\mathrm{d}s_1 + U_{n2}\,\mathrm{d}S_2 + \ldots + U_{nn}\,\mathrm{d}S_n = 0 \end{aligned}\right\} \quad (4.36)$$

$$\overline{S_1\,\mathrm{d}P_1} + \ldots + \overline{S_n\,\mathrm{d}P_n} + P_1\,\mathrm{d}S_1 + \ldots + P_n\,\mathrm{d}S_n = \overline{\mathrm{d}\bar{Y}} + \mathrm{d}M_0 \quad (4.37)$$

The barred terms are to be taken as parameters in this analysis. That is, in order to perform the comparative-statics tests in which the quantity demanded of each product is the endogenous variable, the 'data' must be held constant. These data for the individual are the things we will want to vary in our list $\{(a), (b), (c)\}$ in this set of experiments. The data are the P_i, Y and M_0; a, the Lagrangean term, is the marginal utility of 'money' and is, of course, not taken to be a constant here.

The constants are gathered on the right-hand side of each equation in Equations (4.36) and (4.37) and the exogenous variables are reorganized on the left-hand side, adopting matrix notation for compactness. The result is Equation (4.38):

$$\mathbf{K}\tilde{\mathbf{S}} = \begin{bmatrix} 0 & P_1 & \ldots & P_n \\ P_1 & U_{11} & & U_{1n} \\ \vdots & & & \vdots \\ P_n & U_{n1} & & U_{nn} \end{bmatrix} \begin{bmatrix} \mathrm{d}a \\ \mathrm{d}S_1 \\ \vdots \\ \mathrm{d}S_n \end{bmatrix}$$

$$= \begin{bmatrix} \mathrm{d}Y + \mathrm{d}M_0 - \sum_{i=1}^{n} S_i\,\mathrm{d}P_i \\ -a\,\mathrm{d}P_1 \\ \vdots \\ -a\,\mathrm{d}P_n \end{bmatrix} \equiv \mathbf{R} \quad (4.38)$$

Here the U_{ij} are second partial derivatives of the utility function with respect to its arguments $(S_1, \ldots, S_n)$, as in Equation (4.36), and $\mathbf{K}$ represents the matrix of these values (bordered with prices); $\mathbf{K}$ is $n+1$ by $n+1$; $\mathbf{S}$ is $n+1$ by 1 and $\mathbf{R}$, a vector of constants, is then $n+1$ by 1. Note that $\mathbf{R}$ includes initial nominal wealth.

We are now in a position to apply Cramer's rule directly to Equation (4.38). This exercise produces the following expressions for the income effect and for the effect of a change in nominal balances. To get the dimensions

straight, note that D_s is a cofactor produced by exchanging columns s (or row s) for the constant vector:

$$\frac{\partial S}{\partial Y} = \frac{1}{D} D_s \tag{4.39}$$

$$\frac{\partial S_s}{\partial M_0} = \frac{1}{D} D_s \tag{4.40}$$

The result, clearly, is that both of these effects are the same because if all the other items on the right-hand side are held constant, then the role of Y or M_0, assuming they are the same amount in money terms, must be the same. The rational consumer, we are saying, will change his holdings of commodity S in the same way whether on account of a change in initial income or in initial wealth. All 'money' is the same to him. In this experiment we are not allowed to let the price level vary. This being the case, empirical experiments of the results so far stated ought to be conducted in real terms, and the causal apparatus ought to emphasize M and not the price level in this version of the 'real-balance effect'. In this case the real-balance and wealth effects are identical.

The third experiment, then, that of varying prices, produces some analytical complexity. First, consider the effect of varying any other price (P_r). By Cramer's rule we obtain the following expression for this effect on the demand for commodity S.

$$\frac{\partial S_s}{\partial P_r} = \frac{1}{D}\left[- S_r D_s - aD_{rs} + \frac{\partial P_n}{\partial P_r}(- S_n D_s - aD_{ns}) \right] \tag{4.41}$$

Indeed, this contains a troublesome point for Patinkin's analysis because here it is seen that what we can call the real-balance effect of a change in a price *other* than that of money involves not only the direct income and substitution effects familiar in the Slutsky equation but also a third effect because the change in price is associated with a change in the price *level*. These three effects, listed here for the sake of clarity are an income effect,

$$-\frac{S_r D_s}{D}$$

a substitution effect,

$$-\frac{aD_{rs}}{D}$$

and a derived real-balance effect caused by the necessary change in P_n

$$\frac{\partial P_n}{\partial P_r}\left(- \frac{S_n D_s + aD_{ns}}{D} \right)$$

Referring, firstly, to Equation (4.38) we can now see how the last-named effect arises. Obviously, what we intend is that when the first component in **R**

involving P_r changes, the first two terms of the 'derived real-balance effect' are produced. We also see a change in P_n itself involving an income and a substitution effect because P_n is a function of each price. The two income effects here cannot be signed unless we wish to rule out the case of inferior goods, but we can perform a Slutsky compensation in order to establish the sign of the substitution effect. After the compensation is performed, we would be left with the following equation, consisting of the direct substitution effect and an indirect substitution effect:

$$\frac{dS_s}{dP_r} = -\frac{a}{D}\left(D_{rs} + \frac{\partial P_n}{\partial P_r} D_{ns} \right) \tag{4.42}$$

The first term would be negative (it corresponds to a term from the diagonal of the cross-effects matrix between r and s), but the last effect is not along the diagonal and hence its sign cannot be asserted *a priori*.[8] Even in the case when the income effect is known because of the assumption of non-inferiority, we cannot obtain a sign for this term. Thus we are left with a kind of impossibility theorem that states that the real-balance effect, while existing under these conditions, has no *a priori* sign. On the other hand, if all price changes are equal so that the conditions of the composite goods theorem hold, a signable effect of the obvious sort can be obtained.

Where all this takes us in terms of the macroeconomic version of the real-balance effect is the subject of some dispute. Patinkin wrote down a real consumption function – in which the effect would occur directly – as in

$$c = c\left(y, i, \frac{M_0}{P} \right)$$

where M_0/P represents the potential real-balance effect (of a change in the price level), with an effect that is presumably positive. This would seem appropriate. This function has been tested (see the surveys in D. Fisher, 1978, and Grice, 1981), often with apparent success.

As noted, the reasoning of the microtheoretic part of this chapter would certainly seem to support some such formulation as just given, but, even so, some years ago, Archibald and Lipsey (1958) raised the question of whether the real-balance effect was merely a short-run phenomenon, having no role to play in the long-run. This view has apparently dominated, on the record, since it is rarely challenged. Recently, however, Fischer (1981) has suggested a way of looking at the long-run that clarifies many of the issues of a complex (and, for this study, largely peripheral) literature. In particular, Fischer asks whether there is a real-balance effect in equilibrium (the counter-argument being that in the steady state it is better to describe the situation as one in which there are no forces whatsoever operating on the equilibrium). The reason there is an effect, then, putting aside special characteristics of money, is that the movement from one steady state to another, following a monetary injection, involves the actions of consumers who must be modelled as having

wealth (including real balances) in their consumption functions. To fail to do this is to fail to provide a mechanism whereby the price level alters following a monetary injection. To put it another way, the macroeconomic model of the economy must describe consumers as they actually are, either in or out of equilibrium; this is with a real-balance effect embedded in their consumption function. The effect exists in the short and the long run, but operates (by definition) only in the short run. This observation goes some way toward reconciling the different views on this phenomenon.

4.3.2 Neutrality and net wealth

Monetary economists typically make heavy use of accounting identities in discussions of the role of money, a practice which tends to minimize this role. One commonly reads that *inside* money, i.e. money issued by a privately owned financial institution, is not net wealth simply because the debt of the bank equals in value the asset of the money-holder; also when we aggregate (thus summing over debtors and creditors), this item disappears.[9] This view is the result of approaching the commercial bank by means of its balance sheet, but it is not the only way to proceed. Indeed, an attractive alternative is to think of banks as producers of *real* financial services using *real* resources in the process. Of course, the banking firm actually offers many financial services – information services, lending facilities, safe-deposit facilities, transfer facilities, dealer services and even diversification services – so this admission opens up a very complex problem in the theory of the (aggregate) firm in the banking industry. Chapter 6 will tackle the more microeconomic aspects of the banking industry, but here we will look into a part of this literature involving their creation of net wealth.

Pesek and Saving (1967) have taken a stab at this problem, keeping pretty much to the macroeconomic themes that are required to translate the essentially microeconomic topics just discussed into a possible concern for macropolicy. Pesek and Saving first argue that outside (government *fiat*) money is an asset to its holders and a liability to no one. This paves the way for a wealth effect (on spending) from the issue of outside money. The point is often conceded in the debate. The alternative is to treat outside money as a case parallel to that of outside debt and apply the Ricardian equivalence theorem to both. One possible line to take is to think of money as the limiting case of debt (Johnson, 1970), i.e. to think of it as non-interest-bearing debt, and then to treat it just like debt in the discussion of neutrality. In particular, if the argument goes that individuals expect the government to pay back its 'loan' of money by means of future tax revenues, we will find that individuals will acquire an asset and a liability simultaneously and thus the conditions of the Ricardian equivalence theorem are satisfied. Then, only to the extent that government debt is considered a private liability, while outside money is not, will a clear case for a net wealth effect from, e.g., open market operations, emerge. *Inside money,* being issued by, e.g., a bank to individuals who are

themselves the owners of the bank, requires no such circumlocution to produce a null effect. In this argument what are essentially accounting conventions are employed, and the most we could expect from a wealth effect (produced by an arbitrary change in the quantity of money) would be a contribution from outside money (really from *high-powered money*).

Pesek and Saving also argue that if the charters for commercial banks are rationed by the government, then the charter – as evidence of a limited monopoly in the production of money – is itself valuable. Indeed, to push the matter further, if money production by banks is costless and no interest payments are made on deposits, then the quantity of bank money, the value of the equity of the bank or the net wealth of the bank will reveal the value of the monopoly. Presumably, this value would change when open-market operations are conducted so that an arbitrary change in outside money, operating through the banking multiplier, would affect bank profits (and therefore wealth) and produce an effect on real spending. The presence of significant oligopoly or economies of scale in the banking industry would also be responsible for effects of this sort, although these are never discussed in this context. The impression from the voluminous literature on the wealth effect is that this particular proposition has also been conceded (as by Johnson, 1970), although whether it is an important macroeconomic concern has not been established (even in the further discussion in Chapter 6).

At this point the harmony breaks down over a third proposal by Pesek and Saving, involving an attempt to create a distinction between money and debt that is based on the interest rate. In the words of Friedman and Schwartz, Pesek and Saving are saying:

> The payment of interest on deposits transferable by check converts them into money-debt, which has the property of losing its moneyness (its capacity to serve as a medium of exchange) as the interest rate paid tends to approach the market interest rate. At the limit, it is entirely debt – in no part money – . . . Hence, theory provides a sharp line of demarcation between 'money' and 'debt', money consisting of items used as a medium of exchange which are best regarded as assets to their holders but liabilities to no one. (1970, p. 111)

Friedman and Schwartz dispute this contention and argue that all the relevant financial assets have joint properties in common and that, most especially, these properties cannot be separated by any hard-and-fast rule such as whether they pay interest. They make the point that if for some reason demand deposits pay interest exactly equal to the interest rate, people would then acquire transactions services as a free (but joint) good. The paying of interest as such, say Friedman and Schwartz, does not make a demand deposit any less acceptable in exchange. While this is true, it is possibly beside the point. It is precisely because the owner of the deposit refuses to agree to surrender (tacitly) his claim to liquidity that he gets no interest payments. That is, we can argue that Pesek and Saving discuss an *ex ante* arrangement which, considering the cost of adjustment, is negotiated for a definite (expected) period of time. The technical ability to switch at will

is irrelevant if individuals actually do not do this – as revealed by their financial decisions – and structure their financial plans accordingly. Indeed, Chapter 1 illustrated that technical substitutability appears to have surprisingly little to do with how consumers structure their asset portfolios.

Putting aside the interest-paying problem, the next issue concerns whether or not real-balance or wealth effects can be produced through changes in the quantity of *inside* money. As discussed above, Pesek and Saving distinguish two sorts of wealth effect: the price-induced and the interest-induced wealth effects. The latter is the concept that Pesek and Saving wish to add to standard analysis, and it involves the revaluing of a flow of services (more particularly the services of money) expected to be received in perpetuity as a result of a change in the appropriate discount rate. The effect itself is on consumption (and investment, etc.), and it could be caused initially by an open-market operation. It operates independently of a price-level (real-balance) effect, by which is meant that, even if prices cannot change for institutional reasons, a wealth effect by means of interest-rate changes could operate as the result of, say, an expansionary open-market operation.

The argument over the key features of the Pesek and Saving position that inside money is net wealth has gone on for some time now. Their main positions are that the liability of the bank essentially dissolves upon the issue of demand deposits, and that the interest payment foregone in holding money is a good measure of the services that money provides. The latter is, of course, the notion that lies behind the user-cost of money that first appears in Chapter 1. Further, Pesek and Saving argue that the following will apply once demand deposits start paying interest:

1. Demand deposits will continue serving as money only if interest payments cease.
   Or
2. Interest payments will continue but then demand deposits will cease serving as money.
   Or
3. Some intermediate position will be found.

Friedman and Schwartz (1970) challenge these views and note 'a zero *price* for the transactions services of demand deposits does not mean that the quantity of money in the form of demand deposits is zero' (p. 114); and later, on the ability of money to retain its liquidity and yet pay an interest rate, they say:

> We have seen that the view and shelter are two economic dimensions of the house that cannot be added directly together, though the values attributed to them can be. Likewise, the 'dollar' of moneyness and the 'dollar' of interest-payingness can be two dimensions of the 'dollar' of deposits that cannot be added directly together, though the values attributed to them can be. (p. 116)

Friedman and Schwartz conclude that the logic of the Pesek and Saving position is that money (as net wealth) ought to be high-powered money. This compromise is rejected by Pesek and Saving as too narrow.

Patinkin's work (1965) on the real-balance effect can certainly be rationalized in terms of high-powered money, and that is one way to tie Section 4.3.1 into the present discussion. Patinkin (1969), commenting on Pesek and Saving, argues that we should take the point of view of the banking system and examine its 'net wealth'. A lot depends on how this is done; Pesek and Saving feel that there is a danger, in that 'economists may accept the balance sheets prepared by the banking industry only if they are willing to abdicate their own responsibility for making analytical decisions . . .' (p. 139). Patinkin, however, concludes 'the essential point . . . is that the origin of the net worth of the banking sector is not in the production of money, *per se*, but in the monopoly right which this sector has received' (p. 1143). But this view, widely shared as it is, hardly does justice to the nature of the vigorously growing financial sector. Clearly, it is correct to argue that *if* money is costless to produce (an absurd idea!) and if overproduction is prevented by the need to obtain a monopoly right, then the market value of the monopoly rights (or, equivalently, the market value of the firms that obtain them) will correctly measure the value of the services of money. But the essence of an inside-money economy surely is that it uses private resources to 'manufacture' money. More fundamentally perhaps, the critics of Pesek and Saving, some of them accepting many of the policy implications, are involved in an argument that sounds as if an exchange of money for non-money, in a perfectly competitive economy, including the banking system of course, would be effected without a gain in welfare. As Buchanan warns:

> If pushed to their extreme limits, accounting conventions 'prove' that gains from exchange are impossible . . . Broadly speaking, this procedure is acceptable so long as all transactions are assumed to be made in full equilibrium . . . where there are offsetting transfers of expected present values between contracting parties. The unique feature of the call-loan is that no such offsetting transfer takes place. (1969, p. 814)

Thus, logically, the exact-dollar 'liability' of the commercial bank might be replaced by the expected value of the call-loan (demand deposit in this case) to the bank. The expected value would then be expected to fluctuate with the probability of recall (or 'repurchase', to use the terminology favoured by Pesek and Saving) of the loan. The value of the bank would suffer, for example, in times of bank runs, when the probability of a recall would tend to go up. This seems to get at the fundamental nature of the problem of 'liquidity' which appears to underlie the Pesek and Saving distinction. It also leaves intact a wealth effect from (arbitrary) changes in the volume of both inside and outside money (although the latter is the more likely to occur).

4.4 NEUTRALITY AND SUPERNEUTRALITY: RECENT MACROECONOMIC DISCUSSIONS

The context of discussion so far in this chapter has been mostly short run, static and descriptive of a simple exchange economy (and certainly devoid of

an interesting supply side). It has also been largely microeconomic in tone. However, when we want to consider policy themes, we naturally go to macroeconomics and, of course, naturally think of more dynamic systems; either cycle or growth models are the generic possibilities. What this section will do is look at the growth material on monetary neutrality and superneutrality, partly because it is almost entirely theoretical without the benefit of empirics and partly because it seems to follow the preceding discussion in a logical way. That will leave the more cyclical topics to Chapter 5. Let us attempt some definitions before considering the plan of the section.

By monetary *neutrality* we mean the (null) effect of a once-and-for-all change in the quantity of money on the real variables of the economic system. This is the sense in which we have used the term so far in this chapter, where we have observed that having no real effects implies having an effect only on the price level. *Superneutrality*, then, is generally taken to be the (null) effect of a once-and-for-all change in the *growth rate* of the quantity of money on the real variables of the economic system. Again, under superneutrality, the effect of the change would be felt on the (rates of change of) nominal variables in the system. Note that in both cases (neutrality and superneutrality) there is a short-run and a long-run case and that acceptance of superneutrality does not necessarily imply neutrality. Also note that the short-run non-neutrality of money is often conceded in this literature (e.g. by many classical economists, monetarists, etc.).[10]

Turning to the plan of action in this section, then, we will begin with a short discussion of the standard money-growth model in use in this literature, that of Sidrauski (1967*a*). Here, basically, we will examine the question of superneutrality in a model in which a monetary sector is basically grafted onto a real-sector model. It turns out that money is superneutral in the long run in this framework, but not in the short run. The next section, Section 4.4.2, then offers a somewhat richer model in which an arbitrary change in the growth rate of the money stock (presumably policy-induced) has a non-neutral effect, even in the long run. These results suggest both 'trend' and 'cycle' effects from money. Empirical work will follow in Section 4.5.

4.4.1 The Sidrauski money-growth model

What follows is a summary version of the Sidrauski model, leaving some of the details of the solution to the richer model of Section 4.4.2. Suppose that the individual maximizes the following utility function in real consumption expenditures and real *per capita* money balances:

$$u = U(c, m) \tag{4.43}$$

The individual will face both a *stock* constraint which requires that real non-human wealth (a) be allocated among physical capital (k) and real balances as in

$$a = k + m \tag{4.44}$$

and a *flow* constraint for which after-tax income is equal to consumption plus saving. This latter constraint is

$$y(k) + v = c + s \tag{4.45}$$

Here $y(k)$ is the output from a homogeneous production function and v defines the real value of transfers from the government. Gross savings in this case will equal gross investment (i) plus gross additions to money balances.

In this model capital will accumulate at the rate

$$i = \dot{k} + (\delta + n)k \tag{4.46}$$

where δ is the depreciation rate and n is the growth rate of the labour force (of population); i, of course, is *gross* investment in this formulation, and $\dot{k}$ is the net addition to the capital stock. A second accumulation condition refers to the rate of change of real cash balances and is given by

$$x = \dot{m} + (\pi + n)m \tag{4.47}$$

Again, gross cash balances grow according to newly created real balances and to those created by inflation (π) and population growth. Note that this expression, with $\dot{m}$ and m, provides a means for distinguishing between superneutrality and neutrality respectively. Utilizing the results so far, the flow constraint given in Equation (4.45) can be rewritten as

$$y(k) + v - (\pi + n)m - (\delta + n)k - \dot{m} - \dot{k} - c = 0 \tag{4.48}$$

Thus Equations (4.43), (4.44) and (4.48) represent the structure of the basic Sidrauski money-growth model.

We will not pursue Sidrauski's exact solution here in view of the work on a somewhat richer model given later in this section, but instead will move directly to the neutrality discussion. In the solution to the system of the individual, the following three demand functions result:

$$c = c(a, \pi, v) \tag{4.49}$$

$$m = m(a, \pi, v) \tag{4.50}$$

$$k = k(a, \pi, v) \tag{4.51}$$

where the variables are as defined above. For the individual case, then, equilibrium in the money market is given by

$$\frac{M}{PN} = m(a, \pi, v) \tag{4.52}$$

where the left-hand side measures the *per capita* stock (supply) of money. If the government taxes, transfers and provides money, but does *not* spend on government goods, then the government's budget constraint is given by

$$v = \frac{M}{PN} = \theta m \tag{4.53}$$

where θ, the rate of growth of the money stock, represents the policy parameter in the model; it defines the rate of growth of the money stock. We are, then, assuming that the excess of transfers over taxes is financed by money creation. We can assume that θ grows at the fixed rate θ_0 and population by n, as follows:

$$\theta = \theta_0 \tag{4.54}$$

$$\frac{\dot{N}}{N} = n \tag{4.55}$$

Further, since everything that is not spent in this neoclassical world ends up as consumption, we find that

$$k = y(k) - (\delta + n)k - c(a, \pi, v) \tag{4.56}$$

For our next step, let us substitute Equations (4.44) and (4.53) into Equation (4.52) and then reparameterize to produce

$$\frac{M}{PN} = m^*(k, \theta, \pi) \tag{4.57}$$

This is the money market equilibrium condition and it determines the price level (given k, θ, M and N). We may then combine Equations (4.44), (4.53) and (4.57) into Equation (4.56) to produce the following differential equation:

$$\dot{k} = y(k) - (\delta + n)k - c^*(k, \theta, \pi) \tag{4.58}$$

Here consumption is similarly reparameterized and represents the flow of optimal real consumption expenditures appropriate for the price level determined in the money market (in Equation (4.57)).

Let us assume that price expectations are determined adaptively as in

$$\pi^e = b\left(\frac{\dot{P}}{P} - \pi\right) \tag{4.59}$$

An alternative, of course, would merely be to hold them constant. The final model of the economy, then, consists of Equations (4.54) and (4.55), Equation (4.57) for money-market equilibrium, Equation (4.58) for product-market equilibrium, and Equation (4.59) for adaptive expectations. We can, finally, differentiate the money-market equilibrium condition with respect to time and substitute in Equations (4.54), (4.55), (4.58) and (4.59) to produce a second differential equation.

$$\dot{\pi} = \frac{1}{[1 + b(\partial m^*/\partial \pi)(1/\mathrm{m}^*)]}\{\theta - \pi - \delta - [y(k) - (\delta + n)k - c^*(k, \theta, \pi)]\} \tag{4.60}$$

Thus Equations (4.58) and (4.60), for any given θ (the rate of monetary expansion), describe the time path of the economy. Obviously, experiments on θ are potential (policy-induced) superneutrality experiments.

In the steady state we would set $\dot{\pi}$ and $k = 0$ in which case

$$c^s = y(k^s) - (\delta + n)k^s \tag{4.61}$$

and

$$\pi^e = \theta - n \tag{4.62}$$

That is, consumption equals net output (net of capital accumulation) and inflation is determined as the difference between the policy-determined (and exogenous) rate of money expansion and the exogenous rate of population growth. Clearly, in the steady state superneutrality holds.[11] In the short run, however, when there is a change in θ – say, an increase – then, because the effect of monetary expansion on steady state consumption is positive, there will be a rise in consumption and a reduction in the rate of capital accumulation. Money is non-superneutral in the short run in this model. These are standard results in the money-growth literature initiated by Sidrauski.

4.4.2 An extension of the standard money-growth model[12]

The next step is the construction of a basic money-growth model with dynamically adaptive expectations embedded, in the tradition of Sidrauski.[13] The purpose is to generalize the Sidrauski model by providing a richer framework for the analysis of monetary policy. As it turns out, this version of the model has non-superneutrality, even in the long run. The framework will look a lot like the standard aggregate demand–supply model, with a spending sector (consumption and investment), a financial sector (inside bonds and money) and a supply side (labour supply and demand and a production function). There will be three economic agents, households, firms and the government, with the government's role limited to taking advantage of the non-superneutrality of money.

For *households*, which consume and save, the following represents their *flow constraint*, defined in real terms:

$$C^d + S^d = \frac{W}{P} N^s + rK_f + \left(\frac{\dot{M}}{P} - \pi^e \frac{M}{P} \right) \tag{4.63}$$

Here N^s represents the supply of labour services; rK_f earnings (in real terms) on corporate bonds (K_f is claims on real corporate assets); $\dot{M}/P$ additions to private wealth due in effect to surprise introductions of outside money by the government; and $-\pi^e(M/P)$ the expected inflationary tax on existing money balances. Under rational expectations, the entire term in brackets would presumably be zero.

Individuals, as already noted, will save some of their income and will hold it in the form of either financial assets or money. Indeed, they will also be constrained by

$$\frac{M^d}{P} + K_f^d = \frac{M}{P} + K_f \tag{4.64}$$

which is, of course, a *stock constraint.* In effect, then, when the government introduces money, individuals will be forced to hold it, although we should note here that since P is an endogenous variable their actions to disgorge unwanted money will raise P; they will not be forced to hold a real quantity of money but only a nominal quantity. Nevertheless, Equation (4.64) is stated in real terms. We note that the two constraints will apply simultaneously; i.e. the *flow* of savings in Equation (4.63) must be held in the form of the *stocks* of M/P and K_f in Equation (4.64). Indeed, this forces M/P to $(M/P)^d$ and K_f to K_f^d.

Let us define $y \equiv (W/P)N^s + rK_f$ as *real income from firms* and $Z \equiv y + \dot{M}/P - \pi^e(M/P)$ as *disposable real income*. The consumption function, then, is

$$C^d = (1 - s)Z \qquad (4.65)$$

where s is the propensity to save.

The household sector will have separate demand functions for money and corporate securities with the following forms:

$$M_d = J(Py, PA, r + \pi^e) \qquad (J_1 > 0, 0 < J_2 < 1, J_3 < 0) \qquad (4.66)$$

$$PK_f^d = n(Py, PA, r + \pi^e) \qquad (n_1 < 0, 0 < n_2 < 1, n_3 > 0) \qquad (4.67)$$

These functions are defined in nominal terms, with the variable A measuring real assets $(M/P + K_f)$ and $(r + \pi^e)$ the nominal (*ex ante*) rate of interest (r is the real rate). This is, of course, the Fisher equation. To the right of each equation are the expected signs for the partial derivatives of each equation. Equation (4.66) is perfectly orthodox, with $(r + \pi^e)$ representing the opportunity cost of holding money, while the signs on Equation (4.67) reflect the need to maintain portfolio balance in this model (which is not a disequilibrium model). These constraints, generally recognizable from consumer theory, are that

$$\text{(a)}\ J_1 + n_1 = 0$$

$$\text{(b)}\ J_2 + n_2 = 1$$

$$\text{(c)}\ J_3 + n_3 = 0$$

Most of this is the result that the decision to hold more of one asset requires the decision to hold less of the other, in the exact amount, so long as there are only two assets and a wealth constraint. Basically, n_1 is negative because an increase in corporate cash flow (a rise in Py) will reduce the corporation's need to issue securities. It affects individuals in this way because they own the firms (and $PK^s = PK^d$).

Households also supply labour and we will assume that they do so at the fixed rate δ:

$$\dot{N} = \delta N \qquad \left(\dot{N} = \frac{dN}{dt}\right) \qquad (4.68)$$

The rate δ could be the 'augmented rate of growth of the labour supply' as

defined in Phelps (1968), and, since the other neoclassical restrictions apply to the model discussed here, this could be considered to be a special version of his general neoclassical model. It is a special version, in particular, because we will impose the very non-classical restriction that inflationary expectations are revised adaptively:

$$\dot{\pi}^{e} = \beta(\pi - \pi^{e}) \qquad (0 < \beta < \infty) \tag{4.69}$$

This is a dynamic version of the concept, since $\dot{\pi}^{e} = d\pi^{e}/dt$. In the steady state, we note, $\dot{\pi}^{e} = 0\ (\pi = \pi^{e})$, and so this particular restriction is the source of short-run non-neutrality, but not of long-run non-superneutrality.

Business firms, in this structure, will be presumed to operate the following linear–homogeneous production function:

$$y^{s} = F(K, N^{d})$$

which will be assumed to have positive (but diminishing) marginal products. The firm will face a flow constraint that forces them to pay out all their profits to their owners, as in

$$0 = F(K, N^{d}) - \frac{W}{P}N^{d} - rK_{f} \tag{4.70}$$

and a trivial stock constraint in the form of $K = K_{f}$. The decision to hire labour will be conditioned by $F_{N} = W/P$ and, because of the linear homogeneity of the production function, we will have $F_{K} = r$, with r, as before, the real rate of interest.

Finally, completing the structure of the model, the role of the government is defined as that of picking θ in

$$\frac{\dot{M}}{P} = \theta\left(\frac{M}{P}\right)$$

Note that in this very neoclassical (except for the adaptive expectations) framework, the role of the government is limited to that of flying a helicopter over the countryside and letting bundles of currency drop to the ground. This will, though, have a real (non-neutral) effect.

Equation (4.64) can actually now be given a direct interpretation: it is *Walras's law for stocks*. There is also a flow version of Walras's law which can be derived as follows. If Equations (4.63) and (4.70) are combined along with $N^{s} = N$, we obtain

$$C^{d} + S^{d} = \frac{W}{P}(N - N^{d}) + y^{s} + \frac{\dot{M}}{P} - \pi^{e}\frac{M}{P} \tag{4.71}$$

Noting that real savings must be held in the form of new real-money balances or financial assets (and that $\dot{K}_{f} = dK_{f}/dt$), we have

$$S^{d} = \frac{\dot{M}}{P} - \pi^{e}\frac{M}{P} + \dot{K}_{f}$$

Substituting this into Equation (4.71) and noting that $y^d = C^d + I^d \equiv C^d + \dot{K}_f$, where C^d is consumption demand and I^d is investment demand, we have

$$y^d - y^s = \frac{W}{P}(N - N^d) \tag{4.72}$$

which is *Walras's law for flows.*

The adoption of these two constraints, in a model with four markets (commodities, money, financial claims and labour services), implies that two markets are redundant (although their parameters can be recovered from the constraints). We can, if we impose Walras's laws, eliminate two markets, and we will do so, eliminating the markets for financial claims and labour services. We will specify overall equilibrium, then, in terms of product-market and money-market equilibrium.

Product-market equilibrium is defined in the usual way – consumption plus investment equals income – i.e. as

$$(1 - s)Z + I = F(K, N) \tag{4.73}$$

Taking advantage of the homogeneity of $F(\cdot)$ we can write it in *per capita* form as $f(k)$, where $k = K/N$ and $NF(k, 1) = Nf(k)$. Using this, and the definition of Z given above, we then have

$$(1 - s)[f(k) + m(\theta - \pi^e)] + \dot{k} + \delta k = f(k) \tag{4.74}$$

Here we have also used the facts that $\theta = \dot{m}/m$ and $\dot{k} + \delta k$ represents gross *per capita* investment (δ being the depreciation rate which is equal, arbitrarily, to the rate of growth of the augmented labour force). We are also substituting $f(k)$ for y/N wherever it appears. We will employ Equation (4.74) as the product-market equilibrium curve. It is dynamic by virtue of the presence of $\dot{k}$.

For the *money-market equilibrium* curve, let us return to Equation (4.66). Noting that $r = f'(k)$ and expressing the function in real *per capita* terms (imposing, in effect, the lack of money illusion on the function), we have

$$j[f(k), m + k, f' + \pi^e] = m$$

Here we have made use of the fact that $a = A/N = m + k$ for $A = M/P + k$; m and k, of course, are in *per capita* form. Solving this expression for m results in

$$L(k, f' + \pi^e) = m \qquad (L_1 > 0, L_2 < 0) \tag{4.75}$$

as the money-market equilibrium condition. These two conditions, then, will solve for P and k, given M, N, K and π^e – a sufficient framework for us to investigate superneutrality since we have both a real (k) and a nominal (P) variable as endogenous and the money supply (M) as a control variable.

The foregoing is a short-run specification, and so to move into dynamic mode, we need to differentiate our static short-run conditions with respect to

time. By definition, since $m = M/PN$, we have that $\dot{m}/m = \dot{M}/M - \dot{P}/P - \dot{N}/N$ or, equivalently,

$$\dot{m} = m(\theta - \pi - \delta) \tag{4.76}$$

Differentiating the money-market equilibrium with respect to time, we have

$$\dot{m} = L_1\dot{k} + L_2(f''\dot{k} + \dot{\pi}^e) \tag{4.77}$$

We can combine these two expressions and substitute the result into Equation (4.69) to produce

$$\dot{\pi}^e = \beta\left\{\left[-\frac{L_1\dot{k} + L_2(f''\dot{k} + \dot{\pi}^e)}{m}\right] + \theta - \delta - \pi^e\right\} \tag{4.78}$$

Let us define ε as the 'capital elasticity' of the demand for real money balances; this is calculated as

$$\varepsilon \equiv \frac{\partial m}{\partial k}\frac{k}{m} = \frac{L_1 k}{m} + \frac{L_2 f'' k}{m} \equiv (L_1 + L_2 f'')\frac{k}{m}$$

When this expression is substituted into Equation (4.78), a dynamic form for changes in inflationary expectations results:

$$\dot{\pi}^e = \frac{\beta(-(\dot{k}/k)\varepsilon + \theta - \delta - \pi^e)}{1 + \beta(L_2/m)} \tag{4.79}$$

It is important to notice that in the steady state, when $\dot{\pi}^e = \dot{k} = 0$, the result is that $\pi^e = \theta - \delta$. That is, expected (=actual) inflation equals the difference between the rate of growth of the money-stock and that of the economy. This result is not true by definition, but as a condition of equilibrium in the money market. Note that since we are about to show that changes in θ have real effects, this condition does not imply that the basic quantity theory of money holds, even though velocity is constant, at monetary equilibrium.[14]

In the steady state, we may derive the *dynamic product-market equilibrium condition* as follows. Starting with Equation (4.74) for short-run equilibrium (recall that $\dot{k}$ appears there), letting $\dot{k}=0$ and using the dynamic equilibrium relation from the money market in the form of $\pi^e = \theta - \delta$, we find (by direct substitution) that in the steady state,

$$(1 - s)[f(k) + \delta m] + \delta k = f(k) \tag{4.80}$$

This is the dynamic product-market equilibrium curve in the steady state. This yields, when solved for m,

$$m^r = \frac{sf(k^r) - \delta k^r}{(1 - s)\delta} \equiv w^r(k^r)$$

This is a curve, in the m, k plane, which rises and then falls. Indeed, its slope is $(sf' - \delta)/[(1 - s)\delta]$ which must be negative for stability in the steady state (for $f' > 0$).

The dynamic money-market equilibrium curve in the steady state can be derived from Equation (4.75) with the condition that $\pi^e = \theta - \delta$. This is

$$m = L[k, f'(k) + \theta - \delta] \tag{4.81}$$

The slope of this function in the m, k plane is $L_1 + f''L_2$, which is unambiguously positive. Thus the possibility of overall equilibrium exists, at least if $(sf' - \delta) < 0$ for the product-market equilibrium.

Let us now test for superneutrality. The experiment performed is that of changing θ, the rate of growth of real *per capita* money balances (controlled via nominal balances). Our two dynamic, steady state, equilibrium conditions are

$$-s[f(k) + \delta m] + \delta(k + m) = 0 \tag{4.82}$$

$$L[k, f'(k) + \theta - \delta] - m = 0 \tag{4.83}$$

for $\dot{k} = \dot{m} = 0$ and $\pi^e = \pi = \theta - d$. Both of these equations must be differentiated by θ and the resulting expressions must be solved for the effect of changes in θ on k and m. The result for k is

$$\frac{\partial k}{\partial \theta} = \frac{L_2 \delta(1 - s)}{H} > 0 \tag{4.84}$$

where $H = -[(\delta - sf') + \delta(1 - s)(L_1 + L_2 f'')]$. Here, with $\delta(1 - s)(L_1 + L_2 f'')$ unambiguously positive, with $(\delta - sf')$ also positive (as a stability condition – see above), and with $L_2 < 0$, monetary expansion brings a rise in k (in K/N) and hence in y ($= Y/N$). Money is non-superneutral in this model, and, in particular, increases in the rate of its production stimulate output in the steady state.

The reason for this result is simply that a rise in θ also raises the inflation rate, and this reduces the demand for money. Since there are only two kinds of capital in the model – money and corporate securities – reduction of the demand for money implies an increase, via the portfolio constraint, in the *demand* for financial assets. Firms, owned (of course) by households, can satisfy this demand by increasing their issue of securities. The proceeds from these security issues are utilized in the expansion of the capital stock of firms. An interest-rate story can also go along with this chain of events, but the line just laid down is more consistent with the way our model has been set out. In particular, non-superneutrality can be traced to the asset effect (real-balance effect) mechanism embedded in the model. We note, in passing, that

$$\frac{\partial m}{\partial \theta} = (L_1 + L_2 f'')\frac{\partial k}{\partial \theta} + L_2$$

is actually ambiguous in sign since the first term is *a priori* positive and the second negative. The first term is a 'capital market' effect which increases real per capita money-holdings (as the economy expands), while the second reflects the determination of the value of money-holdings as judged by its

opportunity cost. Thus non-superneutrality has implications for the demand for money in the steady state, since this sign would have been unambiguously negative for $\partial k/\partial\theta = 0$ (i.e. for superneutrality).[15]

4.5 RECENT EMPIRICAL TESTS OF THE QUANTITY THEORY OF MONEY

In the preceding discussion the superneutrality of money appears in the form of two propositions: 'that a given change in the rate of change in the quantity of money induces (i) an equal change in the rate of price inflation; and (ii) an equal change in nominal rates of interest' (Lucas, 1980, p. 1005). These propositions, as we have just demonstrated, flow from the Sidrauski theory and, better in some respects, possess the property that should the predictions of the theory fail, the model could then provide guidance as to why. In Lucas's terminology, this is the property of 'theoretical coherence' that, he feels, the quantity theory of money possesses. Thus, in the Sidrauski (1967*a*, 1967*b*) model, 'both laws appear as explicit, necessary characteristics of the stationary solution of the differential equations which describe equilibrium in the system' (Lucas, p. 1005). The differential equations are Equations (4.58) and (4.60). This superneutrality does not hold in the alternative models either because of the presence of a long-run real-balance effect in the money-demand function or on account of the Mundell–Tobin effect (see Note 15). These are reasonable qualifications and establish the existence of an interesting empirical question.

What we are looking for, then, is contained in Propositions (i) and (ii) in the first quotation just given from Lucas. With respect to the former, Lucas suggests that since the quantity theory is a proposition meant to apply to a variety of economic structures (of monetary economies) for any value of the rate of change of the money stock, it might be useful to look at some long-run averages for the 16 Latin American countries appearing in Vogel's (1974) study of Latin American price dynamics.[16] These numbers are graphed by Lucas and appear here as Figure 4.1. There is also a regression line drawn in Figure 4.1 whose slope (at 1.136) is actually significantly different from that of a 45° line. In his study, Lucas draws in a 45° line through the point of the means and notes how closely this line appears to fit the data. The regression line, however, is

$$\pi = -\,6.544 + \underset{(5.76)}{}\;1.136\,\theta, \qquad \bar{R}^2 = 0.972, \qquad DW = 2.119$$

$$(5.76) \quad (22.10)$$

Vogel also provides some data on the rate of change of real income and the rate of change of velocity for these countries (for the average values, that is to say, for each country). When real income growth (g) is included in the

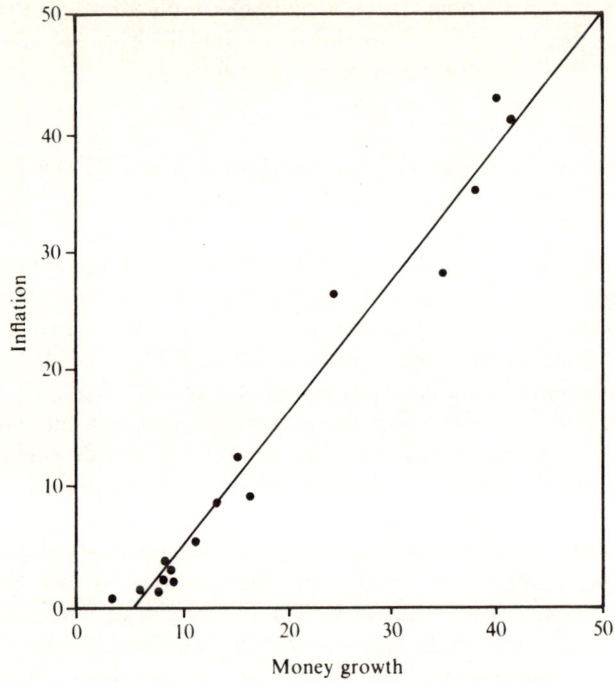

Figure 4.1 Sixteen Latin American countries.

regression, we find that

$$\pi = 1.347 + 1.040\,\theta - 1.380\,g, \qquad \bar{R}^2 = 0.986, \qquad DW = 1.950$$
$$(0.56) \quad (22.31) \quad (3.55)$$

This time money growth (θ) is not significantly different from unity (the numbers in parentheses are t-values), while the growth rate of real income is significant (with the expected negative sign). Indeed, this is what the Sidrauski theory predicts in the steady state. This is not to say that Lucas's procedure is incorrect (by projecting his line through the point of the means and restricting it to a 45° slope he approximates the true line) but to note that the formal statistical test is easier to interpret.

A recent test of the same model by Dwyer and Hafer (1988) covers the annual data from 1979 to 1984 for a sample of 62 countries. What Dwyer and Hafer do is average the rates of growth of money and prices (and income) for the 62 countries over the six years to produce a cross-sectional test comparable to the Lucas test of Vogel's Latin American data. Again, the rationale is that 'monetary regimes' will differ sufficiently across these countries to generate a valid test. The results appear in Figure 4.2 and again

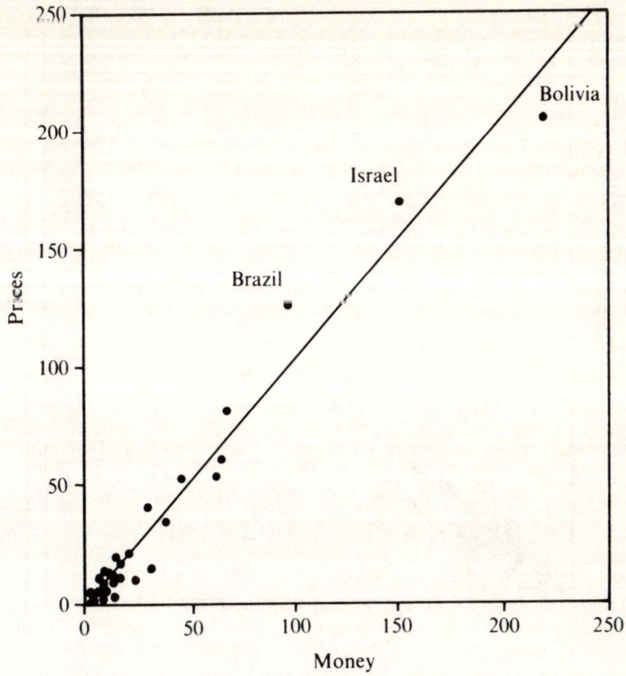

Figure 4.2 Growth rates for *M*, *P* (62 countries).

appear to support the notion of a stable long-run proportionality. Here, again, the regression line is drawn in. The slope of the regression line is 1.030 (with a *t*-value of 40.64), a number very close to the steady state value of 1.0 predicted by the theory (in this case real income is not a significant additional variable). Note, as illustrated in Figure 4.3, that dropping the three 'outliers' named in Figure 4.2 does not alter the conclusions materially. Indeed, a regression of inflation on money for the 59 countries produces a coefficient of 1.011 (*t*-value = 20.52).[17] On the whole, then, the Lucas specification does very well in these two tests.

There is a second test in the Lucas paper, however, which provides yet another way of organizing the data, this time in a time-series context. Lucas argues, again, that what we are looking for is long-run proportionalities between

(a) money growth and inflation; and
(b) money growth and the nominal interest rate.

The latter is the Fisher effect. How the long-run test might be implemented is to *filter* all the data (i.e. smooth the data) by any one of a large number of potential filters. Lucas illustrates the results of using an especially general,

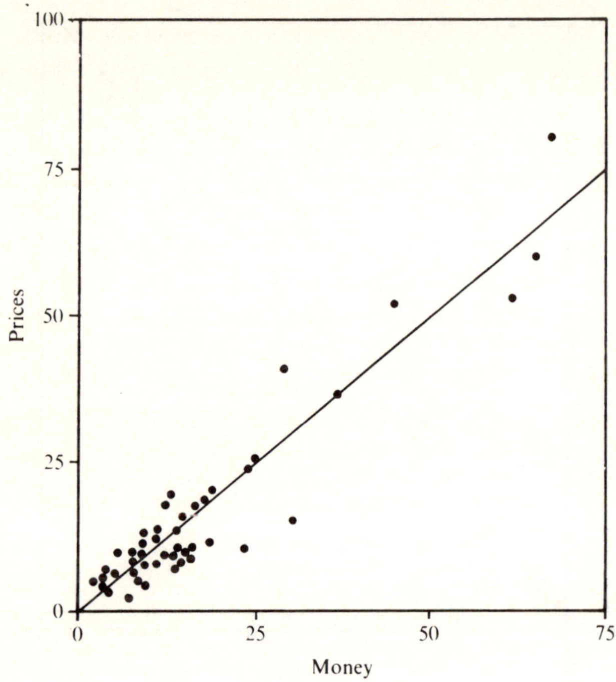

Figure 4.3 Growth rates for M, P (59 countries).

two-sided, exponential filter.[18] This appears as Equation (4.85):

$$x_i(\beta) = \left(\frac{1-\beta}{1+\beta}\right) \sum_{k=-j}^{j} \beta^{|k|} x_{1,t+k} \qquad (0 \leq \beta < 1) \qquad (4.85)$$

In Lucas's test j is taken to be infinity. This construction is designed to filter out short-run noise so that the true long-run signal can be revealed. If the smoothed observations of a pairwise plot (of M against π or M against i) lie along a 45° line, for some relatively high value of β (not equal to unity), then we have uncovered illustrations of the quantity theory at work. Indeed in Lucas's tests for both hypotheses (on smoothed annual US data from 1955–75), this appears to be true for β in the vicinity of 0.9. For $\beta=0.5$, or for the original unsmoothed data, the plots are quite dispersed. Lucas comments that the simple plots of the unsmoothed data just referred to 'seem to capture fairly well what people mean when they say that the quantity theory of money is not a "short-run" relationship' (p. 1007).

We have been working with other (quarterly) data in this study, and since quarterly data, or other data sets, might throw more light on the proposition, it is useful to look at a variation of the test, designed to exploit this more recent set of data. For a value of $\beta=0.5$ and for $j=50$ quarters of data, Figure 4.4 shows a scatterplot of inflation v. money growth on recent US

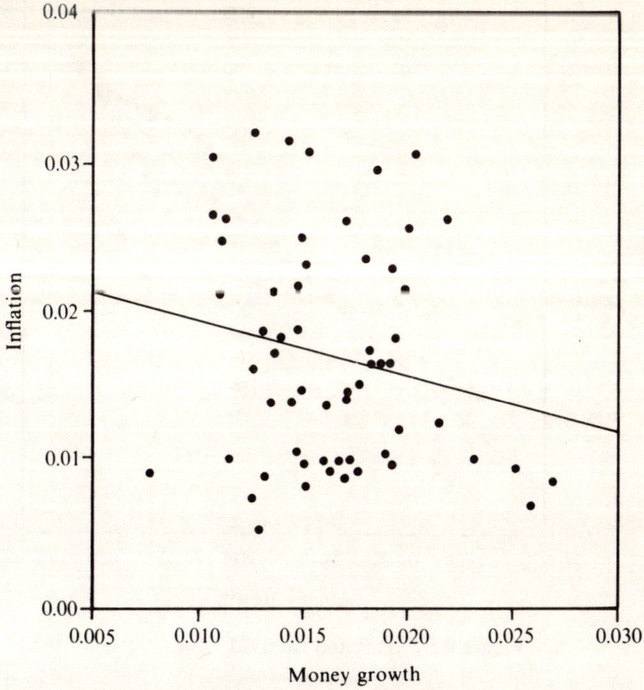

Figure 4.4 Prices and SumM1 ($\beta=0.5$).

SumM1 data. As Lucas suggests for his data, there is considerable short-run variation (a poorly determined regression line is also drawn in).

As the value of β increases in Equation (4.85), the weighting scheme tends to throw more and more weight on distant observations (i.e. smooths the data more). In frequency-domain terms, as β approaches unity, the relationship between money and prices approaches zero frequency (approaches the long-run case); this is explained at length in Lucas's paper.[19] If the smoothed data (either inflation/money growth or interest rate/money growth) lie along a 45° line, the theory is successfully illustrated. But for the quarterly data, with the 50-quarter lag and $\beta=0.95$ for sumM1, Figure 4.5 presents some bad news for the hypothesis. That is, while the data are smoothed, they turn back on themselves in a decidedly non-random way, and the slope of the regression line is not close to unity, as marked.[20] A similar result holds for interest rates (the commercial paper rate was used in this case) as plotted in Figure 4.6, and an even more deviant plot occurs for Divisia M2 (but is not shown).[21] All is not (quite) lost, however, since a regression of inflation on money growth and real income produces a coefficient on the former 'reasonably' near unity:

$$\pi = a + \underset{(14.88)}{1.132\,\theta} + \underset{(5.172)}{1.089\,g}, \qquad \bar{R}^2 = 0.928, \qquad DW = 0.07$$

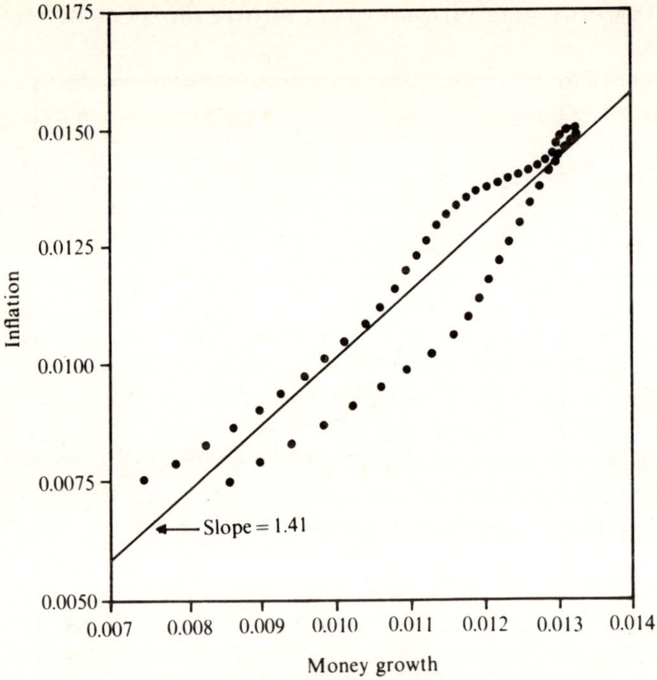

Figure 4.5 Prices and SumM1 ($\beta = 0.95$)

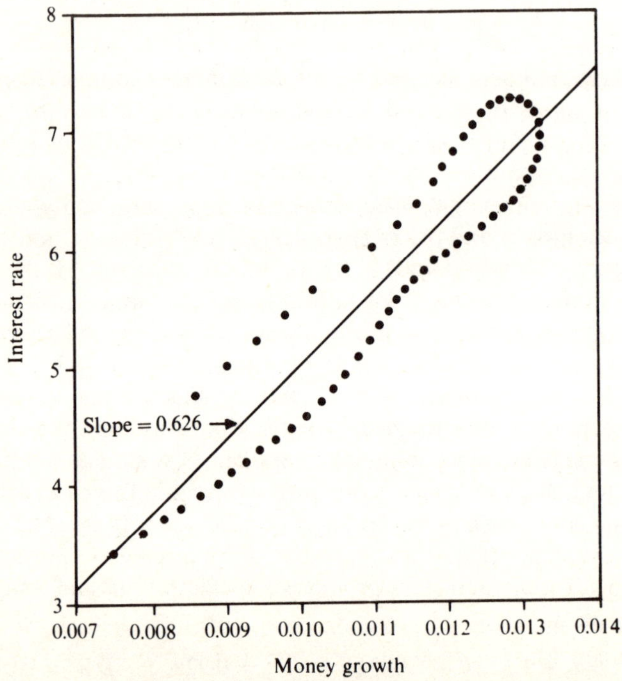

Figure 4.6 Interest and money ($\beta = 0.95$).

There is not a lot of comfort here (consider the Durbin Watson statistic), but perhaps it is asking a little too much for the quantity theory to show up neatly in a world that is affected by 'missing money', collapse of the international payments system, a reversal of the velocity trend (see Chapter 5), several energy crises and increasing financial variability (uncertainty). Lucas actually suggests that such tests must be run over very long data sets (e.g. 100 years of annual data) and so this is just not quite right. The reason it was done here, essentially, aside from the illustration of a technique that we will hear more of, is that he did report success on a short run of recent US data. It is evident, if we accept that the theory does perform on that data (see below), that recent events have tended to obscure the relation, to be most charitable.

To see explicitly how the demand for money ties into this discussion of the quantity theory of money, consider a simple demonstration by Fama (1982). Assuming that the demand for money is

$$\Delta \log m_t \equiv \Delta \log M_t - \Delta \log P_t = \alpha_0 + \alpha_1 \Delta \log y_t + \alpha_2 i_t + e_t \qquad (4.86)$$

a standard form, then if real activity is exogenous to the monetary sector and if in an efficient (and rational) bond market the interest rate is exogenous to the price level (both at time t), then a reduced form equation can be written for the rate of inflation in the form of

$$\Delta \log P_t = -\alpha_0 - \alpha_1 \Delta \log y_t - \alpha_2 i_t + \alpha_3 \Delta \log M_t - e_t \qquad (4.87)$$

Here, α_3 is unity. Thus a decline in income or the interest rate reduces the rate of inflation (stagflation), while an expansion of money-growth raises it. Clearly, if interest rates are a random walk (see Chapter 2), then the determination of inflation depends on the two (assumed to be) exogenous variables y and m.[22]

The quantity theory advanced here is not phrased solely in terms of M but in terms of both M and y (and their exogeneity); this is the result of the reformulation of the theory in terms of the demand for money. Fama suggests that both factors appear to work, with the expected signs, on monthly, quarterly and annual data for the USA over the 1953–77 period. In the regression reported above for Lucas's annual data (for the same period), the sign expectations of Equation (4.87) are confirmed, but, as just noted, for the quarterly 1970–85 period they are not. Several reasons have already been given for this, to which might be added the possibility (as in Keynes, 1936) that the quantity of money is not exogenous. In any event, there is more discussion of the role of the demand for money in the quantity theory of money in Section 5.3.1.

There have been several significant criticisms of these tests which bring up some interesting aspects of this sort of empirical modelling. One important problem concerns the modelling of the interest rate, which (see Chapter 2) may not be a random walk as it must be under Lucas's hypothesis. Furthermore (Mills, 1982), the interest rate probably has too much short-term

fluctuation to it, random or not,' to be treated in a parallel fashion (for $\beta = 0.95$) to the relatively smooth money growth and inflation numbers. Mills performs his own test on quarterly US data, now run out to 1980. He concludes that:

> The long-run response of the inflation signal to a unit change in the money growth signal is 1.05 . . . This result is consistent with the quantity theoretic implication of a unit response.
>
> The response of the interest rate signal to such a change is 1.4, somewhat higher than that implied in the quantity theory, and, in fact, a formal significance test rejected this quantity theoretic null hypothesis. (pp. 1167–8)

Note that the long-run 'signal' in each case is the smoothed data series.

A second problem is raised by Whiteman (1984) who argues that while the Lucas model is fine as, in effect, an illustration, it fails to provide the evidence that Lucas claims for the failure of the Mundell–Tobin effect to occur. That is, says Whiteman, Lucas's 'reduced form' correlations are actually:

> complicated functions of the structure of the economy as well as of the law of motion of processes individuals care about. As such, they are unlikely to provide much evidence about the 'true' model of the economy unless one already has it very much in mind. (p. 748)

In short, says Whiteman, Lucas's tests suffer from the well-known Lucas critique (1976). And, we might add, none of this is drawn up with any formal reference to the underlying money-supply hypothesis (or to questions of separability and monetary aggregation).

NOTES

1. The relevant nineteenth- and early twentieth-century literature on these topics can be found in Sowell (1972).
2. That is, from Equation (4.4), $M = \Sigma PD = P\Sigma D = PT$ for P a price level and T a transaction index.
3. Another device that is often mentioned in this context is the 'homogeneity postulate' (see Patinkin, 1965). The restriction in this case is that the commodity excess-demand functions are homogeneous in (all) money prices.
4. To see this, scale each P_j and the supply of money by β at $X_n = 0$ and observe that β factors out.
5. This statement is not as strong an assumption as that employed above in which the commodity *demand* functions had a similar condition imposed upon them.
6. See the proof in Bernstein (1978*a*); the following discussion is also drawn from that paper.
7. See Bernstein (1978*a*). As straightforward as it is, but contrary to the author's claim, Equation (4.32) is not the most general formulation possible – being in an additively separable form – and can be generalized further. In particular, it can be shown that in the context of the dual budget constraint formulation, the following weakly separable utility function possesses all the neoclassical restrictions:

$$u = U[\phi(X_1, \ldots, X_{n-1}), M, m, P_1, \ldots, P_{n-1}]$$

The nomenclature here is the same as in Equation (4.32). The function (U), with

its weakly separable component $\phi(\cdot)$, retains all the neoclassical restrictions and attendant empirical implications (again see Chapter 2), including, especially, the symmetry property for the commodities that are either demanded or supplied.

8. In the case in which the *r*th good is money and some degree of homogeneity is imposed, it can be signed.
9. This proposition is frequently applied to debt instruments – a bond-holder's loss being identical to the issuer's gain (after an interest-rate change, for example).
10. Actually, acceptance of long-run superneutrality, for example, would imply a restriction that could be applied to studies of the (short-run) influence of money on real variables in order to condition the estimates better. For a discussion of these and many other concerns in neutrality testing, see M. Fisher (1988).
11. If the equilibrium in the model is a stable one.
12. The model of this section is drawn from D. Fisher (1988); it is joint work with J. I. Bernstein in that version.
13. Two other basic papers in this literature are Tobin (1955) and Levhari and Patinkin (1968). See the discussion in Turnovsky (1977*c*), especially Chapter 8.
14. To see this, consider the dynamic version of $MV=Py$ (the equation of exchange); there the rate of change of velocity would be zero for the equilibrium condition just given.
15. We note that in roughly the same context, Lucas (1975) shows that a model with neutrality does not necessarily show superneutrality. The culprit in this case in known as the Mundell (1963)–Tobin (1965) effect. This is similar to what was found in Equation (4.84), although in Lucas's case it works via interest rate changes.
16. The idea is that since the theory is about steady states, a cross-section of the numbers of different countries (averaged) could provide sufficient variation in (exogenously determined) monetary policy to expose the steady state relations among money, interest and prices.
17. In this case, though, real income in significant (and negative) in a regression with money and real income as regressors.
18. The backward-looking part of this filter requires no justification. What Lucas says about the forward-looking part is that individuals '*care* about the future and probably process much more information in forecasting that part of the future relevant to their own decisions than we econometricians can observe' (p. 1009, fn).
19. Indeed, under the assumption that money growth is exogenous, causation presumably runs from money to prices.
20. That is, the plot is generated serially, beginning with 1970 on the far left, above the line, continuing up to the blurry part (1978–82) and then down under the line to 1985. All the graphs generated show this break in the 1978–82 period. We will have some conjectures about this period in Chapter 5.
21. We note that a plot of nominal income growth on money growth also shows the same pattern. This plot is prompted by the monetarist notion that money determines nominal income and not just the price level (since $Y=Py$). Friedman (1971) has such a theory, and the Lucas and Dwyer/Hafer papers report a successful implementation of this proposition (the latter is only done across the 62 countries, not for a time series).
22. Note that there is some discussion in the literature as to whether or not GNP is itself a random walk (West, 1988).

5

MONEY SUPPLY, MONEY DEMAND AND MONETARY POLICY

5.1 INTRODUCTION

This chapter will consider the role of the money-supply relation in the determination of the money stock, although the analyses of Sections 5.2 and 5.3 are more of a blend of money supply and demand. What distinguishes this chapter from Chapter 4 is the emphasis on discretionary monetary policy as a major mover of the money supply. In a sense this is a bridge chapter between the detailed money/supply-side discussion in Chapter 6 and the helicopter-style monetary policy discussed in Chapter 4. Here more attention will be paid to the structure of the economy, with particular reference to money demand. In Chapter 6, then, banks will receive their fair share of the discussion and money demand will (almost) disappear from the scene.

The story begins with a traditional literature – a version of banking-multiplier analysis. This is 'money-determinants' analysis in which a blend of money demand and money supply – modelled in terms of the agents who make the critical financial decisions – is used to explain the money stock in terms of its proximate 'determinants' – the currency-money ratio, the reserves-deposit ratio and the stock of high-powered (base) money. The agents who determine these entities are final money-holders, banks and the government respectively.

The second topic, in Section 5.2, is also macroeconomic (and almost entirely astructural) and involves the determinants of the velocity of money (i.e. of Y/M). Velocity, too, is potentially influenced by both money supply and money demand as well as by any independent influences on income, but in the classical tradition its determination mostly involves money demand. In this respect, Friedman's (1956) model of money demand is a seminal presentation and is discussed here in some detail. The model is tested, as it were, in the course of an attempt to explain the recent behaviour of velocity (in the USA); this experiment is of interest simply because the actual velocity patterns do not correspond with those predicted by the basic money-demand theory. Of most interest is the marked decline in velocity after 1979 (it grew over most of the post-World War II period) as well as the increase in the

variance of velocity (and in a lot of other time series of economic variables). An original explanation on the quarterly US data will be presented here as a way of illustrating some of the other possible explanations (and in order to assess further the relative performance of the different possible monetary definitions). The prime suspect in velocity instability is money-stock variability (i.e. is possibly variable monetary policy), and the method employed is the Granger-causality test.

The analysis in Section 5.2 has only minimal economic structure to it and that in Section 5.3 basically none. Section 5.4 introduces more structure in order to consider more specifically the influence of monetary policy on the economy. We will also briefly discuss the Phillips curve environment lying behind some of the discussion of non-neutrality in Chapter 4, although this chapter is mostly interested in the role of rational expectations in conditioning the influence of monetary policy on real variables (especially in Section 5.4.2). Neutrality issues return, although throughout this chapter there is a standing presumption of non-neutrality. In that sense, in Section 5.5 we will continue by covering recent work on the monetary causes of the real business cycle. This last is a traditional literature that has been mostly on the sidelines in the work of recent years on real business-cycle theory, although the omens are promising for a revival. As illustration of the main technique, new tests in the context of some of the different possible money-stock measures are reported here (with a non-neutrality result). Section 5.5.3 continues this topic with a discussion of how money might affect financial markets (in particular bond and equity markets). The reader does need to notice that it is monetary policy that motivates most of the material in this chapter, especially after Section 5.2.

5.2 MONEY MULTIPLIERS

The approach to money-stock determination that we will be considering in this section generally operates at the 'reduced form' level, in which the money *stock* is assumed to be determined by the contributions of three economic agents:

demanders: the public (I)
suppliers:
banks (II)
the Government (III)

It is a reduced-form approach, formally, because the decisions of the three agents are assumed to be independent of each other and not subject to feedback from other variables in the system. First, the agents determine their desired holdings in the form of

C/M: the ratio of currency to money, as determined by the public (I);
R/D: the ratio of reserves to deposits, as determined by either the banks (II) or the Government (III); [1] and

H: the monetary base (or, sometimes, the stock of high powered money) as determined by the central bank (III).

These, then, become the *proximate determinants* of the money stock itself, as follows. Note, again, that supply forces (R/D and H) and demand forces (C/M) both appear in the list of money-stock determinants.

Assume that $H \equiv C+R$ defines the quantity of high-powered money. Dividing each of these terms by M and then rearranging, we obtain the expression

$$M = \frac{H}{(C/M) + (R/D) - (C/M)(R/D)} \tag{5.1}$$

where the relations among the determinants and the money stock are made more precise. If we take the logs of this expression as in

$$\log M \equiv \log H - \log\left(\frac{C}{M} + \frac{R}{D} - \frac{C}{M}\frac{R}{D}\right) \tag{5.2}$$

and totally differentiate with respect to time, we get

$$\frac{\mathrm{d}\log M}{\mathrm{d}t} = \frac{\mathrm{d}\log H}{\mathrm{d}t} + \frac{M}{H}\left(1 - \frac{R}{D}\right)\frac{\mathrm{d}(-C/M)}{\mathrm{d}t} + \frac{M}{H}\left(1 - \frac{C}{M}\right)\frac{\mathrm{d}(-R/D)}{\mathrm{d}t} \tag{5.3}$$

whereby C/M and R/D are seen to reduce and H to increase the rate of growth of the money stock. The expressions in front of each are the weights attached to the individual influences.[2] Using the end-points of the series, for example, this formulation can be applied directly to pinpoint the proximate influences on the money stock. The estimated growth rates and mean values can also be used to do this. Used in either of these ways, the approach does require that these influences be independent of each other, although there exist viable alternative methods such as multiple regressions or, possibly better, Granger-causality tests, which do that automatically.

Money-stock determination theory is a valid short-cut if the determinants are independent of each other and if the ratios (e.g. C/M) are themselves truly independent variables. If we simply run a regression of M on C/M, H and R/D, we would probably not need to worry about correlations among the independent variables, but we would still have to deal with the problem of inconsistency if any of these terms were correlated with the error term. This source of difficulty, produced possibly by endogeneity in the right-hand variables, also affects the essentially non-stochastic approach described above in that the determinants themselves could be subject to feedback from the determinees. Such will occur, for example, whenever C/M responds to interest rates (or income), whenever currency demand directly influences the quantity of high-powered money or whenever banks hold excess reserves (as they did after 1930, in the USA). Such a situation seems likely in the event

that the country in question has a floating exchange rate or is a member of the gold-standard nations but does not play by the rules.[3]

There is another problem with the money-multipliers approach discussed here, and this involves the behaviour of the monetary authorities. We have not said much about their specific policies to this point, preferring to treat their activities as leading to an exogenously determined monetary base, but the fact is that their choice of 'proximate target' in their policy design is tied up with the question just raised and, in particular, with how the direction of causation must be modelled in the economic system. For example (McCallum, 1986*a*, Hetzel, 1986), if the authorities follow the policy of setting (targeting) the *nominal* stock of money, then the real quantity demanded is determined by the demanders of money and the price level is endogenous and adjusts to equate the real demand for money with the nominal supply (in effect). Causation, *ceteris paribus*, runs from nominal money to prices. This is the mainstream monetarist view (e.g. Friedman, 1956) and has received considerable support in many (but not all) tests around the world, as discussed later in this chapter.

What have not received so much attention in this particular context are the consequences of the authorities targeting the nominal interest rate rather than the nominal money supply.[4] First, as is well known (Friedman, 1968; Sargent and Wallace, 1975), strict maintenance of a nominal interest-rate target would render the price level and the nominal quantity of money indeterminate (unstable, really). If, however, the authorities in fact tie the growth of money to the difference between i^* and r^e, where i^* is the target nominal interest rate (so that actual inflation is equal to expected inflation at that target rate) and r^e is the expected real rate, and if shocks in M_t (due to shocks in r_t) produce a systematic response in M_{t+i} by the authorities, then the price level and the nominal money stock need not be indeterminate. Other explanations, however, are conceivable.

Whatever the rationale, nominal interest-rate pegging (to the extent that it is practised) implies that a shock to the nominal (real) interest rate will be accompanied by a passive (policy) response in H and therefore in M. The (let us say) increase in the price level now equates the *nominal* money demanded with that supplied. Indeed:

> A major source of confusion has been the failure to recognize that the reserves-money multiplier relationship . . . does not summarize behavioural relationships important to the determination of the money stock in a regime of (interest) rate control. (Hetzel, 1986, pp. 4–5)

In particular, the pattern of behaviour of the money stock depends on real and nominal shocks to the system (which induce regular responses in the money stock). Prices (shocks) may cause money responses, but so may real shocks. The real demand for money is simply independent of these considerations and the role of price level changes is to equate the nominal demand to the nominal supply. This is known in the literature as the 'nominal adjust-

ment hypothesis' and is the subject of some empirical testing on the demand for money.[5] The multipliers model goes wrong because the R/D ratio will tend to respond to interest rates (if the authorities let it). That is, if the authorities lend to the commercial banks (or their intermediaries) as their method of responding to the pressure to, for example, increase the nominal supply of money, then R/D would be interest-sensitive. If either R/D or C/M is interest-sensitive for any reason, this (endogenous) feedback response invalidates the working assumptions of the determinants approach.

5.3 MONEY SUPPLY, MONEY DEMAND AND THE VELOCITY OF MONEY

The velocity of money has been of interest to economists since its elevation to the role of a key parameter in I. Fisher's quantity theory of money (1922). Typically, the concept is defined as the ratio of national income (or the volume of transactions) to the quantity of money (Y/M) and is no more than a measure of how many times money is turned over (per year, for example) as a particular flow of spending goes by. Indeed, as it is written, with an endogenous variable in the numerator and (at least by frequent assumption) an exogenous variable in the denominator, it would seem an unlikely candidate for a long-run constant but so it has been taken in some of this literature. In any case, it is obvious even at first glance that both money supply and money demand are involved in the determination of velocity.

5.3.1 Some basic concepts

One particularly apt way to look at the concept of velocity, in view of its development in the neoclassical tradition, is to pursue a model first considered in Chapter 4, that of a monetary, general-equilibrium, exchange economy. In that model (e.g. in Equation (4.17)) we derive the condition listed as Equation (5.4):

$$\bar{M} = k \sum_{j=1}^{n-1} P_j S_j \tag{5.4}$$

Here k is the (assumed) proportionality from the demand for money and S_j defines initial endowments of the $n-1$ commodities; the P_j are money prices. If a consistent price index (P) can be found (as in Chapter 1), then Equation (5.4) can be written as

$$\bar{M} = kP \sum_{j=1}^{n-1} S_j$$

Further, if a consistent quantity index can be found for the expression ΣS_j – and it can be if the price index is consistent, since in that case the quantity index is the dual of the price index (using price weights) – then we

can write

$$\bar{M} = kPnS \tag{5.5}$$

with the *n* coming from the summation. In this form we recognize a concept very much like nominal GNP in *PnS*, the money value of total expenditures. Thus, making the arbitrary substitution of *Y* for *PnS*, we have

$$\frac{\bar{M}}{Y} = k$$

and it is clear that our restriction on the money-demand function (that economic agents hold a fixed proportion of their income in the form of money) actually does produce a parameter $(1/k)$ which defines velocity in this exchange economy. Increases in the quantity of money (recalling its exogeneity in this particular model) then spill onto P and y $(=nS)$ and, in the pure exchange economy, with S fixed, changes in money would presumably *cause* changes in the price level. Velocity itself would not be caused by changes in the quantity of money unless k changes under the influence of policy.

The fact is that income velocity series (everywhere) are certainly not constant (although in some periods they do look like random walks (Gould and Nelson, 1974; Friedman and Schwartz, 1982; Ahking, 1984) and so the strict proportionality view cannot be maintained. This does not leave the quantity theory of money without a foundation, though, if we replace the constant k with a weaker condition – such that 'money demand is a *stable* function of a few key variables'. This familiar monetarist refrain can be explained (following Friedman, 1956) as follows. Suppose that the demand for nominal money balances is written as

$$M^{d} = f\left(P, i_{b} - \frac{1}{i_{b}}\frac{di_{b}}{dt}, r_{e} + \frac{1}{P}\frac{dP}{dt} - \frac{1}{r_{e}}\frac{dr_{e}}{dt}, \frac{1}{P}\frac{dP}{dt}; w; \frac{Y}{r}; u \right) \tag{5.6}$$

Here the corrections to the interest-rates measure capital gains (for bonds (b) and equities (e)); the rate on equities is a real rate (r), while that on bonds is a nominal rate (i); the own-rate on money is $(1/P)$ (dP/dt) as a proxy for expected inflation; Y represents the return to all forms of wealth (so that Y/r is a measure of wealth itself, interpreted as a perpetuity); w is the ratio of non-human wealth to human wealth; and u is a variable representing tastes.[6] Neglecting w and u, equating the nominal rates on assets to each other, referring to the yield on money as i_m and proxying Y/r with Y, we can produce the very familiar $M^d = f(P, i, i_m, Y)$. Then, if the function is homogeneous of degree one in money prices (recall that $Y = Py$), we have

$$\left(\frac{M}{P}\right)^{d} = f^{*}(i, i_m, y) \tag{5.7}$$

If, again, the real income elasticity of the demand for money is unity, we can

factor out that term so that we have

$$\frac{(M/P)^{\mathrm{d}}}{y} \equiv \frac{M^{\mathrm{d}}}{Y} = f^{**}(i, i_{\mathrm{m}}) \tag{5.8}$$

whence it is seen that with the neoclassical assumption of homogeneity and with the *ad hoc* assumption on income, velocity (the left-hand term) still depends on interest rates (at equilibrium).

In terms of the preceding discussion the argument, in effect, is that k, the proportionality factor, should also be taken as depending on interest rates. What Friedman does, then, is transform a proposition about the constancy of velocity to one that requires only that $f^{**}(\cdot)$ be *stable*. In that case any change in the quantity of money will have predictable effects on both prices and velocity:

> The quantity theorist accepts the empirical hypothesis that the demand for money is highly stable . . . the quantity theorist need not, and generally does not, mean that the real quantity demanded per unit of output, or the velocity of circulation of money, is to be regarded as numerically constant over time. (Friedman, 1956, p. 16)

As noted, he expects the demand for money to be stable and, hence, the velocity function to be stable. The reason for the few key variables seems simply to be doubts over achieving stability of the function if a lot of things matter (some at one time and some at another). This should lay to rest any notion that monetarists, at least, regard the velocity of money as necessarily a constant.[7]

The remainder of this section will consider recent discussions of velocity, organized around the debate over the rather surprising decline in velocity in the USA. We will, in the following, consider explanations – including Friedman's – of this phenomenon and then present some simple results from a battery of Granger-causality tests of the hypotheses that emerge from the discussion. The data are basically the same Divisia monetary aggregates employed in other illustrations in this study, the quarterly US data from 1970–85.

5.3.2 Unstable velocity in the 1980s?[8]

In recent years there has been a resurgence of interest in the determinants of the velocity of money in the USA, primarily as the result of a rather substantial decline in the income-velocity series, beginning around 1981 and continuing intermittently since then. This apparent deviation is statistically unusual in that income velocity had generally been growing for a long time prior to 1981. Now obviously if one is interested in the behaviour of income velocity, then the long upward trend is also an interesting empirical regularity, but be that as it may, the present situation has been around long enough to provoke a substantial flurry of scholarly papers.[9]

Let us be perfectly clear, before getting down to details, on the possible determinants of velocity from a money-demand perspective (see Gordon, 1984). Suppose that the short-run money-demand function is (in logs)

$$m_t - p_t = \alpha_0 + \alpha_1 y_t - \alpha_2 i_t + \alpha_3 (m_{t-1} - p_{t-1}) + e_t \tag{5.9}$$

This is the Goldfeld (1973) formulation. When we log-difference the equation of exchange, velocity is given by

$$v_t = p_t + y_t - m_t \tag{5.10}$$

After a direct substitution between Equations (5.9) and (5.10), the following describes velocity:

$$v_t = -\alpha_0 + (1 - \alpha_1) y_t + \alpha_2 i_t - \alpha_3 (m_{t-1} - p_{t-1}) - e_t \tag{5.11}$$

In this form the *variable* determinants of velocity are y_t, i_t and lagged real balances; the *structural* determinants are embedded in α_1, α_2 and α_3; and the random components are measured by e_t, the error term in the money-demand equation. If, in fact, the interest rate is a random walk (or, further, if income is), then this equation can be interpreted as a reduced form; see the discussions in Chapter 2 for the interest rate and in West (1988) for income. Be that as it may, this formulation will put most of the following discussion into perspective.

The debate that has arisen concerns quite a few specific hypotheses about the determinants of velocity. In the first instance it has been suggested that the decline of velocity is the result of changes in the financial (or even non-financial) structure of the US economy. One very popular view, for example, is that the introduction of interest-paying cheque accounts has increased the demand for money (that is for M1 and all broader measures) without, in turn, stimulating any offsetting rise in income. In this event velocity falls, as long as the money-supply process accommodates the pressure. As a result of this influence the demand for money is essentially destabilized and a so-called monetarist-style monetary policy becomes infeasible, at least in so far as the function is shifting erratically.[10] Along somewhat the same lines mention has been made of the possibility that tax cuts have had an influence on velocity.[11]

Another view argues that since velocity is a function of nominal interest rates, any unusual pattern in inflation, which would tend to be captured in the nominal interest rate by means of the Fisher effect, would produce a change in velocity in the same direction.[12] The mechanism here involves the demand for money in that as the inflation rate falls, money becomes more attractive relative to some other assets, an attraction which is captured by the nominal interest rate (an argument in the demand for money function). In so far as the authorities accommodate this increased quantity demanded, the stock of money would rise and velocity would fall (*ceteris paribus*!). Since a positive empirical link between nominal interest rates and velocity has often been reported, this is certainly a mainstream view. It is not, however, a direct causal relation. For that we may well require an explanation of why the

inflation rate itself declined. Note that this argument does not necessarily imply an unstable demand for money, although it could.

An interest-rate variable is included successfully in a test conducted by Tatom (1983) who also includes a long list of other variables that have been suggested as causal agents operating on the money stock, real income or, of course, on their ratio (velocity). Here the determinants of velocity are money growth, the growth rate of high-employment government expenditures, energy prices, the current change in the GNP gap, changes in a key bond interest rate, the inflation rate and even a strike 'dummy'. These tend both to explain velocity up until 1981 and to provide an effective forecasting equation for the early days of the period of unusual velocity behaviour (just as if no structural change had occurred). We note, especially, that money growth is successful in Tatom's test (and is also successful in the tests reported below). Even so, this is clearly not a very useful framework for forecasting (and hence for monetary policy) because there are so many variables involved and, worse, because many of them are more obvious *ex post* than *ex ante*.

Another approach in the literature is that a potential explanatory variable – apparently not obvious at earlier times – is now relevant; this is the 'volatility of money growth' suggested by Friedman (1984). What Friedman argues is that increased uncertainty in financial markets – itself caused by the increased volatility of money after the 1979 change of Federal Reserve policy-operating techniques – produces an increased demand for money for (essentially) precautionary purposes and, assuming the money-supply process accommodates the pressure, a rise in money-holding relative to nominal income. One way of putting this hypothesis (more directly) is that money growth and its variability *Granger-cause* velocity and do so by reducing real income and/or by increasing the demand for money. Money and/or nominal income could also be Granger-caused by these variables, presumably in either of these scenarios.

By all accounts, the change in operating procedures by the Federal Reserve in October 1979 was associated with increased volatility in all measures of the money stock and in all interest rates. By 1981, the decline in velocity that appears to continue beyond the time period studied here was in progress. Commenting not on the behaviour of velocity as such, but on the ability of monetarism to cope with these disorders, Friedman (1984, p. 398) suggests 'the period from 1980 to 1983 . . . has been characterized by a succession of abnormally short cyclical phases . . . Monetarists attribute this result to the corresponding abnormally short and exceptionally volatile gyrations in monetary growth.' (1984, p. 398) This, clearly, links the volatility of money with the real cyclical experiences of this period.

Where *velocity* enters the story is in the transmission mechanism between the increased volatility of the money stock and real income. Friedman's explanation of the linkage comes in two stages. First, Friedman says that the fall in the inflation rate which ultimately occurred in this period was actually greater than the decline in the rate of growth of the money stock. This he

attributes 'not to a pre-announced slowing of monetary growth, but rather to the exceptional volatility of monetary growth, which increased the degree of perceived uncertainty and thereby increased the demand for money' (p. 399). Thus, the authorities willing, the stock of money would increase, and velocity would decrease, *ceteris paribus*. Of course, standard portfolio models of the demand for money also support this reasoning (e.g. Tobin, 1958, and Klein, 1977), so this clearly is a reasonably mainstream view. Second, Friedman says: 'The inertia in inflation and the lengthy lag between monetary change and inflation mean, of course, that the short-run influence of money on nominal income will be reflected primarily in movements in real income'. (p. 400) This, too, would lower velocity when monetary variability increases.

Pretty clearly, then, there are several ways to go. Since the hypothesis apparently involves the demand for money, an important question concerns the effect of the increased volatility of money supply on money demand itself. This topic has been addressed frequently in the recent literature in the form of the effect of inflation volatility (or of interest-rate volatility) on a representative money-demand function. The results are mixed, but even so it is certainly likely that the mechanism postulated by Friedman exists, and it is probable, but far from certain, that inflation uncertainty increased the US demand for money in this period.[13]

It would seem, then, that what might be done, to verify the links in the 'monetary velocity' hypothesis is to test for two things:

1. Does monetary variability *cause* velocity?
2. Does monetary variability *cause* real income?

If the answer to the first question is 'yes', while the answer to the second is 'no', then it is certainly clear that we have an explanation of the determinants of velocity and of inflation that focuses on the demand for money as an integral part of the transmission process without there being any 'distorting' effects on real variables. A parallel test of (2) is offered later in this chapter, but for now we will consider the details of a test of Proposition (1) on the US data.

The data in these first tests are the quarterly measures of the money stock published by the Federal Reserve and MQ, as defined in Chapter 1. In Chapter 2 we determined that differenced-logarithms of the US monetary data would render the data stationary, and the data were so transformed before the following tests were performed; they are referred to as 'money growth' and 'velocity growth' in what follows. The measures of money (and velocity) use the conventional monetary definitions (SumM1, SumM2, M1D, M2D) except for MQ, which is the velocity-weighted index number proposed by Spindt (1985). This index will prove to have some empirical value in our exhibitions here, but recall that a satisfactory theoretical rationale for such a measure is unavailable.

To test the hypothesis that money growth causes velocity growth, we specify an equation where the growth rate of velocity is regressed on lagged

Table 5.1 Tests of Granger-causality from money growth to velocity growth (1970–85)

Effect	Cause	6 lags	4 lags	2 lags	FPE lags	
SumM1 velocity	SumM1	2.550*	3.689*	5.725*	[1, 1]	9.368*
		(0.034)	(0.011)	(0.006)		(0.003)
SumM2 velocity	SumM2	1.729	1.971	1.346	[1, 0]	(*a*)
		(0.274)	(0.139)	(0.114)		
Divisia M1 velocity	Divisia M1	2.367*	2.546*	5.312	[1, 1]	6.110*
		(0.047)	(0.052)	(0.008)		(0.016)
Divisia M2 velocity	Divisia M2	2.570*	1.543	0.306	[1, 0]	(*a*)
		(0.033)	(0.205)	(0.738)		
MQ velocity	MQ	3.420*	2.585*	5.100*	[1, 1]	8.053*
		(0.008)	(0.049)	(0.009)		(0.005)

(*a*) No lag was chosen for the causal variable in these cases.
The numbers in parentheses are *p*-values (significance of 0.05 or better is indicated with an asterisk).

values of velocity growth and lagged values of money growth; this is the procedure commonly used in tests of Granger-causality. The precise specification is

$$\Delta v_t = \alpha_0 + \sum_{i=1}^{r} \alpha_i \Delta v_{t-i} + \sum_{j=1}^{s} \beta_j \Delta m_{t-j} + u_t \qquad (5.12)$$

where v_t and m_t are logarithms of velocity and a money stock measure, respectively, and u_t is a stochastic disturbance. Note that the lengths of the lags (r, s) are not necessarily equal.

In this test we are interested in the effect on velocity of changes in both money growth and its variability. The hypothesis tested successfully by Tatom (but not in a causal framework) is that money growth affects real income. To test to see if money causes velocity in the Granger sense, Equation (5.12) is first estimated by ordinary least squares, and the unrestricted sum of squared residuals, SSR_u, is obtained. Then, by running another regression under the restriction that all βs are zero, the restricted sum of squared residuals, SSR_r, is obtained. If u_t is white noise, then the statistic computed as the ratio of $(SSR_r - SSR_u)/s$ to $SSR_u/(n-r-s-1)$ has an asymptotic F-distribution with the numerator having degrees of freedom of s and the denominator of $n-r-s-1$. Put in the form of the Granger test, we see the results in Table 5.1 for the quarterly US data.

The set-up of Table 5.1 is as follows. First, the main entries given are values of the F-statistic, as described above, comparing the sums of squares between the unrestricted and the restricted regressions. Underneath, in parentheses, are the p-values (probabilities) associated with these F-statistics; a level of 0.05 is set arbitrarily to assert causality. The set of five tests indicates, pretty clearly, that three of these aggregates show a causal influence on the growth of velocity. These causal results occur with the narrowest measures of money (Divisia M1 and SumM1) and with MQ, the transactions-velocity

Table 5.2 The influence of money-stock variability on the velocity of money (changes in the standard deviations of the data)

Effect	Cause	6 lags	4 lags	2 lags	FPE lags	
SumM1 velocity	SumM1	1.976 (0.109)	3.283* (0.032)	1.670 (0.201)	[3, 0]	(*a*)
SumM2 velocity	SumM2	0.670 (0.649)	0.986 (0.410)	1.417 (0.254)	[1, 0]	(*a*)
Divisia M1 velocity	Divisia M1	1.808 (0.139)	3.016* (0.042)	3.961* (0.027)	[3, 0]	(*a*)
Divisia M2 velocity	Divisia M2	1.326 (0.275)	2.478 (0.077)	2.785 (0.074)	[3, 0]	(*a*)
MQ velocity	MQ	2.497* (0.051)	4.103* (0.013)	0.144 (0.866)	[2, 0]	(*a*)

(*a*) There were no significant lags on the causal variables.
The table contains *F*-values and the numbers in parentheses are levels of significance.
*Indicates significance at the 0.05 level or better.

measure of moneyness. Since the narrower measures are intended to be of transactions balances, the evidence here is clearly that the recent behaviour of velocity is related to the behaviour of transactions rather than, say, savings balances, even though most measures of velocity show the decline.

The last column in Table 5.1 presents statistics from an important part of the test just laid out. This concerns the length of the lags, r and s, as specified in Equation (5.10). In the literature, r and s are frequently chosen so that the independent variables have identical lag lengths. This is done, in the other columns in the table, but since it is clearly arbitrary, and since it has been shown that Granger-causality tests are sensitive to the lag structure specified (Hsiao, 1979*a*, *b*), an alternative approach is employed in order to appraise the sensitivity of our results to the lag specification. This involves using Akaike's (1970) final prediction error (FPE) criterion to select (from the data) the optimal lags for each of the independent variables. The FPE is calculated as the product of $(n+r+s+1)/(n-r-s-1)$ and SSR/n, where n is the number of observations and SSR is the sum of squared residuals. This procedure balances the fit of the equation with the degrees of freedom and is judged by an F-test. The results, with the lags chosen appearing in square brackets, are given in the last column of Table 5.1; they show that the optimal lag structures are generally quite short. The Divisia M1, in particular, has only a one-quarter lag on the independent variable. This is a very short lag, although, of course, we are not comparing level figures here. Even so, the results obtained with the arbitrary lags are still upheld, at least in so far as the identification of the causal agent on monetary velocity is concerned.

The second variable recently proposed as an influence on the behaviour of velocity is that of the variability of money growth; this suggestion is Friedman's and is tested by Belongia (1984) and Hall and Noble (1987); the latter use a Granger-causality approach. The formal econometric model is

the same as before (in Equation (5.12)). Table 5.2 presents the results of the test for the influence of money-stock variability on the various possible velocities of money. Again, we present results for three arbitrary lags and for the lags judged as optimal by the Akaike final prediction error test (in the last column).

These results indicate a partial confirmation of the monetary variability hypothesis, although not by the Akaike criterion, where only lagged dependent variables are chosen. In any case, the standard deviations of the narrower measures of money, whether MQ or Divisia, cause the appropriate measure of velocity. These results over both tests indicate that so long as a shorter measure of money (M1 or MQ based) is selected, both the monetary-growth and the monetary-variability hypotheses come through fairly clearly. Variability is a little less obvious here, although in other results on *monthly* data (Fisher and Serletis, 1989) it does show up strongly.

5.4 MONETARY POLICY AND MONEY DEMAND: THE ROLE OF EXPECTATIONS

This section begins with a Phillips-relation explanation of monetary policy in an adaptive-expectations context. The material is both useful and relevant in view of the style of recent monetary policy, and it also provides a backdrop for the consideration of the role of rational expectations in the debate over monetary policy. This material is the subject of Section 5.4.2. Note that in contrast to Chapter 4, monetary policy is thought of here in a much more activist way, generally along Keynesian lines. That is, we have parked the helicopter for the most part and will now look at monetary policy models that involve both a stabilization role for the authorities and a precise role for money demand in the transmission of cyclical and long-run influences.

5.4.1 Adaptive expectations and money demand

To begin with, let us note that two straightforward ways to introduce monetary non-neutrality in the short-run are by means of a Phillips relation or, even more simply, by employing adaptive expectations (perhaps to represent money illusion on the part of economic agents). To see how these notions might be integrated in a useful and general way involving money demand, consider the following result, drawn from Sargent (1979). Suppose that we have a stochastic (hence u_t) expectations-augmented Phillips curve (where all variables are in logs) of

$$y_t = \gamma(p_t - p^*_{t-1}) + \lambda y_{t-1} + u_t \tag{5.13}$$

Here the difference between (the log of) the expected and actual price level contributes to real activity in addition to the persistence in the real income series (contributed by the lagged value of real income). The influence of the

price term exists because errors in predicting overall prices produce mistakes in, e.g., real spending. Assume, also, that there is a 'portfolio balance' equation of

$$m_t - p_t = y_t + e_t \tag{5.14}$$

again written in the logarithms of the variables. This second expression arises from equilibrium in the money/bonds market. The potential non-neutrality of money is contained in the coefficient $\gamma(>0)$ and in a third relation that assumes that inflationary expectations are formed adaptively.

$$p^*_{t-1} = V(L)p_{t-1} \equiv \sum_{i=0}^{\infty} v_i p_{t-i-1} \tag{5.15}$$

Here $V(L)$ is a function describing the v_i – the weights on past (log) prices – and L is the lag operator. Note that the disturbances to the system are real (u_t) or monetary (e_t) where the latter include policy shocks and/or shocks to the money-demand function. Following such a shock, the adaptive Phillips relation produces the cyclical response.

Let us assume, still following Sargent, that the authorities seek to minimize the following loss function by picking particular values of the monetary quantities; they do so in a manner to be described in a moment. Here d is the 'mean square error'.

$$d_t = E(y_t - y^*)^2 \tag{5.16}$$

This function contains the incentive for taking advantage of money's potential non-neutrality. To see this, square the term on the right-hand side of Equation (5.16) and then rearrange to get the following:

$$d_t = E[(y_t - Ey)^2] + (Ey_t - y^*)^2 \tag{5.17}$$

Here the first term is the variance of real income, and the second describes the disutility that arises from missing the target (squared), given the variance in y (given the first term). The second term then provides the incentive just noted.

To pick the optimal time path of m_t, given the real and monetary shocks, we need to solve for the time path of real income expressed as a function of these three exogenous influences. Note the assumption that m_t will be set *before* u_t and e_t are known. If Equations (5.13), (5.14) and (5.15) are combined, we have an expression for real income entirely in exogenous variables (a *reduced form* for y_t):

$$y_t = H(L)m_t + G(L)e_t + F(L)u_t \tag{5.18}$$

where

$$H(L) = \frac{\gamma(1 - LV(L))}{1 + \gamma - (\lambda + \gamma V(L))L} = \sum_{i=0}^{\infty} h_i L^i = -G(L) = -\sum_{i=0}^{\infty} g_i L^i$$

$$F(L) = \frac{1}{1 + \gamma - (\lambda + \gamma V(L))L} = \sum_{i=0}^{\infty} f_i L^i$$

What the authorities will do in this situation is pick their m_t based on the following linear feedback rule, where the *lagged* values of the errors are presumed to be known to them but the current values (at time t) are not.

$$m_t = k + A(L)e_{t-1} + B(L)u_{t-1} \tag{5.19}$$

Note again that the authorities are setting m in period t based on an arbitrary lag in their information. The expressions $A(L)$ and $B(L)$ are defined as follows:

$$A(L) = \sum_{i=0}^{\infty} a_i L^i \quad \text{and} \quad B(L) = \sum_{i=0}^{\infty} b_i L^i$$

The authorities are assumed to know, at time t, all the parameters of the model and all the values of the data for periods up to and including $t-1$. They will pick k (which is, in effect, a monetarist rule), $A(L)$, and $B(L)$ assuming that the structure just laid out remains unchanged. The choice of $A(L)$ and $B(L)$ is the 'fine-tuning' (i.c. activist) part of policy.

To see what happens when they operate policy in this way, substitute Equation (5.19) into Equation (5.18) to get

$$y_t = kH(1) + [G(L) + \phi(L)]e_t + [F(L) + \theta(L)]u_t \tag{5.20}$$

where

$$\phi(L) = \sum_{i=1}^{\infty} \phi_i L^i = H(L)A(L)L$$

$$\theta(L) = \sum_{i=1}^{\infty} \theta_i L^i = H(L)B(L)L$$

Here, assuming a Phillips relation and adaptive expectations, the policy authorities can alter the time path of income by picking suitable values of k, $\phi(L)$ and $\theta(L)$. The latter are achieved by picking the a_i and the b_i, of course. They will do this in an attempt to minimize the contributions of the two variances e_t and u_t to the time path of income. To see this procedure and its limitations more explicitly (still following Sargent), we can calculate the variance of y_t directly from Equation (5.20) – assuming, as we are, that e_t and *ut* are uncorrelated. This produces

$$\text{var}\, y_t = \text{var}\, e_t \left[g_0^2 + \sum_{i=1}^{\infty} (g_i + \phi_i)^2 \right] + \text{var}\, u_t \left[f_0^2 + \sum_{i=1}^{\infty} (f_i + \theta_i)^2 \right] \tag{5.21}$$

whereby a setting of the parameters such that

$$\phi(L) = -\sum_{i=1}^{\infty} g_i L^i \quad \text{and} \quad \theta(L) = -\sum_{i=1}^{\infty} f_i L^i$$

will clearly reduce the variance of y_t in Equation (5.21) to its minimum $(= g_0^2\sigma_e^2 + f_0^2\sigma_u^2)$. This value is then irreducible current noise that the authorities are not in a position to recognize or counteract (by assumption).

The result, clearly, is that any recognizable cycle in y_t is completely eliminated in this ideal policy setting. Of course, this strong result is questionable in practice since the approach ignores rational expectations (in favour of adaptive) and assumes that the authorities know the exact structure of the economy. The approach also assumes that the structure itself does not alter in response to the policy (as is implied by the Lucas, 1976, critique). As we will now see, replacing the word 'adaptive' with 'rational' alters the possible range of monetary policy, at least theoretically.

5.4.2 Rational expectations in the policy/money-demand context

Rational expectations provides a comprehensive reorientation of neoclassical economics that has been dubbed the 'new classical macroeconomics'. Much of the discussion in this literature involves the neutrality of money and so, in the following paragraphs, we will look at some basic – and very simple – results pertaining to the contributions of the rational expectations 'revolution' to these debates. This section and Section 5.5.1 also looks at what almost amounts to a consensus revision of this simple theory and, then, in order to finish off the discussion, the remainder of Section 5.5 considers a sample of recent empirical evidence.

Rational expectations, according to Muth:

> asserts three things: (1) Information is scarce, and the economic system generally does not waste it. (2) The way expectations are formed depends specifically on the structure of the relevant system describing the economy. (3) A 'public prediction' . . . will have no substantial effect on the operation of the economic system (unless it is based on inside information). (1961, p. 316)

Under rational expectations, then, individuals do not knowingly make systematic errors in their predictions but act on the basis of their predictions. The predictions of economic agents are not always correct, of course, but they are the best that individuals can manage under their particular circumstances. If, for example, a change in monetary policy is expected and if economic agents have a clear idea of the effect on them, they will do their best (considering the costs of action and any other constraints that bind them), to try to profit from – or, at least, to avoid any losses from – the policy. Indeed, their reactions to policy might well render the policy ineffective or materially change the timing of its effect either because they are able to offset the effects of policy (e.g. start saving for an expected policy-induced recession) or because their reactions could (in effect) alter the parameters of the authorities' model and cause its predictions to go awry.[14] In any case, rational expectations undermines the case for the short-run non-neutrality of money in so far as the non-neutrality is produced by adaptive expectations and (other kinds of) money illusion which are based on what we are implicitly calling 'irrational' decision-making.

To see a basic rational result in the simplest possible way, let us set down yet another version of the Phillips relation, this one being the Lucas supply

function (1973). This is actually very similar to Equation (5.13) without the built-in persistence. Let us assume that aggregate supply is explained by Equation (5.22), in which output (y_t) depends on the *normal* level of output (y_n) and the difference between the price level in t and that expected in $t-1$ to rule for t; the variables are again assumed to be measured in log form:

$$y_t = y_n + \alpha(p_t - p_t^e) + \varepsilon_t \tag{5.22}$$

Note especially that since the term $(p_t - p_t^e)$ is the error in the prediction of the log of the price level, we are accepting that there could be some potential for nominal events, e.g. a money supply shock, to influence real activity. This potential non-neutrality is on the level of the usual 'mistakes' rationalization for the Phillips trade-off. Here, to provide an example, policy affects aggregate supply by causing workers to make errors (they have to forecast the price level when contracts are drawn up). In particular, if they underpredict the price level, they will end up providing additional labour services for which they did not originally plan, and actual output will, accordingly, be higher. In effect, they will be offering their services at a lower real wage, and more of their services will be demanded (and used).

Because we are assuming rational expectations, we can jump ahead to the solution for the price level after applying the property (mentioned above) that individuals actually do not make systematic mistakes. That is, rational expectations implies that actual prices can be described by

$$p_t = p_t^e + \mu_t \tag{5.23}$$

where the error reflects random elements wherever they arise in the (unspecified) structural model. When we substitute Equation (5.23) into Equation (5.22), we obtain

$$y_t = y_n + \alpha\mu_t + \varepsilon_t \tag{5.24}$$

Thus, under rational expectations, at least as this model (a supply-side model only) is laid out, output deviates from its natural rate only because of the random shocks μ_t and ε_t. Clearly, the scope for policy is not going to be considerable in this model.

Now let us create a somewhat richer structure by including an aggregate demand equation as in

$$y_t = -\beta_1 p_t + \beta_2 m_t \tag{5.25}$$

This has as right-hand variables the log of the price level and the log of an unspecified and exogenous policy variable (in m_t). Here money demand plays an essentially passive role. If the price level is solved for across both aggregate demand, Equation (5.25), and aggregate supply, Equation (5.22), we obtain

$$p_t = \frac{1}{\alpha + \beta_1}(\alpha p_t^e + \beta_2 m_t - y_n - \varepsilon_t) \tag{5.26}$$

which describes the path of the price level in this somewhat richer model. Since price expectations, if they are assumed to be rational, should be based on the same model that actually generates prices, we directly have that the unspecified price expectation in Equation (5.26) is

$$p_t^e = E\left[\frac{1}{\alpha+\beta_1}(\alpha p_t^e + \beta_2 m_t - y_n - \varepsilon_t)\right] \tag{5.27}$$

Taking expectations of Equation (5.27), then, we have the result that price expectations are given by

$$p_t^e = \frac{1}{\alpha+\beta_1}(\alpha p_t^e + \beta_2 Em_t - y_n) \tag{5.28}$$

We define the error in the prediction of prices as the difference between p_t and p_t^e; this calculation produces

$$p_t - p_t^e = \frac{1}{\alpha+\beta_1}[\beta_2(m_t - Em_t) - \varepsilon_t] \tag{5.29}$$

When this expression is substituted into the aggregate supply, Equation (5.22), we have

$$y_t = y_n + \frac{1}{\alpha+\beta_1}[\beta_2(m_t - Em_t) - \varepsilon_t] - \varepsilon_t \tag{5.30}$$

Thus, fluctuations of real output around its natural level depend both on the shocks in the aggregate supply curve (we could also have shocked the demand curve) and on errors in predicting the policy variable(s). This last would have an *expected* value of zero under rational expectations.

To see the role of the authorities in a more concrete way, we can now specify a rule for the money supply. Let this rule be the following policy reaction function:

$$m_t = \delta_1 m_{t-1} + \mu_t \tag{5.31}$$

Here policy can take the form of a change in the reaction coefficient δ_1 or it can take the form of a random shock (a change in μ_t). If it is the former, rational (and observant) individuals will recognize it and re-solve the system for a new p_t^e; in that event p_t will also change. If they get it right, and we are making it part of a systematic (and very naïve) passive feedback policy that is easily recognizable (because the policy is in the coefficient on m_{t-1}), then Equation (5.23) will still hold. Equation (5.24) will also hold so that the policy will produce a neutral result in the sense of not affecting y_t (or unemployment). If the individuals get it wrong, on the other hand, there will be a temporary effect which will disappear as soon as they recognize the systematic error being made. Once again, policy is neutral, although possibly not in the short run. A shock (a change in δ_t) will have an effect but by its unsystematic nature can hardly help the economy in any obvious way. Thus,

in this basic example, money (i.e. monetary policy) is neutral under rational expectations.

5.5 MONETARY EXPLANATIONS OF BUSINESS CYCLES

The next topic concerns an extension of the basic rational expectations result into the area of business-cycle theory. It is not hard to provide explanations of business cycles that emulate what we know about these events, at least in a general sense, but it has proved to be difficult to pick among the various candidates within or across the broad categories. Still speaking generally, the tendency in the literature has been to divide the causes into 'monetary' and 'real' and then, in view of the strong suspicion that monetary forces are less likely to have produced (at least) recent cyclical events, to concentrate on what is sometimes described as the 'real business cycle'. This chapter is not interested in the latter branch of the subject, since it is the monetary-induced real event on which we are working, but we should note that the frequent declarations of the demise of monetary causes seem to be premature – over a longer stretch of data than merely post-World War II – and so there is clearly more than academic interest in the following discussion.

There are three obvious ways in which the quantity of (or the rate of growth of) money might become involved in the generation of business cycles. One of these is simply that the existence of money, or some (institutional) characteristic of the way it operates in the system, makes money part of the *persistence* in the system. Then, following any sort of shock, there could be cycles in which money is part of the continuing story. In a sense, 'money illusion' of some sort – probably represented by a lag in response – is a typical example of this particular role. A second way money might become involved is as an independent *shock* to the system. Thus, a bank failure might trigger responses which economic agents spread over time irrespective of whether money is itself involved in persistence (whether or not money markets clear quickly, for example). A third interesting way in which money is involved is also as a shock, but in this case as a *policy-induced shock*. In this case the authorities administer the shock (or, less controversially, the policy), and money has an effect because of the features of the economic system. The literature pursues these themes, in a somewhat scattered fashion, with a heavy emphasis on monetary-policy shocks. Note, especially, that cycles will not occur without persistence of some sort and that a cause (a shock) is also required. This means that most of our theoretical (and especially empirical) discussion will necessarily blend these two elements.

5.5.1 Persistence in real business cycle models

The first thing we need to do is lay out the rules for persistence in general. What we mean by the term is the influence of an action (or decision) in period

t on variables (or decisions) in periods $t+1$, $t+2$, ... In some ways the most promising possibilities would seem to lie in the behaviour of inventories (held for future sale), in the lags inherent in the durability of consumption and investment goods or even in utilizing real-balance effects, at least if they are spread over time (Minford and Peel, 1981). The investment/capital stock angle has been exploited since the 1930s in the accelerator–multiplier model (e.g. Samuelson, 1939). A recent manifestation of this appears in Lucas (1975) where the inherited capital stock is introduced so that a shock to the system produces both a labour-supply and an investment-demand response. The effect persists, then, so long as the desired capital stock is less than the actual; this adjustment could easily take several periods. The same thing happens in a model with inventories in it (see Blinder and Fischer, 1981) in which several periods are needed to restock or run down inventories following a shock to the system. Indeed, inventory behaviour, with a natural lag embedded in it, provides a possibility that is widely thought to be important in contemporary cycles. Again, what all these devices do is suggest how shocks (in our case to money demand or money supply) are converted to potential cyclical (or at least multiperiod) responses through persistence.

In a paper that has received a lot of attention, Long and Plosser (1983) generate an equilibrium business cycle model in which there is no government *and no money* and in which business cycles are generated by shocks that are spread over time because of the optimizing actions of economic agents who prefer to smooth their consumption and production spending over time. Active monetary policy turns out to be wasteful of resources in the Long–Plosser model, but it is not in an alternative paper by King and Plosser (1984) which adds an internal monetary sector (producing monetary services) to the basic equilibrium business cycle model. In the King and Plosser model 'a positive correlation (comovement) of real production, credit, and transactions services arises from the general equilibrium of production and consumption decisions by firms and households' (p. 367). In particular, bank deposits (the only money in their model) turn out to be positively correlated with real output. King and Plosser argue that a 'higher than average' shock to the output production function will increase transactions, especially in the factor markets, without having much effect on consumption or leisure. This would generate money-demand responses *before* final output responses and therefore produce a *lead* of money over real activity. Below, the point will be made that a frequent result in the causality literature shows money leading real activity (this is also described as possible evidence of non-neutrality). The result of the King and Plosser study is the finding that such a result can occur because the money market reacts first when the actual cause is a shock to, e.g., the production function. This is a real and not a monetary shock.

When the government is introduced into the King and Plosser model as the creator of an alternative 'transactions service' (currency), which is itself not a perfect substitute for bank deposits, whether money is neutral in this model depends on whether the banking system is regulated. It should be recalled

that this is the generally conceded result in systems in which money is produced without any real resources being used, as discussed in Chapter 4 under the heading of the 'net wealth effect'. Otherwise, as King and Plosser point out, in their model there is monetary neutrality. One of the interesting implications of the model is that a rise in real activity produces a fall in the inflation rate, a property that appeals more to monetarists than to Keynesians, although it is a frequent result of Keynesian models such as this one.

Still on the topic of persistence, an 'informational advantage' approach to price setting is another way to proceed, while still operating under rational expectations. For example, Phelps and Taylor (1977) consider the case where firms set their prices in one period $(t-1)$ in advance of the period (t) in which they expect to sell their products. Firms, in this instance, are assumed to know the structure of the economy, including the role of the monetary authorities. Firms, having bound themselves to contracts, cannot react, and real shocks (or monetary policies) thereby acquire some leverage; this mechanism clearly provides persistence and a real (cyclical) role for money. It has a pseudonym, as well, for this is an instance of the venerable 'price stickiness' so often emphasized by Keynesians. Recent versions of this general idea are available in McCallum (1986*b*) and Mankiw (1985); the latter assumes an element of monopoly in firms' price-setting behaviour.[15]

A second approach which considers contracts is the work of Fischer whose 1977 paper provides an accessible model for purposes of elaboration on the basic point about contractually related persistence. Fischer assumes that labour contracts run for two periods so that there is a kind of stickiness to wages. Here we assume monetary policy can be changed more frequently than wages and so, once again, the authorities have an edge that they can take advantage of. The rationale for entering into such contracts is essentially that of cost saving and/or risk sharing. In period t, workers form expectations for $t+1$ and $t+2$ and sign binding nominal wage contracts. In $t+1$ a new set of workers signs contracts (running to $t+3$); these are referred to in the literature as 'staggered contracts'. At any time, there is a stock of contracts, some in their first year and some in their second. At t, both 'new' workers and the central bank face the same information set; under rational expectations there is nothing the central bank can do in period t to affect output since it has no leverage over workers' decisions. Presumably, both future years of the contract initiated at period t will contain rational expectations of the real conditions workers will face in $t+1$ and $t+2$. In $t+1$, by assumption, there will be new, stochastic information available to the central bank. At that point the central bank will be able to produce a change in the money stock based on the new information, which will affect the real conditions of all workers in the second year of their contracts. This, in turn, implies an effect on real output and employment. Thus, even under rational expectations, as long as there are still good reasons for setting up long-term contracts, monetary policy works in the sense of providing a short-

run trade-off between monetary expansion and employment. It is persistence that guarantees an effect; it is monetary policy that causes it.[16]

One such effect occurs because changes in the rate of inflation affect financial contracts that are written in nominal terms (e.g. bond 'contracts'). Such contracts could in principle contain explicit or implicit inflation forecasts, but most do not; if they do not, then economic agents will experience price-induced wealth effects whenever the price level changes. One important asset for which no contract exists is cash. In this case, whether inflation is expected or not, agents will be taxed by inflation as long as cash is at all useful (presumably it is useful for transactions purposes). However its effect is rationalized; this operation of a wealth effect will tend to alter the rate of capital formation in the economy and thus, presumably, employment and output.

Finally, we can build a model in which the authorities' information advantage gives them no ability to control real variables but in which real variables respond to money stock announcements containing new information (Siegel, 1985). That is, assuming that the government has more timely information when the money stock is announced, the private sector, too, is let in on the secret and makes the appropriate real adjustments. So money has a real effect – that is, it is part of the real business cycle – because of its information content, but policy itself is still ineffective. This seems to be an important distinction. It also makes money part of the persistence mechanism.

5.5.2 Money and real income: efforts to determine causality

Let us begin by going over an original Granger-causality test on the link between money growth and real income growth for the USA to see if such an effect exists; this is a continuation of the material introduced in the discussion of velocity. As it turns out, there is no universally accepted definition of causality, but the one most used in economics is known as *Granger-causality* (see Granger, 1969). A useful statement of this in a time series context is by Feige and Pearce: 'Heuristically, Granger's notion of causality states that X "causes" Y if the past history of X can be used to predict Y more accurately than simply using the past history of Y'. (1979, p. 521) It is important to note that this procedure does not deal explicitly with contemporaneous causation but only covers lagged causation (the approach thus measures what is sometimes referred to as 'predeterminedness'). This test is the one applied earlier in this chapter.

C. Sims (1972) is the first to employ this test (on US quarterly data for 1947–69) and finds – for either the monetary base or M1 as determinants of nominal GNP – that money appears to determine nominal income, but not (necessarily) the converse.[17] This is not really the issue here, because the concern is the influence of money on real variables. Be that as it may,

Table 5.3 The influence of money growth on income growth, Granger-causality tests (*F*-values and their significance)

Cause	6 lags	4 lags	2 lags	FPE lags	
SumM1	1.334	1.879	4.533*	[1, 0]	(*a*)
	(0.264)	(0.13)	(0.015)		
SumM2	1.836	2.300*	4.902*	[1, 1]	4.822*
	(0.116)	(0.073)	(0.011)		(0.032)
Divisia M1	1.091	1.710	2.548	[1, 0]	(*a*)
	(0.38)	(0.16)	(0.088)		
Divisia M2	2.111	2.730*	7.093*	[2, 2]	7.093*
	(0.073)	(0.040)	(0.002)		(0.002)
MQ	1.229	1.742	4.124*	[1, 0]	(*a*)
	(0.31)	(0.16)	(0.022)		

(*a*) In this case the Akaike procedure selected only lags of the dependent variable.
*Indicates significance at the 0.05 level or better.

numerous tests have been conducted of the influence of money on nominal income, real income and the price level without there being any universal resolution for any of these variables, at least for the short run (see D. Fisher, 1988). For the long run, there is more agreement that money is neutral (and does not affect real income).

We will calculate several sets of Granger-causality tests of the influence of money growth on real-income growth, to explain and illustrate some of the procedures. What is different here is

(a) that the test is across the different monetary aggregates; and
(b) that there are some money-variability results.

The reader should note that these tests will employ both quarterly and monthly data (the latter are used in Fisher and Serletis, 1989).[18] The first set (Table 5.3) looks at money growth as a 'cause' of income growth on quarterly data. Recall that we are using the first differences of the logs of the data in order to render them stationary. Here we see that most of the measures of moneyness show a causal influence of money growth on real-income growth, with the FPE lags (see the explanation above) on the causal variables being no more than two quarters. Money certainly does not appear to be Granger-neutral here.

Our special concern is in the influence of monetary variability on real-income growth. This influence may be the result of price distortions (and other interferences with market signals) and the general increased costliness of transactions. It also provides an additional explanation of what happened to velocity in the USA, in that a decline of real income leads to a decline of velocity, *ceteris paribus* (see Equation (5.11) above). This, though, is not our interest here. Table 5.4 carries the basic results, this time with a switch to the monthly data simply because nothing showed up in the quarterly data.

Table 5.4 The effect of money variability on income growth, Granger-causality tests (*F*-values and their significance levels in parentheses)

Cause	8 lags	6 lags	4 lags	FPE lags	
Sum M1	1.673	2.288*	1.868	[1, 5]	2.015
	(0.109)	(0.038)	(0.118)		(0.079)
Sum M2	0.917	0.902	1.005	[1, 3]	1.478
	(0.504)	(0.495)	(0.406)		(0.222)
Divisia M1	2.600*	2.837*	1.440	[1, 7]	2.849*
	(0.010)	(0.011)	(0.223)		(0.007)
Divisia M2	1.141	1.105	1.597	[1, 3]	1.228
	(0.339)	(0.361)	(0.177)		(0.301)
MQ	1.691	1.972	3.308*	[1, 4]	2.985*
	(0.104)	(0.072)	(0.012)		(0.020)

*Indicates significance at the 0.05 level or better.

From the set of results given in Table 5.4 it is clear that real-income growth appears to be influenced by the variability of the *transactions* measures of money, quite apart from how they are measured (e.g. as SumM1, Divisia M1 or MQ), although only the Divisia M1 and MQ indices come through in the FPE tests. The lag lengths are not unreasonable, running up to seven months. It seems clear, then, that monetary variability does influence real income, perhaps for the reasons suggested above. There are, of course, many other results in the literature, but we are restricting ourselves here to those connecting the money stock and money demand. Of course, it should be emphasized that we are offering tests on only a small part of the potential hypothesis space.

5.5.3 The systematic and random influences of money: empirical tests

By far the largest volume of recent material on the role of money (given persistence) concerns the influences of money shocks; the survey in Dotsey and King (1988) will get us started in this section. The general idea (Barro, 1977, 1978) is to break the money stock into an anticipated (or predicted) component and an unanticipated (or random) component and then to see if the former has a null effect and the latter a definite effect on real income (or on some other variable presumed to affect real income). What is needed to implement this distinction between anticipated and unanticipated is a *decomposition* that effects a clean separation of the data. Among the many proposals over the years are decompositions such as:

(a) the permanent/transitory distinction (with the permanent component measured by a distributed lag);
(b) the Wold decomposition (see Chapter 2); and
(c) the Beveridge–Nelson (1981) decomposition.

The problem with any of these procedures is that we are automatically involved in a complicated joint hypothesis involving a model of the economy (or a subset of the economy), rational expectations, a money-supply process and the neutrality proposition itself. In addition, there are quite a few potential measures of money. Even with these difficulties, as the following paragraphs will suggest, there is no shortage of empirical material, although what it all means at this stage is not exactly clear.

With reference to effects on real variables, Barro (1977) and Barro and Rush (1980) find *unanticipated* money affects, variously, real output and unemployment, while *anticipated* money affects only prices. These are, basically, neutrality results. These findings are echoed in several British tests (Attfield, Demery and Duck, 1981*a*,*b*). Results running the other way are provided by Mishkin (1982) and Leiderman (1983), who take advantage of certain structural characteristics of the model. More recently, disaggregated tests by Kretzmer (1985) find real wages at the industry level responding to *unanticipated* money – as should be the case – and by Chrystal and Chatterji (1987) find that *anticipated* money affects industry-level real output – as it should not do. Both tests are on US data.

The next place to look, in order to investigate the empirical record on neutrality, is the financial market place because financial markets provide real services (putting aside the questions of financial market stability that we will consider in Chapter 6) and so effects (non-neutralities) here are just as important, at least generically. The literature concentrates on the effects of policy on interest rates (i.e. on bond markets) and on stock markets, and so shall we in what follows. Note, though, that there is also a rapidly growing literature on the effects of monetary policy on particular financial institutions (especially banks), but Chapter 6 is the appropriate place to discuss that work.

When we look to interest-rate effects, we must begin by considering whether the unanticipated effect proposed is:

(a) a *nominal* interest-rate response to a money-stock announcement that is the result of agents revising their prediction of inflation e.g. upward; or
(b) a response that is in *real* interest rates because agents expect the authorities to, e.g., tighten up soon (producing a (real) effect on employment and output).

Let us start with a sample of the literature on (b) before discussing (a).

With respect to having an effect on the real rate of interest, the first question concerns whether or not the *ex ante* real rate of interest can be influenced at all. The question is raised in an empirical context by Fama (1975) who once argued that r^e has actually been constant in the USA since World War II. If this result is itself not the object of recent policy, it would suggest that there is little scope for real effects from short-run policy in the actual numbers. In any event, the case for constancy of the real rate has basically

come unglued. That is, subsequent studies (Nelson and Schwert, 1977; Garbade and Wachtel, 1978; Fama and Gibbons, 1980; and Hafer and Hein, 1982) find evidence against constancy. This is echoed in a recent test by Viren (1987) who runs tests for six OECD countries including the USA.

After 1979 both *ex post* and *ex ante* measures of the real rate of interest seem relatively high, compared with any other post-World War II data, and this result has provoked some discussion to say the least. A sharp increase in interest rate, money stock and velocity volatility, as discussed above several times, has also occurred. The most obvious hypothesis about the higher real rate is that the tighter monetary (and even fiscal) policies instituted at that time by the USA and several other major countries were simply 'unbelievable' and did not succeed in dampening inflationary expectations. Considering that these expectations are probably calculated using short moving-average processes, it is at least conceivable that a measurement error was introduced, at least for a time, in *ex post* real rates. But the relatively high (*ex post*) real interest rates have continued well past 1982 in generally prosperous economies and so this argument seems considerably less persuasive as time passes. In any case, a recent study by Hoffman and Schlagenhauf (1988) for four countries (including the UK and the USA) shows that *anticipated* inflation lowers real interest rates considerably, and *unanticipated* money also has an effect. The latter is consistent with neutrality, but the former is not.

One frequently cited test of the influence of money on *nominal* interest rates is that of Grossman (1981) who looks at private sector forecasts collected from money-market dealers who are sampled two days *before* the money-stock announcement and then again on the day of the announcement itself. Looking first to see if the forecasts and the revisions are not only unbiased but also use all available relevant information (and hence are rational), Grossman concludes that both expectations and weekly revisions are efficient (the prediction errors are orthogonal to an arbitrary but broad set of available information), and that they provide a better forecast of the money stock than an arbitrary extrapolative autoregressive money-stock forecasting equation. With regard to the effect of such monetary surprises on interest rates, Grossman finds interest 'rates respond *only* to monetary surprises, in a way which correctly incorporates the policy rule in operations. Thus the paper lends . . . support to the rational expectations monetary models.' (p. 423) More recently this has been confirmed by Roley and Walsh (1984), and there is further support on long-term interest rates in a study by Cook and Hahn (1987).

The tests just described are questioned by Nichols, Small and Webster (1983) who point out that the money-stock announcement has an effect because it actually contains new information; as such: 'The announcement provides the same, possibly surprising, information about the quantity of money *demanded* as it does about the quantity supplied.'(p. 383, my italics) This basically questions Grossman's orthogonalization. As mentioned above, some studies find *anticipated* money has an influence on real variables.

These findings also occur in the interest-rate literature in studies by Urich and Wachtel (1984), and others, as mentioned in a recent survey by Belongia and Sheehan (1987). The last-cited study also confirms the non-neutrality of money in the USA. Finally, Huizinga and Leiderman (1987) find that the announced *monetary base* has an effect on nominal interest rates exceeding that of the announcement of the money stock itself. This, too, may suggest that additional information is available on announcement dates but is not (as monetary neutrality requires) embodied solely in the money stock.

We have mentioned changes in policy regimes as having the potential for springing surprises on economic agents, and this notion has been extended to a consideration of the 'money-stock announcement' effect both before and after the October 1979 policy-regime change in the USA. Grossman's study referred to above finds a positive response to money announcement surprises solely on pre-October 1979 data. In one test looking at pre- *and* post-1979 data, Evans (*c.*1982) finds that the 1979 shift may have created a 'surprise' for the public, as judged by the behaviour of the bond market. Roley (1983), noting that the variances of both interest rates and announcements increased dramatically after October 1979 and that the authorities seem to have been more committed to a firm and coherent policy thereafter, suggests that a different and non-linear model may help to control for the apparent instability of a Grossman-style test on pre- *and* post-1979 data. He concludes:

> the change in policy regimes has significantly affected the behaviour of the three-month bill yield . . . This change in behaviour apparently reflects the market's assessment that the Federal Reserve will respond more vigorously to deviations in money when money growth is outside of the long-run range. (p. 53)

All this, of course, refers to tests in which *anticipated* money-stock changes do *not* affect interest rates.

With regard to the influence of money on the equity markets, there is a large amount of material, but much of it is less structured than might be desired, at least if the theoretical debates that have dominated so much of the material considered to this point are the standard. In fact, while the following results basically stand by themselves – and they set some interesting questions – it should be emphasized that the theory behind them is exceedingly sketchy.

A common finding in this literature is that money-stock changes simply do not have useful information for equity investors. Representative papers in this literature are by Cooper (1974), Rozeff (1974) and Rogalski and Vinso (1977); the last-named provide results from causality tests that firmly reject unidirectional causality from money to stock prices. If money does not affect stock prices, it is still possible that inflation does. Indeed, studies by Bodie (1976), Nelson (1976) and Fama and Schwert (1977) indicate that inflation in the post-War period has had a *negative* effect on the equity market. Some

of the reasons advanced for this (Feldstein, 1980; Pearce, 1982) can be summarized as follows:

1. Inflation causes the real value of depreciation to fall and real *taxable* profits to increase so that real net profits vary inversely with inflation.
2. Inflation imposes an additional tax on nominal capital gains.
3. Inflation increases the return on assets that are alternatives to equities (e.g. on houses).
4. Inflation confuses economic agents as to the true value of their equity investments.

These factors may be influential, but this sort of work seems to be partly *ex post* rationalizing, and some alternatives need to be considered.

Fama (1981), for one, argues that the negative effect of inflation on stock returns is really a spurious result appearing because the process has several stages to it. That is, stock returns and anticipated real growth rates are positively correlated (or ought to be), while inflation (if unanticipated) affects real activity adversely. Thus, stocks may still be a good hedge against inflation, *ceteris paribus*, but impounded in the *ceteris paribus* is the unpleasant real-world result that inflation affects real activity adversely, and *that* is why stock returns and inflation have a (derived) negative correlation (see Canto, Findlay and Reinganum, 1983, and Benderly and Zwick, 1985, for other explanations).

Students of the equity market have a traditional interest in evaluating the efficient-markets hypothesis, and so it is not surprising to find doubts about the wisdom of using *actual* money-supply changes rather than unanticipated changes as the theory requires (e.g. Pesando, 1974). One early study by Tanner and Trapani (1977) does make this distinction and finds that only the unanticipated change in the money stock matters and that is quickly assimilated just as the efficient-markets theory predicts. Following this line, Bonomo and Tanner (1983) use the capital-asset pricing model along with three different methods of distinguishing the unexpected from the expected money supply. Their results show broad confirmation of the rational expectations theory but with one qualification – forecast *revisions* seem to have relative-price effects. They conclude: 'Such a result is consistent with the Keynesian rational expectations theory that the US is characterized by contracts permitting a minor role for discretionary policies.' (p. 343) A natural extension of this is to try an application of the money-announcements approach that we have already considered to be a useful test of the effect of monetary policy on interest rates. A recent study by Pearce and Roley (1982) finds:

(a) that only unexpected increases in the money stock have an effect on equity prices; and
(b) that revisions in the money stock data also have an effect.

The revisions, presumably, are essentially a presentation of new information to the market, so that neutrality is suggested by these findings.

NOTES

1. When this ratio tends to rest at its minimum (its legal minimum), it is in effect determined by the Government. This is the case, at least, when the commercial banks have no desire to hold excess reserves.
2. In Cagan's (1965) study of the US data (1875–1960), H generally dominates, although there are significant episodes when C/M is important (as in 1929–33).
3. There are some popular 'rules of the games' tests using a similar methodology. Some recent efforts appear in papers by Fratianni and Spinelli (1984) and Jonung (1984).
4. If the nominal interest rate is an instrument for controlling the nominal money supply, then the comments of the preceding paragraph apply (Parkin, 1978; McCallum, 1981). We are assuming in our discussion here that this is not the case, although in practice an element of this must enter the policy in order to avoid the unpleasant consequences described in this paragraph.
5. For example, Serletis (1988*a*) compares nominal to real adjustment, to the advantage of the former, and then compares the different measures of money in the same context. He concludes that over a series of tests none of the measures of money (Divisia or not) dominate. See also Fair (1987) who tests money demand for 27 countries and also comes out strongly in favour of nominal adjustment.
6. Of this list only w is unique to Friedman. Presumably, individuals with a larger proportion of financial assets to human (non-loanable) assets would need to hold smaller balances of money, especially for precautionary purposes. The expected sign of w, then, would be negative. This variable never appears in money-demand studies, although over long runs of data, it is certainly likely to alter. This is especially obvious in the case of (rapidly) developing countries where the financial system is also growing rapidly (and velocity is declining). Examples are Sweden, the USA and Italy in the nineteenth century.
7. We should note that there is a large literature on the determinants of velocity with perhaps the best examples appearing in Bordo and Jonung (1987). They argue, for a sample covering many countries and running back into the nineteenth century, that numerous institutional factors help to explain velocity. This, too, is consistent with a monetarist interpretation of the link between money and real income.
8. The work in both this and the next subsection is based on Fisher and Serletis (1989).
9. We have applied the qualifier 'income' to velocity in this paragraph simply because there are both theoretical and practical reasons for working with transactions velocity (see Selden, 1956). If we were to use transactions velocity, we would undoubtedly find a different pattern for velocity. For example, Cramer (1986) finds an enormous rise in the transactions velocity of bank money over the 1950–79 period. It is, of course, financial market activity that produces this result.
10. Curiously, it is hard to find this view seriously promoted in the professional literature, although it pops up all over the place in passing. At any rate, see the explanations in Hall and Noble (1987) and Judd and Motley (1984).
11. Specifically, a tax cut would increase the demand for money and (thus) money holding and, by shifting the *LM* curve to the left would possibly even reduce the level of real income (ignoring any effects of the tax cuts on the *IS* curve or on

aggregate supply). Both effects would lead to a decline of measured velocity in the event of a series of tax cuts as, speaking casually, we have had in recent years. The argument that tax cuts would affect the demand for money and real income appears in Mankiw and Summers (1986). They take the position that the demand for money (and the velocity measure) is actually mis-specified as it is presently defined (in terms of either an income or wealth scale variable instead of a consumption scale variable). See also H. Taylor (1986) for more on the potential influence of tax cuts and Santoni (1987) on the inability of changes in wealth to explain velocity behaviour.

12. Tests of this influence are reported in Higgins and Faust (1981), Tatom (1983) and Judd and Motley (1984). In the last-named, it is the decline in expected inflation that brings the change after 1981 (and, presumably, during the preceding rise some part was due to an increase in expected inflation).
13. There are studies that support the existence of a link between inflation volatility and interest-rate volatility (e.g. Mascaro and Meltzer, 1983), studies that link interest-rate volatility to money demand (e.g. Artis and Lewis, 1976, and Slovin and Sushka, 1983), and studies that directly link inflation volatility to money demand (e.g. Klein, 1977, and Smirlock, 1982). The upshot of this particular line of research is not particularly clear either in a theoretical or empirical sense (compare Klein with Smirlock).
14. For example, if they start saving, the expected recession could actually arrive earlier.
15. Phelps and Taylor rationalize the existence of such contracts in terms of reducing information costs, of keeping customer loyalty and of bearing some of the risk of price fluctuations (for whatever reason). McCallum (1977) argues that pure price stickiness without the informational advantage will produce an ineffective policy under rational expectations. Price stickiness *per se* will not do the job by itself, although it is widely believed to be sufficient to establish a role for active policy.
16. One such change would be to have indexed-wage contracts where the nominal wage is indexed to the price level *and* to an index of firm profits (because of real wage changes). In this event, monetary policy would again be ineffective (in altering real output and employment). Such contracts are generally not observed in practice, possibly because the computations involved would be difficult (part of the difficulty in any such case is the cost of negotiating complicated contracts), and even price-indexed contracts (COLA) are relatively infrequent. This literature has been extended in recent papers (by J. B. Taylor, 1980, and Fethke and Policano, 1981) and the economics of staggering itself has been examined by Fethke and Policano (1984, 1985). This last is required because:

    (a) in the Fischer model staggering is just 'given'; and
    (b) across countries different types of staggering and synchronization of labour contracts can be observed (Japan and Germany have synchronized contracts, while the UK has shorter staggered contracts (one year, generally) than the USA (three years)).

17. See also C. Sims (1980) and Eichenbaum and Singleton (1987).
18. The data are self-explanatory except for income, which is, of course, not available on a quarterly basis. What we do, following Christiano (1986) in this respect, is construct a synthetic monthly-GNP series by multiplying the industrial-production index by the price level. It should also be noted that the Divisia aggregate data are actually produced by the Fisher ideal index.

6

MONEY-SUPPLY THEORY AND THE BANKING SYSTEM

6.1 INTRODUCTION

This chapter will undertake to extend the discussion of earlier chapters to include the financial services industry. Our main topic will be commercial banks, although in rare instances financial intermediaries of other sorts will come into the story. We will begin with a literature on the demand for money by firms which is only partly germane to our topic. This material is placed here because the techniques, revolving around the production function of the typical firm, are somewhat different from our earlier consumer-demand methods and because we wish to develop some analogies. The most obvious of the latter is simply that this chapter will concentrate on a particular firm, the commercial bank, and it is possible to treat this institution as a 'manufacturer' of the services it offers. The material will be microeconomic – or microfoundation – in much of this chapter, especially in Section 6.2, which deals with the typical firm, and Section 6.3, which extends the production-function technology of Section 6.2 into questions of how aggregation theory might be adapted to deal with the financial firm. The latter is based on recent work by Barnett (1987).

Section 6.4 enters into a discussion of what appears to be the beginning of a promising financial market literature on the various roles of commercial banks in formal macropolicy contexts. We start with the Niehans (1978) money and banking model as an example of a macro framework in which the representative financial firm maximizes expected profits, subject to a deterministic production technology and to stochastic cash withdrawal risks and stochastic defaults on loans. This material is extended in different ways in work by Hancock (1985*a*, 1985*b*) and Williamson (1987*a*, *b*) as discussed in Section 6.4. Here, among other topics we will consider models in which the existence of regulatory wedges and monopoly power in banking suggest real effects (partly in view of the role of intermediaries in the creation of money). Section 6.5 will look at some recent work on the role of banks in financial panics (notably those of the Great Depression) and, to turn the coin over, will consider some work on the effect of monetary policy on financial

intermediaries. Finally, Section 6.6 turns to a last discussion of the effect of monetary policy, this time on commercial banks. This is a discussion of monetary neutrality again, with special emphasis on the effects of policy operating on the lending and borrowing rates of commercial banks.

6.2 THE DEMAND FOR MONEY BY FIRMS

Perhaps the best place to begin the discussion of the firm's demand for money is to return to the general models of Chapter 2. In this section we will present three models of the demand for money by firms – an inventory model (Fischer, 1974), a transactions model (Saving, 1972) and a simultaneous-equations Translog model (Dennis and Smith, 1978). The first two are essentially extensions of the transactions material in Chapter 2 while the third follows the asset approach described in detail in Chapter 3. Note that the first two models will follow and paraphrase an explanation provided by Bernstein (1978*b*).

The most general early money-demand model for firms is not the inventory-theoretic model described earlier (and below), but one derived (loosely) from the general neoclassical model. Nadiri (1969), using an approach modelled on the Jorgenson and Stephenson (1967) investment function, seems to have the earliest clear statement. In the Jorgenson–Stephenson framework, the desired stock of a capital good (such as money) is given by

$$K^* = \alpha \frac{P}{c} X^* \tag{6.1}$$

Here c is the 'user cost of capital'. It is measured by Nadiri as

$$c = \frac{q}{(1-\mu)[d+\delta_0+\delta_1 s-(\dot{q}/q)]} \tag{6.2}$$

where q is the price of capital goods; μ is the corporate tax rate; d is the cost of capital (the interest rate) and s the utilization rate. (δ_0 is a time-related depreciation rate and δ_1 is a usage-related depreciation rate.) If the firm minimizes total costs of

$$c = wL+cK+vm \qquad \left(\text{where } m = \frac{M}{P}\right) \tag{6.3}$$

subject to a production function of

$$X^* = \phi(K, L, m) \tag{6.4}$$

then a demand for real money balances by the firm can be derived directly in the form of

$$m^* = f\left(\frac{C}{w} v, X^*\right) \tag{6.5}$$

Here v is the opportunity cost (interest foregone, etc.) of holding money and w is the wage rate.

Nadiri assumes the following explicit demand for money function, by-passing a formal cost-minimization solution (in his 'restricted' model):

$$m^* = A_0 X^{*\frac{1}{\rho}} v^{\alpha} \left(\frac{c}{w}\right)^{\beta} \tag{6.6}$$

He argues that reasonable signs for the derivatives of Equation (6.5) are

$$\frac{\partial m^*}{\partial X^*}, \frac{\partial m^*}{\partial c/w} > 0; \quad \frac{\partial m^*}{\partial v} < 0$$

as they certainly are in Equation (6.6). His empirical results on quarterly US total manufacturing data for 1948 through 1960 bear out these expectations. We note, though, for later reference, that m^* is not derived directly from the cost-minimization framework, that cost-minimization *per se* is really not the most general assumption about the firm's objective, that money is entered directly into the production function without benefit of a concealing constraint, that there is no explicit allowance for the effect of technological change and, finally, that no advantage has been taken of the cross-equation restrictions (or duality) inherent in this set-up. These are, in fact, topics that have come up in the more recent literature, and no criticism is intended here.

6.2.1 An inventory-theoretic model

Assume, following Fischer (1974), that the firm has a production function defined in terms of two inputs, capital and production labour (L_p), and that the function has the usual convenient mathematical properties.

$$y = \phi(K, L_p) \qquad (\phi_1, \phi_2 > 0) \tag{6.7}$$

Also assume that the firm faces three other constraints which define the role money plays in its operations. These are:

(a) a constraint dividing the total labour force of the firm into a production part and a transactions part,

$$L_p + L_T = L$$

(b) a constraint that relates the number of transactions (n) to the amount of labour used in carrying out the transaction;

$$n = \beta L_T$$

(c) a 'money requirements' condition

$$n\bar{M} = R$$

where $\bar{M}$ defines average money balances (= revenue (R) divided by the number of transactions).

When we substitute these three constraints into Equation (6.7), we obtain

$$y = \phi\left[K, L - \left(\beta\frac{\bar{M}}{R}\right)^{-1}\right] \tag{6.8}$$

which brings money into the production function as a 'proximate input' that helps economize on the use of labour. It is entered here in a specific way, but it does not enter in its own right. This side-steps a considerable theoretical and empirical literature on the pros and cons of putting money into the (aggregate) production function since here it belongs in the function as a consequence of the method of solution and not because it is being taken as a factor of production *per se*.[1]

Continuing with the derivation, the aggregate firm can be assumed to maximize its profits (R_n for net revenue) where profits are defined as

$$R_n = p\phi\left[K, L - \left(\beta\frac{\bar{M}}{R}\right)^{-1}\right] - w_n L - w_k K - w_m\frac{\bar{M}}{R} \tag{6.9}$$

Here w_n is the average cost of holding money (i.e. inventory cost, as discussed in Chapter 2). The following first-order conditions are then calculated directly from this equation:

$$\left.\begin{aligned} \frac{\partial R_n}{\partial K} &= p\phi_1 - w_k = 0 \\ \frac{\partial R_n}{\partial L} &= p\phi_2 - w_n = 0 \\ \frac{\partial R_n}{\partial(\bar{M}/R)} &= \beta^{-1}p\phi_2\left(\frac{\bar{M}}{R}\right)^{-2} - w_m = 0 \end{aligned}\right\} \tag{6.10}$$

Note, first, that there are only two marginal products (ϕ_1 and ϕ_2) for capital and productive labour and, second, that money is only a 'proximate' factor of production and not a direct one.

To see the demand for money in all this, we can eliminate ϕ_2 between the second and third equations in the set of Equations (6.10). This calculation produces

$$\bar{M} = R\left(\frac{w_n}{\beta w_m}\right)^{\frac{1}{2}} \tag{6.11}$$

This is in the form of the familiar 'square-root' formula although, in fact, the arguments are not the traditional ones. It is apparent from this construction that money-holding responds directly to (the square root of) increases in the cost of labour (the wage rate) and inversely to increases in the cost of holding money ($w_m \equiv$ the interest rate). These are familiar results from the 'consumer' demand functions discussed earlier, which clearly carry over to the demand for money by firms. It is worth underscoring again, in this first and simplest of models, that changes in the price of capital do not affect money-holding

(given our constraints), while changes in the price of labour affect both money-holding and capital- and the labour-input decisions. Symmetric changes in the price of money initiate changes in production labour – *through the transactions process* – but do not affect capital. In effect, then, money is separable from capital but not from labour. A general form for the production process that arises here, then, would be as in Equation (6.12):[2]

$$\frac{\bar{M}}{R} = \phi[K, \theta(\bar{M})] \tag{6.12}$$

6.2.2 A general transactions model

The following presentation is based on the discussion in Bernstein (1978*b*) and is a paraphrase of papers by Saving (1972) and Dutton, Gramm and McDonald (1974). Let the firm's production function continue to be defined by Equation (6.7) but with total labour (L) as an input in the place of productive labour:

$$y = \phi(K, L) \tag{6.13}$$

Instead of establishing an arbitrary money-requirements relation, let us assume that there is a transactions-costs function of the general form of

$$c_t = C(K, L, \bar{M}) \tag{6.14}$$

with the usual properties. Here the firm is assumed to be searching for something like the minimum-cost way of carrying out its transactions by juggling capital and labour inputs and by holding money balances.

The firm in this situation will maximize the following profit function with respect to its three choice variables (K, L, M):

$$R_n = p\phi(K, L) - w_k K - w_L L - w_m M - T(K, L, M) \tag{6.15}$$

The result is the following set of first-order conditions:

$$\left.\begin{aligned} \frac{\partial R_n}{\partial K} &= p\phi_1 - w_k - C_1 = 0 \\ \frac{\partial R_n}{\partial L} &= p\phi_2 - w_L - C_2 = 0 \\ \frac{\partial R_n}{\partial \bar{M}} &= -w_n - C_3 = 0 \end{aligned}\right\} \tag{6.16}$$

Immediately we see that since $C_3 < 0$, an increase in money balances decreases transactions costs; money is a cost-saving input with respect to the exchange networks.

Let us manipulate this system in order to illustrate the comparative-equilibrium properties of this general transactions model. First, let us set up a

system in which all the potential effects of a change in the product price are described; the following set of equations represents this in matrix form.

$$\begin{bmatrix} p\phi_{11}-C_{11} & p\phi_{12}-C_{12} & -C_{13} \\ p\phi_{21}-C_{21} & p\phi_{22}-C_{22} & -C_{23} \\ -C_{13} & -C_{23} & -C_{33} \end{bmatrix} \begin{bmatrix} \frac{\partial K}{\partial p} \\ \frac{\partial L}{\partial p} \\ \frac{\partial \bar{M}}{\partial p} \end{bmatrix} = \begin{bmatrix} -\phi_1 \\ -\phi_2 \\ 0 \end{bmatrix} \tag{6.17}$$

Initially, we are interested in the effect of a change in the product price on money-holding (assuming the price is exogenously determined). Solution of that part of Equation (6.17) yields the following expression:

$$\frac{\partial \bar{M}}{\partial p} = \frac{\phi_1[(p\phi_{21}-C_{21})C_{23}+(p\phi_{22}-C_{22})C_{13}]}{D} - \frac{\phi_2[(p\phi_{11}-C_{11})C_{23}+(p\phi_{12}-C_{12})C_{13}]}{D} \tag{6.18}$$

Even with $D < 0$ (D is the determinant of the left-hand matrix in Equation (6.17)), this expression cannot be signed, and thus there is no 'homogeneity' condition in this model of the firm's demand for money analogous to that in the consumer's case. That is, when the price level changes there is actually a price-induced real-balance effect, but it is unsignable as things stand. Note that we are thinking of an aggregate firm (whose product price is the price level) when we say this.

Chapter 2, argues that an increase in the wage rate would raise the demand for money in the consumer version of the transactions model. In the firm version of the model this calculation (again from Equation (6.17)) produces

$$\frac{\partial \bar{M}}{\partial w_L} = \frac{[C_{32}(p\phi_{11}-C_{11})-C_{31}(p\phi_{12}-C_{12})]}{D} \tag{6.19}$$

which also cannot be signed. Neither can the effect of w_k on real-money balances (which is analogous to a real interest-rate effect). What does emerge as signable is the effect of changes in the *own-price* of money on money-holding as the following expression spells out:

$$\frac{\partial \bar{M}}{\partial w_m} = \frac{[p^2(\phi_{11}\phi_{22}-\phi_{12}^2)+(C_{11}C_{22}-C_{12}^2)-p\phi_{22}C_{11}-C_{22}p\phi_{11}+2C_{12}p\phi_{21}]}{D} \tag{6.20}$$

This term is positive. Thus, the firm's demand for money would have the following form:

$$m^* = g(y, w_m) \tag{6.21}$$

where w_m might be proxied by the own rate on money. If we include bonds in the problem, as do Dutton, Gramm and McDonald, then a cross-rate would enter as well.

On net, then, while this model has an appealing structural set-up, it is not a very useful one in the sense that it contains few specific predictions. Indeed, as we have seen before in this study, such results are common whenever the models are especially general, as this one is. In any case, our purpose here is to set up some intuition for later results involving a special sort of firm – the bank – and so we will not linger any further on the details of this particular exercise.

6.2.3 A Translog model

In the Saving (1972) model of the firm's demand for money, money is thought of as a kind of 'indirect' factor of production (providing services to the user, to be sure) but not as fitting originally into the production function. Dennis and Smith (1978) argue that this is a subtle distinction whose value had not (at the time) been assessed, as it must be, on empirical grounds. Instead, they go straight to the neoclassical framework, as described above, with money as a direct factor of production.

The cost function that Dennis and Smith specify is the Translog. They assume four factors of production (production labour, non-production labour, capital and real-money balances) so that there is considerable interaction in the cost function:

$$\log C = \alpha_0 + \alpha_x \log X + \frac{1}{2}\alpha_{xx}(\log X)^2 + \sum_{i=1}^{4} \beta_i \log P_i$$

$$+\frac{1}{2}\sum_{i=1}^{4}\sum_{j=1}^{4} \gamma_{ij} \log P_i \log P_j + \sum_{i=1}^{4} \theta_i \log P_i \log X \tag{6.22}$$

The cost function is homogeneous of degree one in the P_i (factor prices) and the following restrictions are applicable:

$$\sum_{i=1}^{4} \beta_i = 1 \tag{6.23}$$

$$\sum_{i=1}^{4} \theta_i = 0 \tag{6.24}$$

$$\sum_{i=1}^{4} \gamma_{ij} = \sum_{j=1}^{4} \gamma_{ij} = \sum_{i=1}^{4}\sum_{j=1}^{4} \gamma_{ij} = 0 \tag{6.25}$$

If the conditions of maximization are met and Shepherd's lemma applies,

then the indirect cost function can be examined in the form of the 'cost shares' of total costs. The resulting functions are

$$\frac{P_i V_i^*}{C} = \beta_i + \sum_{j=1}^{4} \gamma_{ij} \log P_j + \theta_i \log X \qquad (i = 1, \ldots, 4) \qquad (6.26)$$

where V_i^* is the optimal level of usage of each of the inputs into the production process.

The empirical work by Dennis and Smith is on 11 two-digit US manufacturing industries over the 1952–73 period. Because of the adding-up properties, one equation (non-production labour) is dropped. A Box–Jenkins procedure is adopted to control for serial correlation (it is over 0.9 in general) which is not assumed to be the same for each equation. Both the homogeneity conditions on inputs and symmetry of the cross-price effects are imposed, and homotheticity and linear separability of the inputs are tested for. Homotheticity is rejected in only two of 11 cases while separability, no matter how constructed, is always rejected. This implies that in this framework money is not separable from the other factors of production, although it must be emphasized, in thinking about this result, that this is a test within a *parametric* (Translog) framework which is known to behave poorly for some data sets.

Considering the Allen (partial) elasticities of substitution, then, Dennis and Smith produce results that suggest that real money balances are (generally) substitutes for both types of labour and for capital. There is no (significant) sign of complementarity. The own-price elasticities are correctly signed and significant. They conclude: 'Real cash balances are not separable from the remaining factor inputs. Thus omitting them in previous analyses of the production technology for these industries offers . . . the potential for a serious specification error'. (p. 807) Inputs are generally substitutes for each other, but there is considerable variation across industries. Since it is also known that other production technologies (e.g. CES, VES–variable elasticity of substitution) work better than the Translog in some of these cases and that the Translog itself is far from the most flexible functional form to adopt (partly because it is a local approximation rather than a global), these results have to be considered as provisional. They are, however, apparently the last word on this particular subject at this point.

6.3 AN AGGREGATION-THEORETIC THEORY OF THE FINANCIAL FIRM

This section will discuss a treatment largely due to Barnett (1987) but embedded partially in the earlier Fischer (1974) inventory model. Paralleling our discussion of the consumer in Chapter 3, we can model the firm with a fully specified, intertemporal framework. That is, let the representative *non-financial* firm have an intertemporal production function, written in implicit

form, of

$$\phi(\tilde{\mathbf{x}}_t, \ldots, \tilde{\mathbf{x}}_{t+T}, \tilde{\mathbf{m}}_t, \ldots, \tilde{\mathbf{m}}_{t+T}, \tilde{\mathbf{v}}_t, \ldots, \tilde{\mathbf{v}}_{t+T}) = 0 \qquad (6.27)$$

where $\tilde{\mathbf{x}}_s$ defines a vector of planned outputs (for a multi-product firm) for period s; $\tilde{\mathbf{m}}_s$, a vector of planned monetary holdings (defined in real terms) and $\tilde{\mathbf{v}}_s$, a vector of other planned inputs. The firm will define its discounted present value of variable profits to be

$$\psi_v^* = \sum_{s=t}^{t+T} \tilde{\mathbf{x}}_s' \tilde{\alpha}_s - \sum_{s=t}^{t+T} \tilde{\mathbf{v}}_s' \tilde{\beta}_s - \sum_{s=t}^{t+T} \tilde{\mathbf{m}}_s' \tilde{\pi}_s \qquad (6.28)$$

Here $\tilde{\alpha}_s$, $\tilde{\beta}_s$, and $\tilde{\pi}_s$ represent the discount factors, and the last two sets of terms represent costs; $\tilde{\beta}$ and $\tilde{\pi}$ are user costs in this framework. The latter can be derived from the full dynamic problem (Barnett, 1981, 1987) and, if so, would appear as follows:

$$\pi_{it} = P_t^* \left(\frac{R_t - r_{it}}{1 + R_t} \right)$$

Here R_t is, again, the return on a benchmark asset and P_t^* is the price level of the firm's products.

The set-up here is the same as that described in Chapters 1 and 3. The firm will maximize Equation (6.28) subject to Equation (6.27), the production function, with the familiar definition of a user cost as just given. Money appears in the production function, although whether this is as a direct factor of production or as the result of combining some prior 'transactions time' constraint is simply not important to the development which will be described in this section (Fischer, 1974). In any case, in the form here it is a short step to setting up the conditions for monetary aggregation by the well-known rules for the aggregation of production functions.[3] Finally, note that we might wish to impose separability between the monetary assets and the other entities in Equation (6.27). If $a(\tilde{\mathbf{m}}_t)$ is such a separable function – termed by Barnett the 'category subproduction function' – then the optimizing firm will solve the following problem:

$$\max a(\tilde{\mathbf{m}}_t) \qquad (\text{s.t. } (\tilde{\pi}_t' \tilde{\mathbf{m}}_t = b_t)) \qquad (6.29)$$

where the constraint defines *optimal* real-money balances. In this construction the firm maximizes the output of the monetary services production function subject to the constraint that actual real-money balances are equal to those desired at prevailing user costs. Note, again, that an overall 'producer' equilibrium holds as well.

We have already discussed aggregation theory in some detail in Chapter 1 and need not restate the theorems here. Indeed, consumer aggregation and producer aggregation follow the same procedures.

> The only change is in the interpretation of the quantity aggregator function. With a consumer, the quantity aggregator function is the category subutility function U. With a manufacturing firm, the quantity aggregator function is the

> category subproduction function $[a(\tilde{\mathbf{m}}_t)]$. Clearly, the quantity aggregator function in both cases is the objective function of the corresponding conditional decision problem. (Barnett, 1987, p. 132)

But the structure of the above problem suggests that the firm (*under separability*) can actually decentralize its monetary portfolio decision-making, either using financial advisers employed as consultants or creating a financial decision-making division for the firm. In this case this 'division' would be given a fixed budget (b_t), as the result of the general solution, and then would operate Equation (6.29) in nominal terms. It seems natural, indeed, to study such situations with portfolio models (such as that used by Maddala and Vogel (1969)). Of course, this decision requires feedback between the different levels of the decision-making process since the calculation of optimal b_t presented in the final decision would require knowledge of the user costs, presumably as calculated by the financial division. Barnett presents exact solutions for all this in the context of a multiproduct firm.

The non-financial firm just described is presumed to maximize profits subject to a financial-resources constraint, in effect, and a specific technology. The financial intermediary can, of course, be modelled similarly but it is more instructive to treat the problem of defining this firm, and arriving at an aggregate measure of its services, as analogous to aggregating over the *inputs* of the non-financial firm. That is, there is also (we assume) a two-stage decision problem for the intermediary, but it is a decision framework in which the firm first solves for its profit-maximizing *inputs* and then chooses its revenue-maximizing vector of outputs, assuming that the total amount to be supplied has already been determined in the first stage.

In the first-stage the intermediary selects a vector of non-capital inputs ($\tilde{\mathbf{v}}_t$) at a given set of input prices ($\tilde{\boldsymbol{\beta}}_t$) such that it maximizes net revenue as in

$$R_{\mathrm{n}} = R^*(\tilde{\mathbf{v}}_t, \tilde{\boldsymbol{\pi}}_t, \tilde{\mathbf{K}}_t) - \tilde{\mathbf{v}}_t' \tilde{\boldsymbol{\beta}}_t \tag{6.30}$$

Here $\tilde{\mathbf{K}}_t$ represents reserve requirements (and any other balance sheet restrictions). Holding these requirements fixed in the short-run, there is a linearly-homogeneous *output* price aggregator function δ such that

$$R^*(\tilde{\mathbf{v}}_t, \tilde{\boldsymbol{\pi}}_t; \tilde{\mathbf{K}}_t) = \delta(\tilde{\boldsymbol{\pi}}_t)\, g(\tilde{\mathbf{v}}_t)$$

In this case, the intermediary's *variable* net revenues can be written as

$$R_{\mathrm{n}} = \delta(\tilde{\boldsymbol{\pi}}_t)\, g(\tilde{\mathbf{v}}_t) - \tilde{\mathbf{v}}_t' \tilde{\boldsymbol{\beta}}_t \tag{6.31}$$

The firm will then select its *variable* inputs in order to maximize Equation (6.31) in this first stage. The intermediary's revenue function (an analogue of the cost function) for its second-stage decision is then

$$R^*(\tilde{\mathbf{v}}_t, \tilde{\boldsymbol{\pi}}_i; \tilde{\mathbf{K}}_t) = \max_{\tilde{\mathbf{m}}_t} \{\tilde{\mathbf{m}}_t' \tilde{\boldsymbol{\pi}}_t; f(\tilde{\mathbf{m}}_t; \tilde{\mathbf{K}}_t) = g(\tilde{\mathbf{v}}_t)\} \tag{6.32}$$

Here the firm chooses its optimal vector of outputs (in the second stage), given both a prior decision on optimal inputs and its financial-services

production function. The equation in curly brackets states that the intermediary produces no non-financial products;[4] it also states that the total of financial services supplied is determined in Stage 1. That is, the intermediary will solve its general (Stage 1) problem to select $\tilde{\mathbf{v}}_t^*$. With this it will simultaneously have its *aggregate* monetary asset quantity m_t. This is $f(\tilde{\mathbf{m}}_t; \tilde{\mathbf{K}}_t)$. With this quantity entered into Stage 2, the firm will choose the composition of its financial services supply vector. The exact money supply aggregate is, clearly,

$$m_t = f(\tilde{\mathbf{m}}_t; \tilde{\mathbf{K}}_t) \tag{6.33}$$

where $\tilde{\mathbf{m}}_t^*$ is the profit-maximizing vector of monetary services.

As it turns out, the second-stage decision problem is equivalent to the choice of $\tilde{\mathbf{m}}_t^*$ to *minimize* aggregate factor usage:

$$\mathrm{f}(\tilde{\mathbf{m}}_t; \tilde{\mathbf{K}}_t) \qquad \text{s.t.} \qquad \tilde{\mathbf{m}}_t' \tilde{\boldsymbol{\pi}}_t = \delta(\tilde{\boldsymbol{\pi}}_t) g(\tilde{\mathbf{v}}_t^*)$$

This sort of duality result is common in the theory of the firm. Such a result could lead to a 'cost-share' approach to the estimation of the intermediary's *output*, which seems to be the chief advantage obtained by thinking of the financial firm in this way. We should note that Equation (6.33) is the exact monetary (supply) aggregate for the financial intermediary with the function f defining the aggregator function.

In the discussion of the uses of the ideal index numbers in Chapter 1, the emphasis (for the consumer case) was that such indices provide the best available (second-degree) approximations to the underlying unknown aggregator function. The same theorem applies literally to the manufacturing firm, but for the intermediary, because the solution procedure is not identified, an additional requirement has to be imposed. In particular, in both the consumer and manufacturing firm cases, the primary functions $\phi(\cdot)$ and $u(\cdot)$ are the aggregator functions, while for the intermediary the aggregator function is actually $f(\cdot)$, which is a second-stage function. This is the reason it was argued that the aggregate money supplied is basically a second-stage solution. What is required in continuous time, then, for the Divisia to track m_t without error is the continual selection of $\tilde{\mathbf{m}}_t^*$ (the profit-maximizing vector of financial outputs) to solve the second-stage decision *at each instant in time*. This is required neither of the consumer nor the producer problem. Basically, this requirement occurs because the intermediary's aggregator function depends on $\tilde{\mathbf{K}}_t$, the vector of reserve requirements. These are given, of course, but have an influence on total profits (at each point in time), depending on the mix of financial outputs. Indeed, the Divisia index depends on $\tilde{\mathbf{K}}_t$ both through its effect on $f(\cdot)$ and because of its effect on $\tilde{\boldsymbol{\pi}}_t$ where it appears, properly, as a 'tax' on the user cost of each asset. This is the reason for the continual solution for the firm's offering of optimal financial services.

It is abundantly clear in recent policy discussions that serious consideration must be given to specifying the supply side of the traditional monetary problem. Where the results of this section take us, so far, is to suggest that a

procedure exists, parallel to that for constructing ideal indices of the monetary aggregates for aggregating the monies supplied by the different financial firms. As things stand, the new monetary aggregates in current use in the USA (the Divisia M1, etc.) are justified only as demand-side aggregations. A comparable supply-side aggregation, by the 'amended Divisia' described in this section, would be needed to complete the general equilibrium (microfoundations) picture of (separable) financial equilibrium. This involves stating the reserve requirements of intermediaries as part of the user costs for these firms. This drives a tax-like (regulatory) *wedge* between the consumer/producer and the intermediary and also implies that the aggregates on the supply side might not be the same as those on the demand side. There are, of course, many other regulations and (hence) other potential wedges to consider in the financial services industry, although nothing exists so far in the technical literature at this level.

A follow-up paper to the Barnett study by Barnett, Hinich and Weber (1986) restates the argument just explained and produces some empirical estimates. When no reserve requirements (no 'regulatory wedges') exist, a Divisia index for monetary services can be calculated from either the demand or the supply side. Indeed, these measures will not differ as a consequence of the equality of marginal rates of substitution, marginal rates of transformation and user-cost ratios at equilibrium. On the other hand, when there are reserve requirements, there are two different user costs, with that for the financial firm reflecting the foregone interest on required reserves. The quantities are the same (in equilibrium), but the prices are not.[5] This leads to the possibility that the size of the wedge can be measured, *ceteris paribus*, by comparing the values of the two indices. Comparisons in the Barnett–Hinich–Weber paper involve both frequency-domain and simple time-domain methods. While there are large differences in results using simple-sum indices, the Divisia supply and demand indices show a relatively small difference (the demand index being slightly higher than the supply) in the time domain (in the period studied). The frequency-domain results are similar. As the evidence stands, we can thus proceed with demand-side Divisia indices, forewarned of, but relatively unconcerned with, the regulatory wedge, provided the demand-side index is sufficiently broad. We recall that in some of our experiments in Chapters 1 through 3 broader measures outperform narrower ones.

6.4 THE MODELLING OF BANKING IN THE MACROECONOMY

In the banking models discussed to this point, we have suggested that a useful way to think of commercial banks is in a two-stage framework in which the firm first solves for its profit-maximizing level of operations (or volume of inputs) and then chooses its vector of outputs. Since the input vector includes

optimal deposits, as does the output vector, this two-stage procedure deals rather neatly with what is otherwise a perplexing aspect of banking: deposits are both an input and an output. This section will look at a macroeconomic literature of recent vintage that takes various approaches to try to deal with this complexity, without getting buried in balance-sheet detail. What we are trying to do, in any event, is work towards a framework in which banks are not thought of merely as operating the same sort of production structure as manufacturers of sausages, in producing so much sausage (loans) from ground-up pieces of pig (deposits). But no matter how we slice it, there *are* both real and financial inputs and financial outputs, and therein lie the complications.

Commercial banks are part of a set of financial intermediaries whose role, broadly, is that of providing financial services to both borrowers and lenders. The bank's particular *raison d'être* lies partly in the particular regulatory climate in which it resides and partly in its special role either as a provider of unique services (liquidity being the most obvious) or as an efficient provider of information, especially on the credit-worthiness of its borrowers (see Fama, 1985). It also can be thought of as providing diversification services to its shareholders, in which case it is analogous to a mutual fund. That it does all of these things (and more) makes the modelling of the bank a particularly interesting undertaking. Broadly speaking, much of the literature on banking consists of:

(a) portfolio management models (in which the size of the banking firm is given and (usually) an asset-portfolio problem is solved); and
(b) complete banking models in which the scale of the operation of the firm is included (is endogenous) in the decision framework.

Most generally, one would want to work with models of the sort in (b) with, especially, the inclusion of some accounting for the real resources employed by the banking firm (see the surveys in Baltensperger, 1980, and Santomero, 1984).

In the asset-choice models, the two approaches currently available are inventory-theoretic or mean-variance. By far, the inventory-theoretic material dominates, with representative versions being available in Orr and Mellon (1961) and Niehans (1978), to bracket most of the literature over time. The inventory models, incidentally, more often deal with uncertainty by making deposit withdrawals stochastic, which forces the banking firm to construct asset portfolios that reflect different possible contingencies with regard to their liabilities.

For the mean-variance approach, but with reference to London discount houses rather than commercial banks, an effective treatment is available in Parkin (1970). The latter approach has the advantage of incorporating risk directly into the decision framework and the disadvantage of working with a fixed scale of operations. Pyle (1971) has an early paper in which he argues that banks (really intermediaries) perform the essential function of arbi-

traging away risk for their customers. The reason they do this is that there is a positive covariance between loan and deposit rates. Thus, when intermediaries operate, they reduce overall risk. A second paper by Sealey (1980) is roughly on the same topic.

An alternative way to think of the banking firm is as the supplier of financial services (on both the asset and liability sides) utilizing real resources (notably labour). This is the method that grows out of the Pesek and Saving (1967) approach to the 'net wealth' controversy, as described in Chapter 4; a representative version for commercial banks appears in Saving (1977). In this case, 'the bank has a production function relating different combinations of liabilities and assets to corresponding possible combinations of inputs' (Baltensperger, 1980, p. 30). Here, the banking firm can be thought of as maximizing its profits as in

$$\Pi = \sum_i \pi_{ai} A_i - \sum_j \pi_{dj} D_j - \sum_h W_h V_h \tag{6.34}$$

where the A_i are interest-bearing assets, D_j represents the different types of deposits and V_h are such as (real) labour inputs. This is maximized subject to the following production function:

$$H(A_i, D_j, V_h) = 0 \tag{6.35}$$

which is written in implicit form, and a balance sheet constraint,

$$\sum_i A_i = \sum_j D_j(1 - K_j) \tag{6.36}$$

where K_j is the reserve requirement on asset j. Models which combine the portfolio-management/real-resource problems are presented in Niehans (1978) and Baltensperger (1980).

We have been emphasizing that commercial banks provide services to lenders and borrowers as 'intermediaries' and as evaluators of the borrower's credit-worthiness. They may, indeed, *create* liquidity, which Niehans (1978) calls 'positive asset transformation' as, for example, in the case of money creation. In this instance, the bank's assets are less liquid than its liabilities, in the aggregate. We may go some way toward constructing a general model of the banking sector, as does Niehans (1978), in the following terms.

Suppose, to begin with, that there exists a simple balance sheet constraint of

$$R + L = D + E \tag{6.37}$$

where E is the equity of the bank. We will assume that banks maximize their expected profits (to be defined in a moment) subject to three constraints; in this respect we are extending the model described a moment ago. First, as might be anticipated, there is a deterministic production function, again written in implicit form, of

$$f(K, N, L, D) = 0 \tag{6.38}$$

where K and N are real inputs of capital and labour. This function brings in the real resources.

In addition, the banking firm will be conceived of as being constrained by two stochastic constraints, one referring to its reserve account with the central bank (and depending on stochastic cash withdrawals (W)) and one produced by the possibility of loan defaults (F). For $\phi(W)$ describing the distribution (with mean = zero and variance = σ_W^2) of withdrawals, the expected value of reserve deficits is given by

$$E(W-R) = \int_R^\infty (W-R)\phi(W)\mathrm{d}W = x(D, R) \tag{6.39}$$

Here we suppose that an increase in deposits (D) increases withdrawals so that the derivative $x_D > 0$; x_R is clearly negative. Note that reserves are *total* reserves (required reserves plus excess reserves). For $\theta(F)$ describing the distribution of default losses (with mean β and variance σ_F^2), then the expected loss from default is given by

$$\bar{z} = \int_E^\infty (F-E)\theta(F)\mathrm{d}F = z(L, E) \tag{6.40}$$

Here $z_L > 0$ and $z_E < 0$. In this analysis, to avoid further complication, it is assumed that the banking firm chooses some tolerable limit of losses.

The banking firm's expected profits will depend on the loan rate (i_L), the deposit rate (i_D), the penalty rate on reserve overspills (i_x), the capital goods rental rate (r), the wage rate (w), the expected profit rate (e) and the expected loan default ratio (β). The relation combining these notions is given by

$$E(\pi) = (i_L - \beta)L - i_D D - i_x X - eE - wN - rK \tag{6.41}$$

These can be combined in a Lagrangean, and when this is done, three first-order conditions fall out for the choice variables K (and N), L and D. One of these is a cost-minimization condition that reads

$$\frac{w}{r} = \frac{f_N}{f_K}$$

This is standard for the theory of the firm. A second condition, unique to a lending institution, states that

$$i_L - \beta = -r\left(\frac{f_L}{f_K}\right) - e\left(\frac{z_L}{z_E}\right) - i_P\left[1 - \frac{z_L}{z_E}\right](x_R)$$

This condition, overall, states that the return on loans, net of default costs, should be equal to the marginal cost of making the loans. For the costs, these are the *real* costs (f_L, $f_K > 0$); the equity costs associated with loans (in terms of the marginal loan to equity ratio); and the costs associated with loans, but related to deposit variability. In this case, loans financed out of equity *reduce* the need to borrow reserves while, as before, an increase in reserves directly increases penalty costs ($x_R < 0$).

The third marginal condition accounts for the optimal selection of deposits, given loans. It is

$$-i_P(x_R) = i_D - r\left(\frac{f_D}{f_K}\right) + i_P x_D \tag{6.42}$$

In this case the firm selects a deposit level such that the benefit of a reduction in penalty costs achieved through lower reserves (on the left-hand side of Equation (6.42)) is equal to the cost of acquiring new deposits (i_D could be negative), adjusted both for the factor cost and for the penalty cost (since additional deposits increase withdrawals).

The result of this exercise would be 'demand' functions for deposits and loans (and for the inputs of E, K, and N). These would depend on the (assumed to be) competitively determined interest rates. In the following tabulation the expected signs of these relations are collected:

	Deposits	*Loans*
Loan rate (i_L)	+	+
Deposit rate (i_D)	–	–
Penalty rate (i_P)	?	–

Here the signs are what might be expected, with the penalty rate ambiguous since an increase in this rate would induce an increase in reserves (thus increasing deposits) while reducing bank profits; this would *reduce* the overall size of the operation (and hence deposits).

6.5 RECENT WORK ON MONETARY NEUTRALITY IN A BANKING ECONOMY

One way that commercial banks can be involved in the generation of real business cycles is through the effect of deteriorating business conditions – however triggered – on the balance sheets of their customers. For example, suppose a (real?) shock somewhere produces a decline in real national product and prices; as a result, bank customers will be poorer; their collateral weaker; and their debts larger (in real terms), with the further consequence that there are more loan defaults, fewer new loans originated, and, even, some disruption (panic!) in the credit markets (see Mishkin, 1978*b*). The result will be some downward pressure on bank profits (and on the value and solvency of the typical banking firm). This scenario was invoked by Friedman and Schwartz in their *Monetary History* (1963) in the following terms:

> The bank failures had two different aspects. First, they involved capital losses to both their owners and their depositors, just as the failure of any other group of

> business enterprises involved losses to their owners and creditors. Second, given the policy followed by the Reserve System, the failures were the mechanism through which a drastic decline was produced in the stock of money. (p. 351)

This was, of course, in reference to the Great Depression.

In a widely cited paper, Diamond and Dybvig (1986) set out to try to make the foregoing notions more precise by specifying the nature of the banking industry and by speculating on the causes of (and proposed cures for) instability in the banking sector. Diamond and Dybvig argue that the representative bank provides both asset and liability services, with the former being such services as evaluating and monitoring loans and the latter being such services as clearing transactions, providing currency on demand, etc. Simplistically, this would involve the creation of 'liquidity' in the sense that illiquid loans are converted into liquid deposits (with a smoother distribution of yields), a way of looking at intermediaries that is close to the traditional view, although it is not motivated in precisely the same way.[6]

With regard to its asset services, the commercial bank gathers information (on markets, credit-worthiness, etc.), some of which is not openly available in the market; they also efficiently monitor the loan process. When setting up a regulatory policy, the central bank must take care not to provide banks with the wrong incentives from the point of view either of the optimal allocation of (financial) resources or of the stability of the banking system. The standard example of a policy with such ill-effects is that of a deposit-insurance scheme that does not set the rates in accordance with actuarial principles (as described in Kareken and Wallace, 1978). Thus 'the bank may have an incentive to select very risky assets since the deposit insurers bear the brunt of downside risk but the bank owners get the benefit of the upside risk' (Diamond and Dybvig, 1986, p. 59). The Federal Deposit Insurance Corporation in the USA operates such a scheme, in effect creating a condition known as 'moral hazard' in the banking industry. Monitoring techniques, regulations (restrictions) and special capital requirements could counteract this problem and they actually do exist in the USA. Historically, then, bank failure is related to risky loans. Presumably, regulatory changes that increase bank risk (let us say, significantly) ought to be carefully scrutinized, while additional restrictions (particularly recent ones), such as imposing ceilings on deposits, might be reconsidered. It is suggested by Diamond and Dybvig that constructing a deposit-insurance scheme that is correctly risk-adjusted is not actually feasible. On net, then, this literature is wary of the recent wave of deregulation in American banking if only because too little thought might have been directed toward the nature of the banking business and the particular regulatory climate in which it resides.

There is yet another version of the 'information' problem just discussed, in this case proposed by Bernanke (1983), which involves the claim that such (real) financial effects occur (and occurred during the Great Depression) on account of the *incompleteness* of the market for financial claims. By a

complete market, Bernanke means one in which bankruptcy could not occur because all loan contracts are written in such a way as to define each party's obligations in all possible circumstances (i.e. for all possible 'states' of the economy). There would be no role in such a world for a financial intermediary, at least if the *raison d'être* for intermediaries is searching out the credit-worthiness of the borrower on behalf of the ultimate lender. Incompleteness, then, is clearly the rule, since it is normally more expensive to write and enforce complete 'state-contingent contracts' than it is to employ simple-loan contracts (with collateral, as available) and then use bankruptcy procedures to deal with mistakes.

In the 1930s, to think about application for a moment and, for that matter, possibly at any time, the erosion of borrowers' collateral (it fell sharply after the first wave of bank failures in October 1930, for example) put banks in the position of dealing with increasingly risky loans. Bankers had their choices, says Bernanke: they could

(a) write 'state-contingent' contracts;
(b) raise interest rates to cover their risks; or
(c) stop making loans to some customers.

Presumably it is the last that occurred in the 1930s, since the first is too expensive (if, indeed, even possible) and the second involves further increases in default risk (at the higher interest-rate payments). The customers thus squeezed out would include many who would have been eligible for loans in better times; this generates a situation that other writers have termed 'credit rationing'. Not making loans helps banks remain solvent simply because they can alter the mix of loans in favour of greater average safety. They would do this, in effect, because the *real* costs of credit intermediation had risen. (These costs include the expected value of the losses caused by customer defaults.)[7]

What this 'disintermediation' does, basically, is to extend and deepen the real cycle by adversely affecting both aggregate supply and aggregate demand. *Aggregate supply* is affected because 'if credit flows are dammed up, potential borrowers in the economy may not be able to secure funds to undertake worthwhile activities or investments; at the same time savers may have to devote their funds to inferior uses' (Bernanke, 1983, p. 267). These effects would limit the economy's productive capacity.[8] With respect to *aggregate demand*, the argument is simply that the higher effective cost of borrowing combined with the unchanged rate of earnings on their savings would induce demanders to shift from present-period consumption/investment to future. This would produce a 'liquidity-constrained' downward shift of the aggregate demand curve (see Bernanke, 1981). In any event, while the style of the Bernanke explanation might not be attractive to all tastes, it is very likely that something like this process works during recessions. The Great Depression seems to provide a good example, in particular, with its waves of bank failures and other credit disruptions and with its, possibly abundant, stock of potential loanable funds (at least technically).

A model is now available for the preceding discussion which spells out a possible role for intermediaries (such as banks) in the transmission process of real business cycles; this is the work of Williamson (1987*a*, *b*). Williamson points out that many of the existing real-cycle models simply do not include a financial sector in a way that could possibly provide it with a real role to play. Williamson provides one such, along the lines suggested by Bernanke.

In Williamson's model, as above, the financial intermediary provides diversification services, produces an asset transformation (i.e. creates 'substitutes') and assumes the role of acquiring information on credit-worthiness. As in Bernanke, the intermediary responds to actual default by rationing credit to (formerly) credit-worthy customers. These constraints on the lending behaviour of intermediaries are *solved for* (i.e. are endogenous) instead of (essentially) arbitrary, as in much of the voluminous credit-rationing literature. In particular, they are not disequilibrium properties of the system, but are essentially equilibrium responses to changes in the cost of doing business when (in effect) state-contingent contracts cannot be written. The tradition on which this model is written is that of Long and Plosser (1983), especially in the sense that the intertemporal substitution hypothesis of the latter is included here. Intertemporal substitution itself is not, however, required to produce real-shock or money-shock real business cycles.

The Williamson framework is an 'overlapping generations' one in which some individuals are lenders and some borrowers. Entrepreneurs contemplate investment projects with an attached probability of success; these projects yield returns to the entrepreneurs, but returns which are only directly known to the entrepreneur. Other agents can observe this return, but only by paying a monitoring cost. We are thus justifying the existence of the intermediary in terms of 'costly state verification' (as in Townsend, 1979). Assuming that agents live only two periods, Williamson argues that it would be 'rational' for an entrepreneur to borrow and lie to the lender and simply consume the proceeds of the loan. Under these circumstances of 'moral hazard' there would be no lenders. This society would invent courts, lawyers, jails and intermediaries.

In the absence of information-sharing (or collusion) among lenders, it might be advantageous for the lenders to delegate the responsibility of monitoring the loan contracts to one of their ilk. In this case, though, the 'moral hazard' problem resurfaces since this lender might lie to his colleagues and split the proceeds with the entrepreneur(s). This happens, of course, but where the intermediary differs is that, in exploiting the law of large numbers for his anticipated profit, he faces free entry in his industry. Intense competition among numerous intermediaries for many lenders and many borrowers forces an equilibrium potentially free of moral hazard. The intermediary, it should be emphasized, does the monitoring on the loan/investment side; deposits are 'non-contingent liabilities' not themselves dependent on outcomes (unless, of course, the intermediary fails). Clearly, then, in equilibrium there will always exist entrepreneurs who cannot borrow at the going rate.

They will, for instance, not be able to pay the intermediary enough interest to cover the cost of monitoring because of a low expected payoff. Furthermore, borrowers with different monitoring costs pay different interest rates. This feature itself will produce a kind of 'credit rationing' in this model.

Suppose, then, that the 'state of the world' can be described by a positively serially correlated Markov process.[9] Then let there be a technology shock (a real shock) which alters the probability of success for entrepreneurs. Williamson presents solutions for small changes in project risks in one of his recent papers (1987*b*) and provides an example in another (1987*a*). These real shocks produce serially correlated output. Furthermore, *nominal* money and real output are correlated at all leads and lags, and there is the appearance of something quite like Granger-causality running from nominal money to real income in this model. As we pointed out in Chapter 4, this result often occurs in the empirical literature. Indeed, *credit* Granger-causes real output in the same sense. The mechanisms which are jointly producing these effects are, of course, those such as intertemporal substitution, etc., on the real side and the 'credit-rationing effect' on the financial side. With regard to the latter, what happens is that the real shock raises the cost of monitoring loan contracts and causes intermediaries to squeeze off some of their customers. Williamson also notes that *both* anticipated and unanticipated money-stock changes will Granger-cause real income, that prices will move pro-cyclically (real cycle models produce contra-cyclical prices) but that shocks in *fiat* money production do not produce reasonable results.[10] Williamson concludes that all of this argues against monetary explanations of the *causes* of real business cycles although, in truth, his model does not capture all the real aspects of money creation as described, for example, in Section 6.4. Williamson's casual empiricism is generally acceptable, but it could be argued equally well that the failure to give money a *reasonable* chance to produce real cycles is a deficiency in his set-up, complicated as it is. In any case, this is a model-specific result, casually compared with the real world, which may well turn out to be important in the continuing debate over the relative influence of money on real activity. The endogenous explanation of credit rationing is especially appealing here, as are the conjectures about how Granger-causality might appear without there being a causal interpretation.

6.6 MONETARY POLICY AND FINANCIAL INTERMEDIARIES

Anything that monetary policy does to affect interest rates will affect financial intermediaries, and thus this is the natural place to start a discussion of this aspect of non-neutrality. In order to provide a little structure to the problem, however, we begin with a model that presents some of the analysis of the theoretical possibilities of an effect of monetary policy on financial intermediaries. We will look at a model of the effect on commercial banks in

particular, since that is as far as the formal theoretical work (of Hancock in this case) has gone. When we discuss banks, of course, we will obviously be making most of the points that relate to savings banks, since much of the structure of the commercial bank resembles that of the savings bank. However, we will not dig into the popular and/or unstructured literature in our discussion, but will deal solely with work that fits the kind of structural modelling that we have been engaged in in this study. In particular, the following material is not meant to be a survey of the topic (some will be referred to), but is a progress report on certain aspects that fit into the framework of this book.

6.6.1 Monetary policy and the commercial bank

This section looks at some theory related to the effect of monetary policy on the commercial bank and does this with two topics, beginning with a Translog model of the banking firm, in which monetary policy is represented by changes in interest rates. The second stage will continue the discussion of the 'regulatory wedge' initiated in Section 6.3. Both these discussions – the work of Hancock (1985*a*, *b*) – involve the modelling of the financial 'transmission process' that provides explanations of how monetary non-neutrality might arise.

Let us assume, then, following Hancock (1985*a*), that the technology of the bank is represented by

$$T(x_1, \ldots, x_{k-1}, x_k) = 0 \tag{6.43}$$

where x_k is capital fixed during the production period and the other entities are outputs and other inputs. Each of the $k-1$ inputs and outputs has a user cost associated with it $(u_1, \ldots, u_{k-1})$. To distinguish inputs from outputs, Hancock adopts the convention of calling any item with a net expenditure on it an input (with a *positive* user cost), and any item generating net revenue an output (with a *negative* user cost). Thus we have the following scheme for

$$\text{Outputs:} \quad x_i > 0 \quad \text{if} \quad u_i < 0$$

$$\text{Inputs:} \quad x_i < 0 \quad \text{if} \quad u_i > 0$$

for $i = 1, \ldots, k-1$. Furthermore, prices for these entities are defined as $p_i \equiv |u_i|$. This scheme deals with a potentially troublesome problem for which practice varies considerably.[11] Hancock prefers to work with a profit function of the commercial bank since banks can pick both inputs and outputs; the alternative is a cost function, for which a choice has to be made as to how to handle earnings assets, loans and deposits. The profit function which is dual to Equation (6.43) is

$$\pi(\tilde{\mathbf{p}}, x_k) = \max_{x} \left\{ \sum_{i=1}^{k-1} p_i x_i : T(\tilde{\mathbf{x}}, x_k) = 0 \right\} \tag{6.44}$$

The demand function for inputs/outputs are then given by

$$x_i = \frac{\partial \pi(\tilde{\mathbf{p}}, x_k)}{\partial p_i} \tag{6.45}$$

where one good (the $k-1$st) has had its price set to unity (as a numeraire) since after application of the balance sheet constraint there remain $k-2$ independent variables (inputs/outputs). The rate of return on capital can also be calculated; it is

$$R_k(\tilde{\mathbf{p}}, x_k) = \frac{\partial(\tilde{\mathbf{p}}, x_k)}{\partial x_k} \tag{6.46}$$

Monetary policy affects this rate of return by affecting interest rates and bank reserve requirements.

Since commercial-bank financial balance sheets are not written to provide the concepts needed to implement such a model, certain adjustments must be made. The user cost of the services of the ith asset is defined by Hancock to be

$$u_i = 1 - \frac{(1 + r_i + c_i + s_i - d_i)}{1 + R} \tag{6.47}$$

Here we have the discounted value of certain revenues (interest (r_i), service charges for late payments (s_i), capital gains (c_i) and losses (i.e. loan losses and insurance premiums (d_i)). This formula would return the standard user cost formula if only r_i were relevant. The user cost of the ith liability is then given by

$$u_i = -1 + \frac{(1 + r_i + b_i + Rk_i - s_i)}{1 + R} \tag{6.48}$$

Here b_i identifies deposit insurance, and s_i (as before) defines service charges; k_i represents the reserve requirement. Recall that these entities are defined as outputs or inputs in terms of the rules laid down above.

The last thing to be done before producing estimates is to set down a specific functional form for the (variable) profit function. That done, estimation can follow a well-worn track. The functional form that Hancock picks is the Translog (this is actually as close to flexibility as any of the banking literature has gone). This is

$$\log \pi = \alpha_0 + \sum_i \alpha_i \log p_i + \alpha_k \log x_k + \frac{1}{2}\sum_i \sum_j \beta_{ij} \log p_i \log p_j + \sum_i \beta_{ik} \log p_i \log x_k + \frac{1}{2} \beta_{kk} (\log x_k)^2 \tag{6.49}$$

This requires a measure of capital. With the demand functions for inputs/outputs of

$$\frac{\partial \log \pi}{\partial \log p_i} = \frac{p_i x_i}{\pi} = \alpha_i + \sum_j \beta_{ij} \log p_j + \beta_{ik} \log x_k \tag{6.50}$$

a complete system comprises Equation (6.49) and the $k-2$ demand functions just written.[12]

In her empirical work on the US data, Hancock looks at cash (x_1), demand deposits (x_2), time deposits (x_3), loans (x_4), labour (x_5) and materials (x_6) as inputs (1, 3, 5, 6) or outputs (2, 4); x_k measures the capital stock, and x_6, the materials input, is the residual. Note that loans (an asset) are an *input*, while demand deposits (an output) and time deposits (an input) fall on different sides of the fence. This is interesting. Finally, for the effect of monetary policy (almost an afterthought after all this theoretical finesse), Hancock finds that increases in interest rates (induced, presumably, by monetary policy) will increase bank profits. In particular, a 100 basis point *increase* in the loan rate raises bank profits by 33.36%, and a 100 basis point *decrease* in the time deposit rate raises bank profits by 26.46%. This suggests the following:

1. This is another reason for the real effects of monetary policy (recall that banks are real resource-using entities in this model).
2. The popular use of the spread between time deposits and loan rates to judge bank profitability effects (of changing interest rates) is potentially ambiguous. This is the case since profits *increase* even when the spread remains constant (the result of a higher estimated elasticity of profits to changes in the loan rate).

Finally, Hancock suggests that her model could be worked on different data with different functional forms (such as the Fourier); we agree.

In a second paper of the same vintage (1985*b*), Hancock applies roughly the same model to the same sample of New York and New Jersey banks. The basic findings differ only narrowly, although results are given in this case with and without individual bank dummy variables (these were included above). In this test Hancock reports on three monetary 'policy' experiments (in terms of their effects on the estimated coefficients at the 1978 means). In the first of these a 0.5 of 1% increase in the interest rate is estimated to increase the own price on time deposits by 9.4% and reduce the time deposit demand (by banks) of somewhat less than that. There is also a slight (1.5–2.3) percentage reduction in loans. The complete elimination of reserve requirements (a 'tax' equal to a rate of 0.452%) reduces the user costs on demand deposits, and under these conditions banks would supply more demand deposits (by 4.6%) – assuming the reserve requirement is a pure tax. Hancock also calculates that if the deposit insurance premium is raised – by eliminating the customary rebate – banks' user costs will fall and deposits will rise. These last two effects are not really macropolicy options as things stand, but they are 'non-market' aspects of bank regulation that provide conduits (as it were) for the real effects of monetary policy (since real resources are involved).

6.6.2 Some empirical notes

There are several possible ways one might evaluate the impact of monetary policy on financial intermediaries, but aside from a host of conjectures in the literature, the recent empirical work seems to be almost entirely devoted to a discussion of interest-rate effects. It is, of course, possible that interest rates do not respond to policy, but, as seen in Chapter 5, where our orientation was slightly different, there is at least some reason to believe that both nominal and real interest rates respond to policy pressures. Further, in the case of monetary policy there is good reason to suppose that discount rate changes will affect the borrowing behaviour of commercial banks (Goodfriend, 1983); this, too, is reason enough to look at this topic. What is missing in this literature, though, is a really rigorous implementation of the kind of effects sought here.

With respect to the interest-rate effects, there is a long-standing tradition, implemented in several papers by Flannery (1981*a*, *b*), which suggests that commercial banks actually insulate themselves against sharp interest changes by matching the term to maturity of their assets with that of their liabilities. In the first of the aforementioned papers Flannery studies a group of large 'money centre' banks – presumably those most likely to feel the impact, at least, of open-market operations – and observes the effect of changes in the market interest rate on their operating income (and on their revenues and costs). The results suggest that there is no effect, although, to be sure, this is not generated in a 'monetary surprises' environment. This is roughly what one might expect.

The large commercial banks just discussed are the main dealers in government securities, and thus they 'move the paper' pretty quickly on behalf of their customers. Very broad – and annual or quarterly – studies may not pick up the effects sought here. On the other hand, small banks and savings and loan associations may have greater exposure to monetary policy for several reasons. For one thing, their business is basically retail and, especially for the savings and loan banks, their portfolios of assets have clearly longer maturities on average, being loaded with longer-term loans and mortgages. This may not produce profit effects, of course, if their customers ignore changes in market interest rates and keep their funds in these institutions, but the well-known problems of the US savings and loan industry of recent years suggests that this is not to be counted upon. The commercial banks, large and small, do not appear to have had the same problem. Flannery repeated the test just described on a sample of 60 smaller US banks (1981*b*). The results suggest somewhat more interest rate sensitivity than for large banks, although comparisons are somewhat perilous here in view of the different nature of their product mixes; however, on net, the interest-rate risk exposure of these banks, too, seems slight.

In a later paper, Flannery and James (1984) recant slightly on the earlier work of Flannery and argue that the accounting data used in those (and

other studies) do not correctly measure the *effective maturity* of certain (apparently) short-term deposits. This concern involves demand, savings and small time deposits. The upshot is that banks may not be as completely insured against risk as an accounting view of their position would suggest.

Following up on this idea in some respects, Aharony, Saunders and Swary (1986) look at the effect on bank profits and risks of the October 1979 change in the Federal Reserve operating strategy. The idea is to look at the behaviour of the prices of bank equity, assuming that the change in procedure affects expected bank earnings and/or the riskiness of banks. With hindsight we would easily suspect at least an increase in riskiness (and hence a fall in bank stock prices), since financial variances went up dramatically around this time, but the point of the test is to see if the (assumed) new information was impounded into stock prices around the time of the announcement. The results indicate that apparently (expected) interest-rate variability had a quick *and negative* effect on the returns that an investor could get from investing in bank stocks. Incidentally, the effect of greater (expected) volatility was greater on large, money-centre banks than on smaller banks.[13]

NOTES

1. See the discussion in D. Fisher (1978, 1983). A recent paper by Nguyen (1986) runs against much of the existing empirical literature on this effect, in suggesting that the role has been overstated (on account of misspecification).
2. Exact solutions for this problem, but with firms also able to hold a bond, appear in Bernstein (1978*b*).
3. See, especially, Coen and Hickman (1970) for important qualifications concerning such an aggregation.
4. In the USA there is legislation and a lively debate over exactly what products commercial banks should offer. At present, the trend seems to be for the authorities to permit activities that are traditionally non-financial. This is not a problem for the description of the intermediary posed here, although it certainly would be if it were proposed to sum only across banks and leave out rival producers of some important services now offered by banks (e.g. discount brokerage services).
5. An exception exists when both of the aggregator functions are linearly homogeneous and the wedge is constant over time.
6. An earlier paper by the same authors (1983) provides a precise model for these liquidity services, in a somewhat narrower framework.
7. Other intermediation costs, not much affected by cycles, are screening, monitoring and accounting costs.
8. Bernanke suggests that this idea is similar to that of Gurley and Shaw (1960) whose reference is to immature (and financially fragmented) underdeveloped countries. Indeed, Bernanke asks if the financial crisis of the 1930s might have turned the USA into a 'temporarily underdeveloped economy'.
9. In this sense the Long and Plosser (1983) framework is a valid predecessor.
10. In particular, shocks in *fiat* money production (producing unemployment) would be associated with a high volume of loans and a low level of business failures. This certainly seems reasonable.

11. In the literature other approaches are taken. Benston (1965), for example, in his classic 'economies-of-scale' paper treats both loans and deposits as outputs, while Pesek (1970), following the procedure in Pesek and Saving (1967), treats deposits as output. In contrast, Mullineaux (1978) treats loans as outputs. This last is certainly the standard approach in the literature (with deposits as inputs, if they appear at all).
12. To get the parameters for input/output $k-1$,we must use the adding up conditions of

$$\alpha_{k-1} = 1 - \sum_i \alpha_i \quad \text{and} \quad \beta_{i,k-1} = -\sum_j \beta_{ij}$$

13. This does not really fit well with the results of the two Flannery studies discussed above since in these the money-centre commercial banks were thought to be more insulated against interest-rate risk than small banks, but we note that the samples are different and, in any case, this is a very small set of studies on which to base any firm conclusions.

REFERENCES

Afriat, S. (1967). 'The construction of utility functions from expenditure data', *International Economic Review* (Feb.).

Aharony, J., A. Saunders and I. Swary (1986). 'The effects of a shift in monetary policy regime on the profitability and risk of commercial banks', *Journal of Monetary Economics* (May).

Ahking, F. W. (1984). 'The predictive performance of the time series and the regression model of the income velocity of money', *Journal of Banking and Finance* (Sept.).

Akaike, H. (1970). 'Statistical predictor identification', *Annals of the Institute of Statistical Mathematics* (**22**, 203–17).

Archibald, G. C. and R. E. Lipsey (1958). 'Monetary and value theory: a critique of Lange and Patinkin', *Review of Economic Studies* (Oct.).

Arrow, K. J. and F. Hahn (1971). *General Competitive Analysis* (San Francisco: Holden-Day).

Artis, M. J. and M. K. Lewis (1976). 'The demand for money in the United Kingdom: 1963–1973', *Manchester School* (June).

Attfield, C. L. F., D. Demery and N. W. Duck (1981*a*). 'Unanticipated monetary growth, output and the price level: UK 1946–1977', *European Economic Review* (June/July).

Attfield, C. L. F., D. Demery and N.W. Duck (1981*b*). 'A quarterly model of unanticipated monetary growth, output and the price level in the UK, 1963–1978', *Journal of Monetary Economics* (Nov.).

Baltensperger, E. (1980). 'Alternative approaches to the theory of the banking firm', *Journal of Monetary Economics* (Jan.).

Barnett, W. A. (1978). 'The user cost of money', *Economics Letters* (1, No. 2).

Barnett, W. A. (1980). 'Economic monetary aggregates: an application of index number and aggregation theory', *Journal of Econometrics* (Sept.).

Barnett, W. A. (1981). *Consumer Demand and Labour Supply: Goods, Monetary Assets and Time* (Amsterdam: North-Holland).

Barnett, W. A. (1983). 'New indices of money supply and the flexible Laurent demand system', *Journal of Business and Economics Statistics* (Jan.).

Barnett, W. A. (1984). 'Recent monetary policy and the Divisia monetary aggregates', *The American Statistician* (Aug.).

Barnett, W. A. (1987). 'The microeconomic theory of monetary aggregation', in *New Approaches to Monetary Economics*, W. A. Barnett and K. Singleton (eds) (Cambridge: The University Press).

Barnett, W. A. and P. Spindt (1979). 'The velocity behaviour and information content of Divisia monetary aggregates', *Economic Letters* (**4**, No. 1).

Barnett, W. A., M. J. Hinich and W. E. Weber (1986). 'The regulatory wedge between the demand-side and supply-side aggregation-theoretic monetary aggregates', *Journal of Econometrics* (Annals, No. 2).

Barnett, W. A., E. K. Offenbacher and P. A. Spindt (1984). 'The new Divisia monetary aggregates', *Journal of Political Economy* (Dec.).

Barro, R. J. (1976). 'Integral constraints and aggregation in an inventory model of money demand', *Journal of Finance* (Mar.).

Barro, R. J. (1977). 'Unanticipated money growth and unemployment in the United States', *American Economic Review* (Mar.).

Barro, R. J. (1978). 'Unanticipated money, output, and the price level in the United States', *Journal of Political Economy* (Aug.).

Barro, R. J. and M. Rush (1980). 'Unanticipated money and economic activity', in S. Fischer (ed.) *Rational Expectations and Economic Policy* (Chicago: University of Chicago Press).

Baumol, W. (1952). 'The transactions demand for cash: an inventory-theoretic approach', *Quarterly Journal of Economics* (Nov.).

Belongia, M. T. (1984). 'Money growth variability and GNP', *Review*, Federal Reserve Bank of St Louis (April).

Belongia, M. T. and J. A. Chalfant (1989). 'The changing empirical definition of money: some estimates from a model of the demand for money substitutes', *Journal of Political Economy*, forthcoming.

Belongia, M. T. and R. G. Sheehan (1987). 'The informational efficiency of weekly money announcements', *Journal of Business and Economics Statistics* (July).

Benderly, J. and B. Zwick (1985). 'Inflation, real balances, and real stock returns', *American Economic Review* (Dec.).

Benston, G. J. (1965). 'Branch banking and economies of scale', *Journal of Finance* (May).

Bernanke, B. S. (1981). 'Bankruptcy, liquidity, and recession', *American Economic Review* (May).

Bernanke, B. S. (1983). 'Non-monetary effects of the financial crisis in the propagation of the Great Depression', *American Economic Review* (June).

Berndt, E. R. and L. R. Christensen (1973). 'The internal structure of functional relationships: separability, substitution and aggregation', *Review of Economic Studies* (July).

Bernstein, J. I. (1978*a*). 'Household behaviour and the demand for money', in D. Fisher, *Monetary Theory and the Demand for Money* (London: Martin-Robertson).

Bernstein, J. I. (1978*b*). 'The demand for money by the firm', in D. Fisher, *Monetary Theory and the Demand for Money* (London: Martin-Robertson).

Beveridge, S. and C. R. Nelson (1981). 'A new approach to decomposition of economic time series into permanent and transitory components with particular attention to measurement of the "business cycle"', *Journal of Monetary Economics* (Mar.).

Bhattacharyya, D. K. (1979). 'On measuring the nearness of near-moneys: an econometric experiment with the UK personal sector data', University of Leicester, *Discussion Paper* (No. 9, Aug.).

Blackorby, C., D. Primont and R. R. Russell (1978). *Duality, Separability and Functional Form* (Amsterdam: North-Holland).

Blinder, A. S. and S. Fischer (1981). 'Inventories, rational expectations, and the business cycle', *Journal of Monetary Economics* (Nov.).

Bodie, Z. (1976). 'Common stocks as hedges against inflation', *Journal of Finance* (May).

Bomhoff, E. J. (1980). *Inflation, the Quantity Theory, and Rational Expectations* (Amsterdam: North-Holland).

Bomhoff, E. J. (1982). 'Predicting the price level in a world that changes all the time', *Carnegie–Rochester Conference Series on Public Policy* (No. 17).

Bonomo, V. and J. E. Tanner (1983). 'Expected monetary changes and relative prices: a look at evidence from the stock market', *Southern Economic Journal* (Oct.).

Bordo, M. D. and L. Jonung (1987). The long-run behaviour of the velocity of circulation: the international evidence (Cambridge: Cambridge University Press).

Boughton, J. (1981). 'Money and its substitutes', *Journal of Monetary Economics* (Nov.).

Brainard, W. C. and J. Tobin (1968). 'Pitfalls in financial model building', *American Economic Review* (May).

Brock, W. A. (1974). 'Money and growth: the case of long-run perfect foresight', *International Economic Review* (Oct.).

Brunner, K. (1971). 'A survey of selected issues in monetary theory', *Schweizerische Zeitschrift für Volkswirtschaft und Statistik* (No. 1).

Brunner, K. and A. Meltzer (1967). 'Economies of scale in cash balances reconsidered', *Quarterly Journal of Economics* (Aug.).

Brunner, K. and A. Meltzer (1971). 'The uses of money: money in the theory of an exchange economy', *American Economic Review* (Dec.).

Buchanan, J. M. (1969). 'An outside economist's defence of Pesek and Saving', *Journal of Economic Literature* (Sept.).

Cagan, P. (1965). *Determinants and Effects of Changes in the Stock of Money, 1875–1960* (New York: Columbia University Press).

Canto, V. A., M. C. Findlay and M. R. Reinganum (1983). 'The monetary approach to stock returns and inflation', *Southern Economic Journal* (Oct.).

Carr, J. and M. J. Darby (1981). 'The role of money supply shocks in the short-run demand for money', *Journal of Monetary Economics* (Sept.).

Chetty, V. (1969). 'On measuring the nearness of near-moneys', *American Economic Review* (June).

Christensen, L. R., D. W. Jorgenson, and L. J. Lau (1975). 'Transcendental logarithmic utility functions', *American Economic Review* (June).

Christiano, L. J. (1986). 'Money and the US economy in the 1980s: a break from the past?', *Quarterly Review*, Federal Reserve Bank of Minneapolis (Summer).

Chrystal, K. A. and M. Chatterji (1987). 'Money and disaggregate supply in the United States, 1950–1982', *European Economic Review* (Aug.).

Clower, R. (1967). 'A reconsideration of the microfoundations of monetary theory', in R. Clower (ed.), *Monetary Theory: Selected Readings* (London: Penguin).

Clower, R. and P. Howitt (1978). 'The transactions theory of the demand for money: a reconsideration', *Journal of Political Economy* (June).

Coen, R. M. and B. G. Hickman (1970). 'Constrained joint estimation of factor demand and production functions', *Review of Economics and Statistics* (Aug.).

Cook, T. and T. Hahn (1987). 'The reaction of interest rates to unanticipated Federal Reserve actions and statements: implications for the money announcements controversy', *Economic Inquiry* (July).

Cooley, T. F. and S. F. Leroy (1981). 'Identification and estimation of money demand', *American Economic Review* (Dec.).

Cooper, R. V. L. (1974). 'Efficient capital markets and the quantity theory of money', *Journal of Finance* (June).

Cramer J. S. (1986). 'The volume of transactions and the circulation of money in the United States, 1950–79', *Journal of Business and Economic Statistics* (Apr.).

Cuthbertson, K. M. (1986). 'Monetary anticipations and the demand for money: Some UK evidence', *Bulletin of Economic Research* (Sept.).

Cuthbertson, K. M. and M. P. Taylor (1987). 'Monetary anticipations and the demand for money: some evidence for the UK', *Weltwirtschaftliches Archiv* (No. 3).

Davidson, P. (1972). *Money and the Real World* (London: Macmillan).

Deaton, A. and J. Muellbauer (1980). *Economics and Consumer Behaviour* (Cambridge: Cambridge University Press).

Dennis, E. and V. K. Smith (1978). 'A neoclassical analysis of the demand for real cash balances by firms', *Journal of Political Economy* (Oct.).

Denny, M. and M. Fuss (1977). 'The use of approximation analysis to test for separability and the existence of consistent aggregates', *American Economic Review* (June).

Diamond, D. W. and P. H. Dybvig (1983). 'Bank runs, deposit insurance, and liquidity', *Journal of Political Economy*, (June).

Diamond, D. W. and P. H. Dybvig (1986). 'Banking theory, deposit insurance, and banking regulation', *Journal of Business* (Jan.).

Dickey, D. A. and W. A. Fuller (1979). 'Distribution for the estimators for autoregressive time series with a unit root', *Journal of the American Statistical Association* (June).

Diewert, W. E. (1974*a*). 'Intertemporal consumer theory and the demand for durables', *Econometrica* (May).

Diewert, W. E. (1974*b*). 'Applications of duality theory', in M. Intriligator (ed.), *Frontiers of Quantitative Economics*, **2** (Amsterdam: North-Holland).

Donovan, D. J. (1978). 'Modeling the demand for liquid assets: an application to Canada', IMF *Staff Papers* (Dec.).

Dotsey, M. and R. G. King (1988). 'Rational expectations business cycle models: a survey', *Economic Review*, Federal Reserve Bank of Richmond (Mar./Apr.).

Dutton, D. S. and W. P. Gramm (1973). 'Transactions costs, the wage rate, and the demand for money', *American Economic Review* (Sept.).

Dutton, D. S., W. P. Gramm and J. McDonald (1974). 'Transactions costs, the wage rate, and the firm's demand for money', mimeo, University of Iowa.

Dwyer, G. P., Jr and R. W. Hafer (1988). 'Is money irrelevant?' *Review*, Federal Reserve Bank of St Louis (May/June).

Eichenbaum, M. and K. Singleton (1987). 'Do equilibrium real business cycle theories explain post-War US fluctuations?', *NBER Macroeconomic Annual* (Cambridge, MA: MIT Press).

El Badawi, I., A. R. Gallant and G. Souza (1982). 'An elasticity can be estimated consistently without *a priori* knowledge of functional form', mimeo, Northwestern University Center for Mathematical Studies in Economics and Management Science (No. 542, Nov.).

Evans, P. (*c.* 1982). 'Monetary policy and the determination of interest rates', mimeo, Stanford University.

Ewis, N. A. (1982). *Nonlinear Monetary Assets Demand System in the Context of Flexible Functional Forms*, PhD Dissertation (Raleigh, NC: North Carolina State University).

Ewis, N. A. and D. Fisher (1984). 'The Translog utility function and the demand for money in the United States', *Journal of Money, Credit, and Banking* (Feb.).

Ewis, N. and D. Fisher (1985). 'Toward a consistent estimate of the demand for monies: an application of the Fourier flexible form', *Journal of Macroeconomics* (Spring).

Fair, R. C. (1987). 'International evidence on the demand for money', *Review of Economics and Statistics* (Aug.).

Fama, E. F. (1970). 'Efficient capital markets: a review of theory and empirical work', *Journal of Finance* (May).

Fama, E. F. (1975). 'Short-term interest rates as predictors of inflation', *American Economic Review* (June).
Fama, E. F. (1981). 'Stock returns, real activity, inflation, and money', *American Economic Review* (Sept.).
Fama, E. F. (1982). 'Inflation, output, and money', *Journal of Business* (Apr.).
Fama, E. F. (1985). 'What's different about banks?', *Journal of Monetary Economics* (Jan.).
Fama, E. F. (1987). 'International evidence on the demand for money'. *Review of Economics and Statistics* (Aug.).
Fama, E. F. and M. R. Gibbons (1980). 'Inflation, real returns, and capital investment', mimeo, Graduate School of Business, University of Chicago (Aug.).
Fama, E. F. and G. W. Schwert (1977). 'Asset returns and inflation', *Journal of Financial Economics* (Nov.).
Farr, H. T. and D. Johnson (1985*a*). 'Revisions in the monetary services (Divisia) indexes of monetary aggregates', *Special Studies Paper* (No. 59), (Washington: Board of Governors of the Federal Reserve System).
Farr, H. T. and D. Johnson (1985*b*). 'Revisions in the monetary services (Divisia) indexes of the monetary aggregates', *Staff Study* (No. 147), (Washington: Board of Governors of the Federal Reserve System).
Fayaad, S. K. (1986). 'A microeconomic system-wide approach to the estimation of the demand for money', *Review*, Federal Reserve Bank of St Louis (Aug./Sept.).
Feenstra, R. C. (1986). 'Functional equivalence between liquidity costs and the utility of money', *Journal of Monetary Economics* (Mar.).
Feige, E. L. (1964). *The Demand for Liquid Assets* (Englewood Cliffs, NJ: Prentice-Hall).
Feige, E. L. (1974). 'Alternative cross-section specifications of the demand for demand deposits', in H. G. Johnson and A. R. Nobay (eds), *Issues in Monetary Economics* (Oxford: Oxford University Press).
Feige, E. L. and D. K. Pearce (1977). 'The substitutability of money and near monies: a survey of time series evidence', *Journal of Economic Literature* (June).
Feige, E. L. and D. K. Pearce (1979). 'The casual causal relationship between money and income: some caveats for time series analysis', *Review of Economics and Statistics* (Nov.).
Feldstein, M. S. (1980). 'Inflation and the stock market', *American Economic Review* (Dec.).
Fethke, G. C. and A. J. Policano (1981). 'Long-term contracts and the effectiveness of demand and supply policies', *Journal of Money, Credit, and Banking* (Nov.).
Fethke, G. C. and A. J. Policano (1984). 'Wage contingencies, the pattern of negotiations, and aggregate implications of alternative contract structures', *Journal of Monetary Economics* (Sept.).
Fethke, G. C. and A. J. Policano (1985). 'Monetary policy and the timing of wage contract negotiations', mimeo, University of Iowa (May).
Fischer, S. (1974). 'Money and the production function', *Economic Inquiry* (Dec.).
Fischer, S. (1977). 'Long-term contracts, rational expectations, and the optimal money supply rule', *Journal of Political Economy* (Feb.).
Fischer, S. (1979). 'Capital accumulation on the transition path in a monetary optimizing model', *Econometrica* (Nov.).
Fischer, S. (1981). 'Is there a real-balance effect in equilibrium?', *Journal of Monetary Economics* (July).
Fisher, D. (1970). 'Real balances and the demand for money', *Journal of Political Economy*, (Nov./Dec.).
Fisher, D. (1978). *Monetary Theory and the Demand for Money* (London: Martin-Robertson).

Fisher, D. (1983). *Macroeconomic Theory: A Survey* (London: Macmillan).

Fisher, D. (1988). *Monetary and Fiscal Policy* (London: Macmillan).

Fisher, D. and A. Serletis (1989). 'Velocity and the growth of money in the United States, 1970–1985', *Journal of Macroeconomics* (Summer).

Fisher, I. (1922). *The Purchasing Power of Money* (New York: Augustus M. Kelley, 1963).

Fisher, M. (1988). *Time Series Implications of the Long-Run Neutrality and Superneutrality of Money*, PhD Thesis (Chicago: University of Chicago).

Flannery, M. J. (1981*a*). 'Market interest rates and commercial bank profitability: an empirical investigation', *Journal of Finance* (Dec.).

Flannery, M. J. (1981*b*). 'The impact of market interest rates on small commercial banks', mimeo, University of Pennsylvania (May).

Flannery, M. J. and C. M. James (1984). 'Market evidence on the effective maturity of bank assets and liabilities', *Journal of Money, Credit, and Banking* (Nov., Pt 1).

Flavin, M. (1981). 'The adjustments of consumption to changing expectations about future income', *Journal of Political Economy* (Oct.).

Fratianni, M. and F. Spinelli (1984). 'Italy in the gold standard period, 1861–1914', in A. J. Schwartz and M. D. Bordo (eds), *A Retrospective on the Classical Gold Standard, 1821–1931* (Chicago: University of Chicago Press).

Friedman, M. (1956). 'The quantity theory of money – a restatement', in *Studies in the Quantity Theory of Money*, Milton Friedman (ed.) (Chicago: University of Chicago Press).

Friedman, M. (1968). 'The role of monetary policy', *American Economic Review* (Mar.).

Friedman, M. (1971). 'A monetary theory of nominal income', *Journal of Political Economy* (Mar./Apr.).

Friedman, M. (1977). 'Time perspective in demand for money', *Scandinavian Journal of Economics* (Dec.).

Friedman, M. (1983). 'Monetary variability: United States and Japan', *Journal of Money, Credit, and Banking* (Aug.).

Friedman, M. (1984). 'Lessons from the 1979–82 monetary policy experiment', *American Economic Review* (May).

Friedman, M. and A. J. Schwartz (1963). *A Monetary History of the United States, 1867–1960* (Princeton: Princeton University Press).

Friedman, M. and A. J. Schwartz (1970). *Monetary Statistics of The United States* (New York: Columbia University Press).

Friedman, M. and A. J. Schwartz (1982). *Monetary Trends in the United States and the United Kingdom* (Chicago: University of Chicago Press).

Gallant, A. R. (1981). 'On the bias in flexible functional forms and an essentially unbiased form: the Fourier flexible form', *Journal of Econometrics* (Feb.).

Garbade, P. J. and P. Wachtel (1978). 'Time variation in the relationship between inflation and interest rates', *Journal of Monetary Economics* (Nov.).

Goldfeld, S. M. (1973). 'The demand for money revisited', *Brookings Papers on Economic Activity* (No. 3).

Goodfriend, M. (1983). 'Discount window borrowing, monetary policy, and the post-October 1979 Federal Reserve operating procedure', *Journal of Monetary Economics* (Sept.).

Goodhart, C. (1975). *Money, Information and Uncertainty* (London: Macmillan).

Gordon, R. J. (1984). 'The 1981–82 velocity decline: a structural shift in income or money demand?', NBER Working Paper Series, No. 1343 (May).

Gordon, R. J. (1986). *The American Business Cycle* (Chicago: University of Chicago Press).

Gould, J. P. and C. R. Nelson (1974). 'The stochastic structure of the velocity of money', *American Economic Review* (June).

Gramlich, E. M. and D. T. Hulett (1972). 'The demand for and supply of savings deposits', in E. M. Gramlich and D. M. Jaffee (eds), *Savings Deposits, Mortgages, and Housing* (Lexington, MA: Lexington Books).

Granger, C. W. J. (1969). 'Investigating causal relationships by econometric models and cross-spectral methods', *Econometrica* (July).

Green, H. A. J. (1964). *Aggregation in Economic Analysis* (Princeton: Princeton University Press).

Grice, J. W. (1981). 'Wealth effects and expenditure functions: a survey of the evidence ' in M. J. Artis and M. H. Miller (eds), *Essays in Fiscal and Monetary Policy* (Oxford: Oxford University Press).

Grossman, J. (1981). 'The "rationality" of money supply expectations and the short-run response of interest rates to monetary surprises', *Journal of Money, Credit, and Banking* (Nov.).

Gurley, J. G. and E. S. Shaw (1960). *Money in a Theory of Finance* (Washington, DC: Brookings).

Hafer, R. W. and S. E. Hein (1982). 'Monetary policy and short-term real rates of interest', *Review*, Federal Reserve Bank of St Louis (Mar.).

Hall, R. E. (1978). 'Stochastic implications of the life cycle permanent income hypothesis: theory and evidence', *Journal of Political Economy* (Dec.).

Hall, T. E. and N. R. Noble (1987). 'Velocity and the variability of money growth: Evidence from Granger-causality tests', *Journal of Money, Credit, and Banking* (Feb.).

Hancock, D. (1985*a*). 'Bank profitability, interest rates, and monetary policy', *Journal of Money, Credit, and Banking* (May).

Hancock, D. (1985*b*). 'The financial firm: production with monetary and non-monetary goods', *Journal of Political Economy* (Oct.).

Harvey, A. C. (1981).*Time Series Models* (New York: Wiley).

Harvey, A. C. and A. M. J. Todd (1983). 'Forecasting economic time series with structural and Box–Jenkins Models', *Journal of Business and Economics Statistics* (Oct.).

Heller, H. R. and M. Khan (1979). 'The demand for money and the term structure of interest rates', *Journal of Political Economy* (Feb.).

Hetzel, R. L. (1986). 'A critique of theories of money stock determination', mimeo (Federal Reserve Bank of Richmond).

Hicks, J. (1946). *Value and Capital* (Oxford: Clarendon Press).

Higgins, B. and J. Faust (1981). 'Velocity behaviour of the new monetary aggregates', *Economic Review*, Federal Reserve of Kansas City (Sept.–Oct.).

Hoffman, D. L. and E. Schlagenhauf (1988). 'Real interest rates, anticipated inflation, and unanticipated money: a multi-country study', *Review of Economics and Statistics* (May).

Hsiao, C. (1979*a*). 'Autoregressive modelling of Canadian money and income data', *Journal of the American Statistical Association* (Sept.).

Hsiao, C. (1979*b*). 'Causality tests in econometrics', *Journal of Economic Dynamics and Control* (Nov.).

Huizinga, J. and L. Leiderman (1987). 'The signalling role of base and money announcements and their effect on interest rates', *Journal of Monetary Economics* (Dec.).

Johnson, H. G. (1970). 'Recent developments in monetary theory – a commentary', in D. Croome and H. G. Johnson (eds), *Money in Britain, 1959–1969* (Oxford: Oxford University Press).

Jonung, L. (1984). 'Swedish experience under the classical gold standard, 1873–1914', in A. J. Schwartz and M. D. Bordo (eds), *A Retrospective on the Classical Gold Standard, 1821–1931*' (Chicago: University of Chicago Press).

Jorgenson, D. W. (1963). 'Capital theory and investment behaviour', *American Economic Review* (May).

Jorgenson, D. W. and L. J. Lau (1979). 'The integrability of consumer demand functions', *European Economic Review* (Apr.).

Jorgenson, D. W. and J. A. Stephenson (1967). 'Investment behaviour in the US manufacturing sector, 1947–1960', *Econometrica* (Apr.).

Judd, J. P. and B. Motley (1984). 'The great velocity decline of 1982–83: A comparative analysis of M1 and M2', *Economic Review*, Federal Reserve Bank of San Francisco (Summer).

Kalman, P., R. Dusansky, and B. Wickstrom (1974). 'On the major Slutsky properties when money is the sole medium of exchange', *International Economic Review* (Oct.).

Kareken, J. and N. Wallace (1978). 'Deposit insurance and bank regulation: a partial equilibrium exposition', *Journal of Business* (July).

Karni, E. (1974*a*). 'The value of time and the demand for money', *Journal of Money, Credit, and Banking* (Feb.).

Karni, E. (1974*b*). 'The transactions demand for cash: incorporation of the value of time into the inventory approach', *Journal of Political Economy* (Sep./Oct.).

Karni, E. (1975*a*). 'The value of time and the demand for money: a rejoinder', *Journal of Monetary Economics* (Oct.).

Karni, E. (1975*b*). 'The value of time and the demand for money: evidence from the UK time series data', *Australian Economic Papers* (Dec.).

Keran, M. W. (1971). 'Expectations, money, and the stock market', *Review*, Federal Reserve Bank of St Louis (Jan.).

Keynes, J. M. (1936). *The General Theory of Employment, Interest, and Money* (London: Macmillan).

King, R. G. and C. I. Plosser (1984). 'Money, credit, and prices in a real business cycle', *American Economic Review* (June).

Klein, B. (1974). 'Competitive interest payments on bank deposits and the long-run demand for money', *American Economic Review* (Dec.).

Klein, B. (1977). 'The demand for quality-adjusted cash balances: price uncertainty in the US demand for money function', *Journal of Political Economy* (Aug.).

Kretzmer, P. E. (1985). 'Cross-industry tests of an equilibrium business cycle model with rational expectations', mimeo, Board of Governors of the Federal Reserve System (Nov.).

Laidler, D. E. W. (1969). 'The definition of money: theoretical and empirical problems', *Journal of Money, Credit, and Banking* (Aug.).

Laidler, D. E. W. (1985). *The Demand for Money* (New York: Harper and Row).

Lancaster, K. (1966). 'A new approach to consumer theory', *Journal of Political Economy* (Apr.).

Lee, T. H. (1966). 'Substitutability of non-bank intermediary liabilities for money: the empirical evidence', *Journal of Finance* (Sept.).

Lee, T. H. (1972). 'On measuring the nearness of near-monies: comment', *American Economic Review* (Mar.).

Leiderman, L. (1983). 'The response of real wages to unanticipated money growth', *Journal of Monetary Economics* (Jan.).

Levhari, D. and D. Patinkin (1968). 'The role of money in a simple growth model', *American Economic Review* (Sept.).

Lindsey, D. E. and P. A. Spindt (1986). 'An evaluation of monetary indices', *Special Studies Paper* (No. 195) (Washington: Board of Governors of the Federal Reserve System).

Lloyd, C. (1964). 'The real balance effect and the Slutsky equation', *Journal of Political Economy* (June).

Lloyd, C. (1968). 'Two classical monetary models', in J. Wolfe (ed.), *Value, Capital, and Growth* (Edinburgh: Edinburgh University Press).

Lloyd, C. (1971). 'Preferences, separability, and the Patinkin model', *Journal of Political Economy* (May/June).

Long, J. B. and C. I. Plosser (1983). 'Real business cycles', *Journal of Political Economy* (Feb.).

Lucas, R. E. (1975). 'An equilibrium model of the business cycle', *Journal of Political Economy* (Dec.).

Lucas, R. E. (1976). 'Econometric policy evaluation: a critique', in K. Brunner and A. H. Meltzer (eds), *The Phillips Curve and Labour Markets* (New York: North-Holland).

Lucas, R. E. (1980). 'Two illustrations of the quantity theory of money', *American Economic Review* (Dec.).

Lucas, R. E. and N. L. Stokey (1987). 'Money and interest in a "cash-in-advance" economy', *Econometrica* (May).

MacDonald, R. and D. A. Peel (1986). 'On lagged adjustment, permanent income, expectations formation and the demand for money', *Oxford Institute of Statistics Bulletin* (Feb.).

MacKinnon, J. G. and R. D. Milbourne (1984). 'Monetary anticipations and the demand for money', *Journal of Monetary Economics* (Mar.).

Maddala, G. S. and R. C. Vogel (1969). 'Estimating lagged relationships in corporate demand for liquid assets', *Review of Economics and Statistics* (Feb.).

Mankiw, N. G. (1985). 'Small menu costs and large business cycles: a macroeconomic model of monopoly', *Quarterly Journal of Economics* (May).

Mankiw, N. G. and L. H. Summers (1986). 'Money demand and the effects of fiscal policies', *Journal of Money, Credit, and Banking* (Nov.).

Mascaro, A. and A. H. Meltzer (1983). 'Long- and short-term interest rates in a risky world', *Journal of Monetary Economics* (Nov.).

McCallum, B. T. (1977). 'Price-level stickiness and the feasibility of monetary stabilization policy with rational expectations', *Journal of Political Economy* (June).

McCallum, B. T. (1981). 'Price level determinacy with an interest rate policy rule and rational expectations', *Journal of Monetary Economics* (Nov.).

McCallum, B. T. (1986*a*). 'Some issues concerning interest rate pegging, price level determinacy, and the real bills doctrine', *Journal of Monetary Economics* (Jan.).

McCallum, B. T. (1986*b*). 'On "real" and "sticky price" theories of the business cycle', NBER Working Paper No. 1933 (June).

McKenzie, G. W. and I. F. Pearce (1976). 'Exact measures of welfare and the cost of living', *Review of Economic Studies* (Oct.).

McKenzie, G. W. and I. F. Pearce (1980). 'How to write real consumption (production), cost of living indices, consumer surplus, or the equivalent and compensating variations all with one formula', mimeo, University of Southampton (No. 8015).

Metzler, L. (1951). 'Wealth, saving, and the rate of interest', *Journal of Political Economy* (Apr.).

Mill, J. S. (1848). *Principles of Political Economy* (New York: Kelley, 1987).

Miller, M. and D. Orr (1966). 'A model of the demand for money by firms', *Quarterly Journal of Economics* (Aug.).

Miller, M. and D. Orr (1968). 'The demand for money by firms: extension of analytic results', *Journal of Finance* (Dec.).

Mills, T. C. (1982). 'Signal extraction and two illustrations of the quantity theory of money', *American Economic Review* (Dec.).

Minford, P. and D. A. Peel (1981). 'The role of monetary stabilization policy under rational expectation', *Manchester School* (March).

Mishkin, F. S. (1978*a*). 'Efficient markets theory: implications for monetary policy', *Brookings Papers* (No. 3).

Mishkin, F. S. (1978*b*). 'The household balance sheet and the Great Depression', *Journal of Economic History* (Dec.).

Mishkin, F. S. (1982). 'Does anticipated monetary policy matter? an econometric investigation', *Journal of Political Economy* (Feb.).

Morishima, M. (1973). 'Consumer behaviour and liquidity preference', in M. Morishima, *et al.*, *Theory of Demand, Real and Monetary* (Oxford: Oxford University Press).

Moroney, J. R. and B. J. Wilbratte (1976). 'Money and money substitutes: a time series analysis of household portfolios', *Journal of Money, Credit, and Banking* (May).

Muellbauer, J, (1983). 'Surprises in the consumption function', *Economic Journal* (Supplement).

Mullineaux, D. J. (1978). 'Economies of scale and organizational efficiency in banking: a profit-function approach', *Journal of Finance* (Mar.).

Mundell, R. A. (1963). 'Inflation and real interest', *Journal of Political Economy* (June).

Muth, J. F. (1961). 'Rational expectations and the theory of price movements', *Econometrica* (July).

Nadiri, M. I. (1969). 'The determinants of real cash balances in the US total manufacturing sector', *Quarterly Journal of Economics* (May).

Nelson, C. R. (1976). 'Inflation and rates of return on common stocks', *Journal of Finance* (May).

Nelson, C. R. and C. I. Plosser (1982). 'Trends and random walks in macroeconomic time series: some evidence and implications', *Journal of Monetary Economics* (Sept.).

Nelson, C. R. and G. W. Schwert (1977). 'Short-term interest rates as predictors of inflation: on testing the hypothesis that the real rate of interest is constant', *American Economic Review* (June).

Nguyen, H. V. (1986). 'Money in the aggregate production function: re-examination and further evidence', *Journal of Money, Credit, and Banking* (May).

Nichols, D. A., D. H. Small and C. E. Webster (1983). 'Why interest rates rise when an unexpectedly large money stock is announced', *American Economic Review* (June).

Niehans, J. (1978). *The Theory of Money* (Baltimore: Johns Hopkins University).

Obstfeld, M. (1984). 'Multiple stable equilibria in an optimizing perfect-foresight model', *Econometrica* (Jan.).

Offenbacher, E. (1979). *The Substitutability of Monetary Assets* (PhD Thesis, University of Chicago).

Orr, D. and W. G. Mellon (1961). 'Stochastic reserve losses and expansion of bank credit', *American Economic Review* (Sept.).

Parkin, M. (1970). 'Discount house portfolio and debt selection', *Review of Economic Studies* (Oct.).

Parkin, M. (1978). 'A comparison of alternative techniques of monetary control under rational expectations', *Manchester School* (Sept.).

Patinkin, D. (1965). *Money, Interest, and Prices* (2nd edn) (New York: Harper and Row).

Patinkin, D. (1969). 'Money and wealth: a review article', *Journal of Economic Literature* (Dec.).

Pearce, D. K. (1982). 'The impact of inflation on stock prices', *Economic Review*, Federal Reserve Bank of Kansas City (Mar.).

Pearce, D. K. and V. V. Roley (1982). 'The reaction of stock prices to unanticipated changes in money', mimeo, Federal Reserve Bank of Kansas City (Sept.).

Pesando, J. E. (1974). 'The supply of money and common stock prices: Further observations on the econometric evidence', *Journal of Finance* (June).

Pesando, J. E. (1979). 'On the random walk characteristics of short- and long-term interest rates in an efficient market', *Journal of Money, Credit, and Banking* (Nov.).

Pesek, B. P. (1970). 'Bank's supply function and the equilibrium quantity of money', *Canadian Journal of Economics* (Aug.).

Pesek, B. P. and T. R. Saving (1967). *Money, Wealth, and Economic Theory* (New York: Macmillan).

Phelps, E. S. (1968). *Golden Rules of Economic Growth* (New York: Norton).

Phelps, E. S. and J. B. Taylor (1977). 'Stabilizing powers of monetary policy under rational expectations', *Journal of Political Economy* (Feb.).

Phiips, L. (1974). *Applied Consumption Analysis* (Amsterdam: North-Holland).

Phlips, L. (1978). 'The demand for leisure and money', *Econometrica* (Sept.).

Pyle, D. H. (1971). 'On the theory of financial intermediation', *Journal of Finance* (June).

Rogalski, R. J. and J. D. Vinso (1977). 'Stock returns, money supply and the direction of causality', *Journal of Finance* (Sept.).

Roley, V. V. (1983). 'Response of short-term interest rates to weekly money announcements', *Journal of Money, Credit, and Banking* (Aug.).

Roley, V. V. (1985), 'Money demand predictability', *Journal of Money, Credit, and Banking* (Nov., Pt 2).

Roley, V. V. and C. E. Walsh (1984). 'Unanticipated money and interest rates', *American Economic Review* (May).

Rossiter, R. and T. H. Lee (1984). 'Statistical tests of relative substitutabilities of near-monies over time', *Journal of Macroeconomics* (Summer).

Rozeff, M. S. (1974). 'Money and stock prices: market efficiency and the lag in effect of monetary policy', *Journal of Financial Economics* (Sept.).

Samuelson, P. A. (1939). 'Interaction between the multiplier analysis and the principle of acceleration', *Review of Economic Studies* (May).

Samuelson, P. A. (1947). *The Foundations of Economic Analysis* (Cambridge, MA: Harvard University Press).

Samuelson, P. A. (1970). 'The fundamental approximation theorem of portfolio analysis in terms of means, variances, and higher moments', *Review of Economic Studies* (Oct.).

Samuelson, P. A. and S. Swamy (1974). 'Invariant economic index numbers and canonical duality: survey and synthesis', *American Economic Review* (Sept.).

Santoni, G. J. (1987). 'Changes in wealth and the velocity of money'. *Review*, Federal Reserve Bank of St Louis (Mar.).

Santomero, A. M. (1984). 'Modelling the banking firm, a survey', *Journal of Money, Credit, and Banking* (Nov.).

Sargent, T. (1979). *Macroeconomic Theory* (New York: Academic Press).

Sargent, T. (1987). *Dynamic Macroeconomic Theory* (Cambridge, MA: Harvard University Press).

Sargent, T. J. and N. Wallace (1975). 'Rational expectations, the optimal monetary instrument, and the optimal money supply rule', *Journal of Political Economy* (Apr.).

Saving, T. R. (1971). 'Transactions cost and the demand for money', *American Economic Review* (June).

Saving, T. R. (1972). 'Transactions costs and the firm's demand for money', *Journal of Money, Credit, and Banking* (May).

Saving, T. R. (1976). 'Transactions cost functions and the inventory-theoretic approach to money demand', *Journal of Money, Credit, and Banking* (Aug.).

Saving T. R. (1977). 'A theory of money supply with competitive banking', *Journal of Monetary Economics* (July).

Schmidt, J. R. (1978). 'Economically rational expectations and the demand for money', mimeo, University of Nebraska-Lincoln (May).

Sealey, C. W. (1980). 'Deposit rate-setting, risk-aversion, and the theory of depository financial intermediaries', *Journal of Finance* (Dec.).

Selden, R. T. (1956). 'Monetary velocity in the United States', in M. Friedman (ed.), *Studies in the Quantity Theory of Money* (Chicago: University of Chicago Press).

Serletis, A. (1987*a*), 'Monetary asset separability tests', in W. A. Barnett and K. Singleton (eds), *New Approaches to Monetary Economics* (Cambridge: University Press).

Serletis, A. (1987*b*). 'On the demand for money in the United States', *Empirical Economics* (No. 4.)

Serletis, A. (1987*c*). 'The demand for Divisia M1, M2, and M3 in the United States', *Journal of Macroeconomics* (Autumn).

Serletis, A. (1988*a*). 'Translog flexible functional forms and substitutability of monetary assets', *Journal of Business and Economic Statistics* (Jan.).

Serletis, A. (1988*b*). 'The empirical relation between money, prices, and income revisited', *Journal of Business and Economics Statistics* (July).

Serletis, A. and A. L. Robb (1986). 'Divisia aggregation and substitutability among monetary assets', *Journal of Money, Credit, and Banking* (Nov.).

Sidrauski, M. (1967*a*), 'Rational choice and patterns of growth in a monetary economy', *American Economic Review* (May).

Sidrauski, M. (1967*b*). 'Inflation and economic growth', *Journal of Political Economy* (Dec.).

Siegel, J. J. (1985). 'Money supply announcements and interest rates: does monetary policy matter?' *Journal and Monetary Economics* (Mar.).

Sims, C. A. (1972). 'Money, income, and causality', *American Economic Review* (Sept.).

Sims, C. A. (1980). 'Macroeconomics and reality'. *Econometrica* (Jan.).

Sims, G. and A. Takayama (1980). 'Currency substitution and the Translog function', mimeo, Econometrics Society meetings.

Slovin, M. B. and M. E. Sushka (1983). 'Money, interest rates and risk', *Journal of Monetary Economics* (Sept.).

Smirlock, M. (1982). 'Inflation uncertainty and the demand for money', *Economic Inquiry* (July).

Souza, G. and A. R. Gallant (1979). 'Statistical inference based on M-estimators for the multivariate nonlinear regression model in implicit form', mimeo, North Carolina State University (Department of Statistics).

Sowell, T. (1972). *Say's Law* (Princeton: Princeton University Press).

Spindt, P. A. (1985). 'Money is what money does: monetary aggregates and the equation of exchange', *Journal of Political Economy* (Feb.).

Swofford, J. L. and G. A. Whitney (1986). 'Flexible functional forms and the utility approach to the demand for money: a non-parametric analysis', *Journal of Money, Credit, and Banking* (Aug.).

Swofford, J. L. and G. A. Whitney (1987). 'Non-parametric tests of utility maximization and weak separability for consumption, leisure and money', *Review of Economics and Statistics* (Aug.).

Swofford, J. L. and G. A. Whitney (1988). 'A comparison of non-parametric tests of weak separability for annual and quarterly data on consumption, leisure and money', *Journal of Business and Economic Statistics* (Apr.).

Tanner, J. E. and J. M. Trapani (1977). ' Can the quantity theory be used to predict stock prices – or is the stock market efficient?', *Journal of Finance* (Oct.).

Tatom, J. A. (1983). 'Was the 1982 velocity decline unusual?', *Review*, Federal Reserve Bank at St Louis (Aug./Sept.).

Taylor, H. (1986). 'What has happened to M1?', *Business Review*, Federal Reserve Bank of Philadelphia (Sept./Oct.).

Taylor, J. B. (1980). 'Aggregate dynamics and staggered contracts', *Journal of Political Economy* (Feb.).

Tobin, J. (1955). 'A dynamic aggregative model', *Journal of Political Economy* (Apr.).

Tobin, J. (1956). 'The interest elasticity of transactions demand for cash', *Review of Economics and Statistics* (Aug.).

Tobin, J. (1958). 'Liquidity preference as behaviour toward risk', *Review of Economic Studies* (Feb.).

Tobin, J. (1965). 'Money and economic growth', *Econometrica* (Oct.).

Townend, J. C. (1972). 'Substitution among capital-certain assets in the personal sector of the UK economy: 1963–1971', mimeo, Bank of England (Sept.).

Townsend, R. M. (1979). 'Optimal contracts and competitive markets with costly state verification', *Journal of Economic Theory* (Oct.).

Turnovsky, S. J. (1977*a*). 'On the formation of continuous time macroeconomic models with asset accumulation', *International Economic Review* (Feb.).

Turnovsky, S. J. (1977*b*). 'Structural expectations and the effectiveness of government policy in a short-run macroeconomic model', *American Economic Review* (Dec.).

Turnovsky, S. J. (1977*c*), *Macroeconomic Analysis and Stabilization Policy* (Cambridge: Cambridge University Press).

Urich, T. J. and P. Wachtel (1984). 'The effects of inflation and money supply announcements on interest rates', *Journal of Finance* (Sept.).

Varian, H. R. (1982). 'The non-parametric approach to demand analysis', *Econometrica* (July).

Varian, H. R. (1983). 'Non-parametric tests of consumer behaviour', *Review of Economic Studies* (Jan.).

Viren, M. (1987). 'Inflation and interest rates: some time series evidence from 6 OECD countries', *Empirical Economics* (No. 1).

Vogel, R. C. (1974). 'The dynamics of inflation in Latin America, 1950–1969', *American Economic Review* (Mar.).

Vogel, R. C. and G. S. Maddala (1967). 'Cross section estimates of liquid asset demand by manufacturing corporations', *Journal of Finance* (Dec.).

West, K. D. (1988). 'On the interpretation of near random walk behavior in GNP', *American Economic Review* (Mar.).

Whalen, E. L. (1966). 'A rationalization of the precautionary demand for cash', *Quarterly Journal of Economics* (May).

Whiteman, C. (1984). 'Lucas on the quantity theory: hypothesis testing without theory', *American Economic Review* (Sept.).

Wicksteed, P. (1933). *The Common Sense of Political Economy* (London: Routledge and Kegan Paul).

Williamson, S. D. (1987*a*). 'Recent developments in modelling financial intermediation', *Quarterly Review*. Federal Reserve Bank of Minneapolis (Summer).

Williamson, S. D. (1987*b*). 'Financial intermediation, business failures, and real business cycles', *Journal of Political Economy* (Dec.).

Yeager, L. (1968). 'Essential properties of the medium of exchange', *Kyklos* (No. 1).

Zellner, A. (1962). 'An efficient method of estimating seemingly unrelated regressions and tests for aggregation bias', *Journal of the American Statistical Association* (June).

INDEX